Woodworking from Ze

The Only Step-by-Step Guide You'll Ever Need to Master Essential Skills, Boost Your Confidence from Day One, and Quickly Build Show-Stopping Wood Projects on a Budget

Copyright © 2024 All rights reserved

No part of this book may be reproduced, distributed, or transmitted in any form or by any means, including photocopying, recording, or other electronic or mechanical methods, without the prior written permission of the publisher, except in the case of brief quotations embodied in critical reviews and certain other noncommercial uses permitted by copyright law.

This book is for informational and educational purposes only. The author and publisher make no representations or warranties with respect to the accuracy or completeness of the contents and disclaim any implied warranties of merchantability or fitness for a particular purpose. The author and publisher shall not be liable for any damages or injuries arising from the use or misuse of the information in this book.

Table of Contents

CHAPTER 1: WOOD FUNDAMENTALS ... 5

1.1 Introduction to Wood Types ... 5
- Hardwood vs. Softwood: Characteristics and Applications ... 5
- Sustainable Wood Choices ... 7

1.2 Properties of Wood ... 10
- Grain, Density, Hardness, and Flexibility ... 10
- How Wood Reacts to Moisture and Temperature ... 13

1.3 Selecting the Right Wood for Your Project ... 14
- Determining the Best Wood Based on Project Type ... 14
- Wood Grades, Cost, and Availability ... 15

CHAPTER 2: ESSENTIAL TOOLS TO START WOODWORKING ON A BUDGET ... 18

2.1 Hand Tools ... 18
- Must-Have Hand Tools for Beginners: Chisels, Saws, Hammers, etc. ... 18
- Essential Measuring and Marking Tools ... 20
- How to Properly Maintain and Sharpen Hand Tools ... 23

2.2 Power Tools ... 25
- Basic Power Tools: Drills, Sanders, and Circular Saws ... 25
- Choosing Cost-Effective Tools for Efficiency ... 28

2.3 Machine Tools ... 30
- Introduction to Machines (e.g., Planers, Jointers, Bandsaws) for Those Ready to Invest ... 30
- Safety Tips and Maintenance Basics ... 33

CHAPTER 3: PROJECT DESIGN ESSENTIALS ... 36

3.1 Project Ideation and Conceptualization ... 36
- Generating Ideas and Planning Out Your Project ... 36
- **Choosing Design Styles: Traditional, Modern, Rustic, etc.** ... 37
- Choosing Hardware: Hinges, Handles, Screws, and Brackets ... 38

3.2 Creating Sketches and Plans ... 42
- Translating Ideas into Sketches ... 42
- Introduction to CAD and Digital Design for Woodworking ... 44

3.3 Prototyping and Testing ... 46
- Building Small-Scale Models ... 46

CHAPTER 4: SQUARING, MARKING, & CUTTING STOCK ... 50

4.1 Stock Preparation ... 50

Selecting and Preparing Wood for Accuracy and Stability 50

Squaring and Flattening Lumber 52

4.2 Measuring and Marking Techniques 54

Essential Techniques for Accurate Measurement and Layout 54

4.3 Cutting Techniques 57

Using Handsaws vs. Power Saws 57

Techniques for Rip Cuts, Crosscuts, and Angled Cuts 60

Avoiding Common Cutting Mistakes 63

CHAPTER 5: JOINERY TECHNIQUES AND ESSENTIAL JOINTS 66

5.1 Introduction to Joinery 66

Overview of Joinery Principles 66

Choosing Joints Based on Project Type and Durability 66

5.2 Essential Joints for Beginners 68

Butt Joint 68

Miter Joint 69

Dado Joint 70

Mortise and Tenon Joint 71

Dovetail Joint 72

Finger Joint 74

Rabbet Joint 76

When to Use Glued Joints vs. Mechanical Fasteners 77

5.3 Advanced Joinery Techniques 78

Dowel Joint 78

Biscuits Joint 79

Pocket-Hole Joint 80

Bridle Joint 80

Half Lap Joint 81

Box Joint 81

Tongue and Groove Joint 82

CHAPTER 6: FINISHING TECHNIQUES 84

6.1 Surface Preparation 84

Sanding Techniques and Tools 84

Filling, Planing, and Preparing Wood for a Smooth Finish 85

6.2 Choosing Finishes for Different Wood Types 86

Understanding Various Finishes 86

    How to Match Finishes with Wood Types 88

    Enhancing Wood Grain and Color with Different Finishes 89

6.3 APPLICATION TECHNIQUES 92

    Best Practices for Brushing, Spraying, and Wiping Finishes 92

    Tips for Layering and Polishing Finishes 94

6.4 MAINTENANCE OF FINISHED WOODWORK 95

    Protecting and Maintaining Finished Projects 95

    Repairing Damaged Finishes Over Time 96

CHAPTER 7: DIY PROJECTS **99**

    DIY HEADPHONE STAND 99

    DIY COFFEE TABLE 105

    DIY PLANT STAND 113

    DIY BIRDHOUSE 124

    DIY CHICKEN FEEDER 128

    DIY PICNIC TABLE 134

    DIY OUTDOOR CHAIR 142

    DIY STORAGE CABINET 147

EXTRA CONTENT **160**

Chapter 1: Wood Fundamentals

1.1 Introduction to Wood Types

Hardwood vs. Softwood: Characteristics and Applications

Wood is the primary material of any woodworking project, and understanding its characteristics is essential for choosing the right type for each task. There are two main classifications of wood: **hardwood** and **softwood**. Despite their names, these terms don't always refer to the hardness of the wood; rather, they are based on the type of tree the wood comes from and its cellular structure. This classification affects the wood's properties, workability, appearance, and ideal applications in woodworking projects.

Hardwood: Characteristics and Applications

Characteristics of Hardwood:
1. **Source**: Hardwoods come from angiosperm trees, which are deciduous, meaning they lose their leaves annually. Common hardwood trees include oak, maple, walnut, mahogany, and cherry.
2. **Cellular Structure**: Hardwoods have a dense, complex structure with smaller pores, which often gives them a tighter grain pattern and greater strength. This structure generally makes hardwoods more durable and resistant to wear.
3. **Grain Pattern**: Hardwood typically has distinct, intricate grain patterns. These patterns add aesthetic value and make hardwood a popular choice for fine furniture and decorative items.
4. **Density**: Most hardwoods are denser than softwoods, making them heavier and, in many cases, more challenging to work with, as they require sharper tools and more precision.
5. **Cost**: Hardwoods are generally more expensive than softwoods due to their slow growth rate and higher density. The cost is also influenced by their desirable appearance and durability.

Applications of Hardwood:
- **Furniture Making**: Hardwoods like oak, maple, and walnut are commonly used for crafting furniture pieces, including tables, chairs, cabinets, and desks. Their durability and visual appeal make them ideal for high-quality, long-lasting furniture.
- **Flooring**: Hardwoods such as oak, maple, and hickory are often chosen for flooring due to their hardness, which withstands heavy foot traffic and resists dents and scratches over time.
- **Cabinetry and Decorative Trim**: The intricate grain patterns and smooth finishing quality of hardwoods like cherry and mahogany make them popular for cabinetry and trim work. These woods add elegance and sophistication to interiors.
- **Musical Instruments**: Some hardwoods, such as maple and mahogany, are used in musical instruments because of their tonal qualities and resonance, which produce a rich sound.

- **Outdoor Furniture**: Certain hardwoods, like teak, are naturally resistant to moisture and pests, making them suitable for outdoor furniture. Teak, in particular, is known for its weather resistance and is often used in patio furniture and boat decking.

Softwood: Characteristics and Applications

Characteristics of Softwood:

1. **Source**: Softwoods come from gymnosperm trees, which are generally conifers, or evergreen trees, such as pine, cedar, spruce, and fir.
2. **Cellular Structure**: Softwoods have a simpler cell structure with larger pores and fewer fibers, making them less dense than hardwoods. This lower density generally gives softwood a lighter weight and makes it easier to cut, shape, and carve.
3. **Grain Pattern**: The grain pattern in softwood is typically more uniform and straight, which can result in a simpler, more consistent appearance compared to the intricate patterns of hardwood.
4. **Density**: Softwoods are less dense than hardwoods, which means they are often more susceptible to scratches, dents, and wear over time. However, this lower density also makes them easier to handle and work with, especially for beginners.
5. **Cost**: Softwoods grow faster than hardwoods, making them more widely available and generally more affordable. This accessibility and lower price make them a popular choice for many DIY and construction projects.

Applications of Softwood:

- **Construction and Framing**: Softwoods like pine and fir are widely used in construction and framing due to their availability, ease of handling, and affordability. They are ideal for structural work, where aesthetics are less of a concern.
- **Interior Paneling and Trim**: Softwoods such as cedar and pine are often used for interior paneling, baseboards, and moldings. Their lighter color and uniform grain can complement various interior styles.
- **Furniture**: While less common than hardwood, softwoods like pine are used to make rustic or budget-friendly furniture. Pine furniture, for example, is popular for items like shelves, dressers, and beds where cost-effectiveness and ease of construction are priorities.
- **Carving and Decorative Work**: Due to their lower density, softwoods like cedar and pine are easier to carve, making them suitable for decorative woodwork, such as sculptures, picture frames, and other artistic projects.
- **Outdoor Structures**: Certain softwoods, like cedar and redwood, contain natural oils that make them more resistant to decay and insects, making them popular choices for outdoor structures like decks, fences, and garden furniture.

Key Differences Between Hardwood and Softwood

Feature	Hardwood	Softwood
Tree Type	Deciduous (e.g., oak, maple, walnut)	Coniferous (e.g., pine, fir, cedar)
Growth Rate	Slow-growing	Faster-growing
Density	Generally denser and heavier	Less dense, lighter
Grain Pattern	Intricate, varied grain	Uniform, straight grain
Durability	More durable, resistant to wear	Generally less durable, more susceptible to dents
Workability	Requires sharper tools, more skill	Easier to cut and shape
Cost	More expensive	Generally more affordable
Common Uses	Furniture, flooring, cabinetry, instruments	Framing, paneling, budget furniture

Choosing Between Hardwood and Softwood

When selecting wood for a project, consider the following:

1. **Purpose**: For projects where durability and visual appeal are key, hardwood is often the preferred choice. For framing or less-visible structural work, softwood may be ideal due to its cost-effectiveness and ease of handling.
2. **Budget**: Hardwood is generally more expensive, so if you're working with a tight budget, softwood can be a practical alternative, especially for functional pieces that don't require intricate details.
3. **Aesthetics**: Hardwood offers unique, natural beauty in its grain, making it ideal for furniture and decorative items. If the project requires a simple, uniform look, softwood can provide a clean and minimalist appearance.
4. **Skill Level**: Softwood is easier to work with, making it a good choice for beginners. For more advanced projects requiring precision and durability, hardwood is often worth the investment in both time and materials.

Sustainable Wood Choices

As woodworking grows in popularity, it's crucial to consider the environmental impact of the materials we use. Sustainable wood choices ensure that future generations will have access to natural resources without harming our planet.

What Makes Wood Sustainable?

1. **Responsible Sourcing**: Sustainable wood is harvested from forests where logging is managed to preserve biodiversity and ecosystem health. These forests are often certified by organizations like the Forest Stewardship Council (FSC) or the Programme for the Endorsement of Forest Certification (PEFC).
2. **Renewability**: Sustainable woods are typically from fast-growing tree species, ensuring a quicker renewal cycle and less strain on forest ecosystems.
3. **Reduced Carbon Footprint**: Responsibly managed forests absorb more carbon dioxide, reducing overall greenhouse gases. Harvesting wood responsibly also limits the need for deforestation.
4. **Alternative Sources**: Some sustainable wood options come from recycled wood, reclaimed wood, or rapidly renewable resources like bamboo.

Common Sustainable Wood Types for Woodworking

1. **Bamboo**
    - **Characteristics**: Bamboo is technically a grass, but its hardness and durability make it a great alternative to traditional hardwoods. It grows incredibly fast, sometimes reaching maturity in as little as 3-5 years, making it one of the most renewable materials.
    - **Applications**: Used for flooring, furniture, and decorative items, bamboo's light color and unique grain pattern bring a modern aesthetic to projects.
2. **Cork**
    - **Characteristics**: Cork is harvested from the bark of cork oak trees, which can regrow their bark, allowing for repeated harvests without harming the tree. Cork is lightweight, resistant to moisture, and has excellent insulating properties.
    - **Applications**: Commonly used for tabletops, furniture inlays, and flooring, cork is also valued for decorative applications.
3. **Reclaimed Wood**
    - **Characteristics**: Reclaimed wood is salvaged from old buildings, barns, and factories. It offers unique, weathered appearances and helps reduce demand for newly harvested wood.
    - **Applications**: Ideal for furniture, wall paneling, and décor, reclaimed wood has natural character and often unique grain patterns and colors, adding rustic charm to projects.
4. **Lyptus**
    - **Characteristics**: Lyptus is a hybrid of Eucalyptus trees, grown specifically for fast harvesting. It matures in about 15 years, making it a highly renewable alternative to traditional hardwoods.

- **Applications**: Lyptus is similar to mahogany in color and workability, making it suitable for fine furniture, cabinetry, and flooring.

5. **Black Cherry**
    - **Characteristics**: Black cherry trees grow relatively fast for a hardwood, reaching maturity in around 30 years. They are often responsibly harvested in North America, making them a more sustainable choice than imported hardwoods.
    - **Applications**: Black cherry's rich color and smooth grain are ideal for furniture, cabinetry, and trim work.

6. **Maple**
    - **Characteristics**: Maple is commonly grown in North America and managed under sustainable forestry practices. It grows faster than many other hardwoods and offers excellent durability and a lighter color.
    - **Applications**: Frequently used for furniture, flooring, and cabinetry, maple's smooth grain makes it versatile and adaptable to many designs.

7. **Acacia**
    - **Characteristics**: Acacia trees grow quickly, making them more sustainable than many other hardwoods. Acacia is durable and moisture-resistant, often with a distinctive grain pattern.
    - **Applications**: Acacia is ideal for outdoor furniture, cutting boards, and decorative items, as it's naturally resistant to the elements and rot.

8. **Rubberwood**
    - **Characteristics**: Rubberwood is sourced from rubber trees that are no longer viable for latex production, typically after about 25-30 years. Using rubberwood reduces waste and maximizes the life cycle of the trees.
    - **Applications**: Commonly used in furniture, cabinetry, and smaller decorative items, rubberwood has a light, neutral appearance and is relatively easy to work with.

Certifications to Look For in Sustainable Wood

1. **Forest Stewardship Council (FSC)**: FSC certification ensures that wood is harvested in an environmentally responsible, socially beneficial, and economically viable manner. It's the gold standard for sustainable wood.
2. **Programme for the Endorsement of Forest Certification (PEFC)**: PEFC certification promotes sustainable forest management by ensuring that forests are managed responsibly and with minimal environmental impact.

3. **Sustainable Forestry Initiative (SFI)**: Particularly common in North America, the SFI certifies wood that meets specific sustainability and conservation standards.
4. **Rainforest Alliance Certified**: This certification focuses on wood from tropical forests and ensures that forests are managed to support biodiversity, protect indigenous rights, and reduce carbon emissions.

Tips for Making Sustainable Choices in Woodworking
1. **Choose Local Woods**: Using locally sourced woods helps reduce the carbon footprint associated with shipping and supports sustainable forest management practices close to home.
2. **Opt for Fast-Growing Species**: Whenever possible, use woods like bamboo, cork, and acacia, which mature quickly and are often grown under sustainable practices.
3. **Reuse and Reclaim**: Incorporating reclaimed wood into your projects can add character while reducing the demand for newly harvested wood.
4. **Avoid Endangered Species**: Certain exotic hardwoods, such as teak and rosewood, are endangered or vulnerable due to overharvesting. Opt for certified sustainable sources or look for alternative woods that offer similar qualities.
5. **Check for Certification Labels**: When buying wood, check for certification labels from the FSC, PEFC, or SFI. These labels confirm that the wood has been responsibly sourced.

1.2 Properties of Wood

Grain, Density, Hardness, and Flexibility

Understanding wood properties is fundamental to making informed choices for your woodworking projects. The properties of wood directly impact its strength, durability, ease of work, and appearance. Let's dive into four critical characteristics—grain, density, hardness, and flexibility—and how they influence the wood's performance in various applications.

---

1. Grain

The grain of wood refers to the direction, texture, and appearance of the wood fibers. It results from the natural growth patterns of the tree and is visible as lines, curves, or even swirls in the wood. Grain patterns vary widely between tree species and even within individual trees, adding unique aesthetics to each piece.

Types of Grain Patterns
- **Straight Grain**: Fibers run parallel to each other, making the wood easy to cut and shape. Common in woods like pine, this grain is ideal for structural and decorative uses.

- **Curly or Wavy Grain**: Irregular wave-like patterns add visual interest but can be more challenging to work with due to unpredictable fiber directions.
- **Cross Grain**: Fibers intersect in varied directions, creating a unique look but also increasing the risk of splitting or tearing during cutting.
- **Interlocked Grain**: Common in hardwoods like mahogany, interlocked grain resists splitting but can be challenging for planing or sanding.

Impact on Workability and Aesthetics: Grain affects not only the wood's beauty but also how it behaves under tools. For instance, straight-grain woods are easier to plane and sand, while wavy or interlocked grains can add depth to the wood's appearance but require more skill to work with effectively. Grain also influences how wood absorbs stains and finishes, with tighter grains offering a smoother, even finish.

---

2. Density

Density measures how tightly packed the wood fibers are, influencing the wood's weight and strength. Denser woods are heavier and often harder, making them suitable for applications where strength is critical, while less dense woods are lighter and easier to handle.

Common Density Ranges

- **High Density**: Dense woods like oak, hickory, and maple are highly durable and resistant to wear, making them ideal for flooring, cabinetry, and furniture.
- **Low Density**: Woods like pine, spruce, and fir have a lower density, making them lighter and easier to work with, especially for beginners or when creating large structures that need to be moved easily.

Impact on Durability and Usability: High-density woods are more resistant to dents, scratches, and wear, but they may also be more challenging to cut or shape due to their toughness. Low-density woods are easier to work with but may require protective finishes if used in high-traffic or load-bearing applications.

---

3. Hardness

Hardness reflects the wood's resistance to surface wear and denting. It is an essential factor when selecting wood for items that will endure frequent use or heavy loads. Hardness in wood is measured using the Janka hardness test, which quantifies the force required to embed a steel ball halfway into the wood surface.

Typical Hardness Levels

- **Hardwoods**: Generally, woods like oak, maple, and cherry have high hardness ratings, making them ideal for floors, furniture, and cabinetry. Hardwood durability means that these items will withstand heavy use over time.

- **Softwoods**: Softwoods, such as pine and cedar, are lower on the hardness scale. They're better suited for decorative projects or pieces that won't encounter much wear.

Impact on Application and Wear: Hardness is a primary consideration for functional pieces that will bear weight or frequent impact. Hardwood floors, for example, maintain their appearance longer than softer wood floors due to their resilience. However, harder woods can be more challenging to work with, requiring sharper tools and more skill to avoid splintering.

4. Flexibility

Flexibility is the wood's ability to bend without breaking. It varies significantly across wood types and plays an important role in applications requiring bending or shaping, such as creating curves in furniture, constructing boat hulls, or crafting archery bows.

Factors Influencing Flexibility

- **Species**: Some wood species, such as ash, hickory, and oak, are more flexible due to their grain structure and cellular composition. These woods are commonly used in applications requiring elasticity and strength.
- **Moisture Content**: Wood flexibility can increase with moisture. Steaming wood, for instance, allows it to bend more easily, which is essential in bentwood furniture making.
- **Cut and Grain**: The grain direction also affects flexibility, with some grain orientations allowing more bending without fracturing.

Impact on Projects Requiring Curves and Bends: Flexible woods are ideal for projects needing intricate shaping. For example, ash is often used in creating curved furniture legs and handles because it bends well without splitting. Conversely, woods with low flexibility, such as walnut, are more likely to snap or crack under pressure, so they are more suited for straight, solid components.

Summary Table of Wood Properties

Property	Key Factors	Impact on Projects
Grain	Direction, texture, pattern	Influences appearance, workability, and finishing quality
Density	Fiber tightness	Determines weight, strength, and ease of handling
Hardness	Janka rating	Impacts durability and resistance to dents and wear
Flexibility	Grain structure, moisture content	Essential for projects involving curves or bending

How Wood Reacts to Moisture and Temperature

Wood is a natural, hygroscopic material, meaning it has the ability to absorb or release moisture from its environment. This interaction with moisture and temperature affects the wood's stability, shape, and durability, which can have a significant impact on woodworking projects. Understanding how wood behaves under varying environmental conditions helps woodworkers make better choices regarding wood types, finishes, and storage.

Moisture Content and Wood Movement

Wood expands and contracts in response to changes in its moisture content, influenced by the humidity levels in the surrounding air. This characteristic, known as "wood movement," can affect the shape and size of wood, potentially leading to warping, splitting, or swelling if not managed properly.

1. **Expansion and Contraction:** When exposed to high humidity, wood absorbs moisture, causing it to expand. Conversely, in dry conditions, wood releases moisture and contracts. This expansion and contraction happen across the grain (width) rather than along the grain (length), which can lead to dimensional changes that need to be accounted for during project design and assembly.
2. **Equilibrium Moisture Content (EMC):** Wood eventually reaches a balance between its moisture content and the ambient humidity, known as the Equilibrium Moisture Content (EMC). Achieving EMC is important, as wood that has not yet reached this balance will continue to expand or contract after a project is completed, risking gaps, cracks, or misalignments in the final product.

To avoid this, wood should be allowed to acclimate to the workshop's humidity levels before starting any major work. EMC varies depending on the climate and season, so allowing for these factors can make projects more durable.

Temperature's Effect on Wood

While wood itself is not highly sensitive to temperature changes, the effect of temperature on moisture is crucial. Higher temperatures increase wood's tendency to lose moisture, while cooler temperatures can retain moisture. For woodworkers, this is especially important when heating or cooling a workspace.

1. **Heat and Drying:** Heating a workshop in the winter, for instance, can lower the humidity, causing wood to shrink. Similarly, storing wood near heating sources can dry it unevenly, potentially leading to warping. Wood should be stored in moderate, consistent temperatures to prevent sudden shifts in moisture levels.
2. **Cold and Condensation:** In colder environments, wood can be more prone to surface condensation, especially if moved suddenly from a cold storage area to a warmer workspace. Condensation can increase the wood's surface moisture, which might interfere with finishing processes and can lead to warping or mildew growth.

Managing Moisture and Temperature for Wood Stability

Storage and Acclimatization: To minimize wood movement, wood should be stored in a controlled environment before use. Allowing wood to acclimate to the workshop climate helps stabilize it, making it less likely to expand or contract once assembled.

Using Proper Finishes: Finishes such as varnishes, oils, and sealants help create a barrier that limits moisture absorption and loss. Applying an even finish on all sides of a piece helps stabilize it, slowing down the rate of moisture exchange and reducing the likelihood of warping or swelling.

Wood Selection: Some woods are naturally more stable in response to moisture and temperature changes. Quarter-sawn woods, for example, exhibit less movement across the grain, making them ideal for furniture and cabinetry. Additionally, hardwoods like oak and maple are generally more dimensionally stable than softwoods.

1.3 Selecting the Right Wood for Your Project

Determining the Best Wood Based on Project Type

When selecting the right wood for your project, it's crucial to consider the type of project you're working on. Different woods offer unique properties that make them more suitable for specific uses, whether you're building furniture, outdoor structures, or decorative pieces. Understanding the nature of your project will help you make the right wood choice, ensuring durability, aesthetics, and ease of work.

1. Furniture Construction: For furniture pieces like tables, chairs, and cabinets, you need wood that combines strength, stability, and beauty. **Hardwoods** like **oak, maple, and cherry** are commonly used due to their durability and ability to take on fine finishes. These woods are resistant to wear and can handle the stresses furniture pieces face, making them ideal for items that will see regular use. **Maple** and **cherry** offer a smooth surface that responds well to stains, while **oak** has an attractive grain that adds character and texture to finished pieces.

2. Outdoor Projects: Outdoor projects, such as garden furniture, decks, or fences, require wood that can withstand exposure to moisture, temperature fluctuations, and sunlight. **Pressure-treated wood**, such as **pine**, is a popular choice due to its resistance to rot and insects, making it suitable for outdoor use. **Cedar** and **redwood** are also excellent choices for outdoor furniture or structures because of their natural resistance to decay and pests. These woods also have a pleasant aroma, adding to their appeal for outdoor environments. For added durability, consider sealing these woods with protective finishes to help preserve their appearance and strength.

3. Decorative Pieces and Carving: If you're creating intricate carvings, sculptures, or smaller decorative pieces, you need a wood that's easy to shape but still holds detail. **Softwoods** like **pine, basswood, and cedar** are favored by carvers due to their workability. These woods are softer, making them easier to carve and detail, and they offer a clean finish when sanded. However, they may not be as durable as hardwoods, so they're better suited for decorative items that won't face heavy wear or exposure to elements.

4. Flooring: When choosing wood for flooring, it's essential to select a wood that can withstand heavy foot traffic and is durable over time. **Hardwoods** like **oak, maple, and walnut** are commonly used for flooring because they're dense and resilient. These woods resist dents and scratches and are relatively easy to maintain. **Cherry** is another option for flooring, although it's softer than oak and may require more care to avoid damage. It's important to select a wood species with a grain pattern that matches the aesthetic you want for the space, as well as one that will hold up under regular use.

5. Shelving and Storage: For shelving units or storage solutions, strength and stability are key. **Oak** and **maple** are solid choices for shelves that will bear heavy loads, as their high density and durability make them resistant to sagging. Lighter woods like **pine** or **fir** may be suitable for shelves that won't carry heavy weight, but they should be properly supported. **Birch** and **poplar** are also commonly used for their balance of strength and affordability.

6. Crafts and Small Projects: If you're building smaller items like picture frames, jewelry boxes, or small crafts, you can often choose from a variety of woods, depending on your desired finish and ease of work. **Pine** and **poplar** are often chosen for smaller items because they're relatively inexpensive, easy to work with, and provide a smooth finish. For more delicate projects, **cherry** or **walnut** may be better choices, as they offer fine grain patterns and take stains and finishes well, giving your craft an elegant, polished look.

Wood Grades, Cost, and Availability

When selecting wood for your project, it's important to understand how wood grades, cost, and availability can affect your choices. These factors will influence both the overall outcome of your project and your budget. Let's explore each of these aspects in detail.

Wood Grades:

Wood grades determine the quality and appearance of the wood you're purchasing. These grades are typically based on factors such as defects, knots, grain patterns, and overall appearance. Higher grades are usually smoother, with fewer imperfections, making them suitable for fine furniture or visible areas. Lower grades may be more affordable but might contain imperfections or irregular grain patterns that are more noticeable.

- **Clear Grade:** This is the highest grade of wood, free of defects like knots, splits, or discoloration. It's ideal for fine furniture, cabinetry, and high-end projects where appearance is critical. Woods of this grade are often used for visible surfaces.

- **Select Grade:** This grade contains a few minor imperfections, but the wood is still relatively smooth and defect-free. It is suitable for projects like furniture, shelving, and other functional applications where a slightly lower level of perfection is acceptable.
- **Common Grade:** This grade is often used for construction, framing, and projects where appearance is less of a concern. The wood may contain knots, checks, or other imperfections, but it's still functional for most structural or non-visible uses. It is typically more affordable than higher grades.

Cost:

The cost of wood varies widely depending on the type, grade, and region where it is sourced. For instance, **hardwoods** like **cherry, walnut, and maple** tend to be more expensive than **softwoods** like **pine, cedar, or fir** due to the slower growth rate and greater density of hardwood trees. Additionally, rare or imported wood species, such as **mahogany** or **teak**, can be quite expensive.

Several factors influence wood costs:

- **Wood Species:** Exotic or rare woods tend to cost more due to limited availability and higher shipping costs. Common woods, like **pine** or **oak**, are more widely available and therefore less expensive.
- **Grade:** As discussed, higher-grade woods with fewer defects are more expensive than lower-grade options.
- **Sourcing and Processing:** Locally sourced and processed wood is often less expensive due to lower shipping and handling costs. Wood that needs to be imported or specially treated can significantly increase the overall cost.
- **Finishing and Treatment:** Wood that is pre-finished or treated (e.g., pressure-treated wood for outdoor use) often costs more due to the additional processes involved.

Availability:

The availability of certain types of wood can vary based on location, demand, and environmental factors. Some woods are more readily available in specific regions due to local forests or plantations. For example, **pine** is abundant in North America and is therefore easier to source and typically less expensive, while tropical hardwoods like **teak** and **mahogany** might only be found in certain regions of the world.

- **Regional Availability:** Local woods such as **oak, ash, and maple** are often available at lumber yards or woodworking suppliers, making them easier to find and purchase. Imported woods like **rosewood** or **ebony** may require special ordering, which can add time and cost.
- **Demand and Seasonality:** Popular woods, such as **oak** or **pine**, are generally more readily available and are often stocked year-round at most lumber yards. However, specialty woods or

those in high demand, like **walnut** or **mahogany**, may have limited availability due to their slower growth or harvesting cycles. Seasonal fluctuations can also affect availability, as certain types of wood are harvested at specific times of the year.
- **Sustainable Sourcing:** Increasing awareness of deforestation and environmental sustainability has led to greater demand for responsibly sourced wood. Woods certified by organizations such as the **Forest Stewardship Council (FSC)** ensure that they are harvested sustainably. However, certified wood can be more expensive due to the additional measures required to ensure sustainability.

Impact on Your Project:

When planning your woodworking project, understanding the interplay between wood grades, cost, and availability can help you make an informed decision that fits your project's needs and budget.
- **Budget Considerations:** For larger projects or ones with functional rather than aesthetic purposes (e.g., framing, decking, or shelving), it may be best to opt for lower-grade, more affordable wood like **construction-grade pine** or **cedar**. If the project demands higher-quality finishes or will be highly visible, it's worth investing in higher-grade wood like **maple** or **cherry**.
- **Long-Term Value:** While premium wood may cost more upfront, it can offer greater durability, strength, and appearance, which is important for furniture, cabinetry, or decorative pieces. Lower-cost wood may not perform as well in terms of longevity or may need more frequent maintenance, especially if exposed to wear and tear.
- **Sustainability:** If sustainability is a priority for your project, consider choosing wood that is FSC-certified or sourced from local suppliers that use responsible harvesting methods. This helps reduce the environmental impact of your project, ensuring that the materials are replenished and responsibly managed.

Chapter 2: Essential Tools to Start Woodworking on a Budget

2.1 Hand Tools

Must-Have Hand Tools for Beginners: Chisels, Saws, Hammers, etc.

When you're starting out in woodworking, it's important to build a basic toolkit with essential hand tools. While power tools may seem appealing, hand tools can be more affordable, versatile, and easier to control, making them a great option for beginners. The right hand tools not only enable you to work efficiently but also give you a deeper connection to your craft. Here, we'll explore the must-have hand tools every beginner should consider, starting with the essentials like chisels, saws, hammers, and more.

Must-Have Hand Tools for Beginners:

1. **Chisels:**

   Chisels are one of the most essential tools in any woodworking kit. They are used for shaping and carving wood, making precise cuts, and cleaning up joints. Beginners should start with a basic set that includes a few different sizes to tackle various tasks.
   - **Choosing Chisels:** Opt for a **set of 4 to 6 chisels** that range from 1/4" to 1" wide. This range of sizes will allow you to tackle most beginner projects, such as cleaning out dovetail joints, carving shapes, or making fine adjustments to fit.
   - **Quality Considerations:** It's better to buy a good-quality chisel that holds its edge well rather than going for a cheap set that requires frequent sharpening. Look for chisels with durable steel blades that can be easily honed and sharpened.
   - **Use:** Chisels are used for tasks like **paring** (removing small amounts of wood), **squaring corners**, **cleaning up joints**, and **detailed carving**. They are especially useful in fine furniture making and detailed woodworking projects.

2. **Saws:**

   A good saw is an essential tool for cutting wood into various shapes and sizes. There are several types of saws that beginners should consider, each suited to different types of cuts.
   - **Crosscut Saw:** A **crosscut saw** is used for cutting across the grain of the wood. It's the most versatile saw for making clean, straight cuts in most types of wood. For beginners, a **hand saw** is sufficient for most tasks. It's affordable and allows for more control when cutting.
   - **Rip Saw:** A **rip saw** is used for cutting along the grain of the wood, typically in the direction of the wood fibers. It has a different tooth pattern than the crosscut saw, with larger, deeper teeth designed for efficient ripping.

- **Coping Saw:** If your projects require more intricate cuts or curves, a **coping saw** is a great tool to add to your toolkit. This saw features a thin, flexible blade that allows you to make curved or detailed cuts with precision.
    - **Selection Tips:** If you're on a budget, start with a **general-purpose saw** that can handle both rip and crosscut tasks. As you gain experience, you can invest in specialized saws. Look for saws with comfortable handles and sharp, durable teeth.
3. **Hammers:** A hammer is another essential hand tool in woodworking. It's used for driving nails, pins, and other fasteners into wood, as well as for general tapping and adjusting of parts.
    - **Type of Hammer:** For general woodworking, a **claw hammer** is a great choice. It has a flat face for driving nails and a curved claw on the opposite side for pulling them out. **Ball-peen hammers** are useful for shaping metal, but for basic woodworking tasks, a good **16-ounce claw hammer** is perfect.
    - **Comfort and Grip:** When choosing a hammer, make sure the handle is comfortable in your hand, and that the weight feels balanced. For beginners, it's often easier to work with a hammer that has a wooden or fiberglass handle, as these offer a good balance of weight and control.
    - **Use:** Hammers are typically used for **driving nails** into wood, **tapping joints into place**, and **light adjustment work** on parts during assembly.
4. **Files and Rasps:**
Files and rasps are used for shaping and smoothing rough edges of wood. These tools are particularly useful for refining joints and making sure edges are smooth and well-fitting.
    - **Rasp:** A **rasp** is a rougher version of a file and is used to remove material quickly. It's great for coarse shaping, particularly on end grain or where more material needs to be removed.
    - **File:** A **wood file** has finer teeth and is ideal for smoothing rough surfaces or edges after using a rasp. A **half-round file** is versatile and can handle both flat and curved edges, making it a great option for beginners.
5. **Screwdrivers and a Screwdriver Set:**
While you may not rely heavily on screws in the beginning, it's still important to have a reliable screwdriver or screwdriver set to assemble parts and hold pieces in place temporarily.
    - **Types of Screwdrivers:** You'll need a **flathead screwdriver** for basic screws, as well as a **Phillips-head screwdriver** for cross-slot screws. A **multi-bit screwdriver** can save you money and space by offering interchangeable bits.
    - **Considerations:** Look for screwdrivers with comfortable, ergonomic handles that won't tire your hands during use. A good screwdriver should also have a strong, durable shaft that won't bend under pressure.

Essential Measuring and Marking Tools

Accurate measurement and marking are the foundation of any successful woodworking project. Whether you're cutting, joining, or assembling, the precision of your measurements directly impacts the final result. In this section, we'll explore the essential measuring and marking tools you'll need to build a solid foundation for your woodworking toolkit.

1. Tape Measure:

A **tape measure** is one of the most essential measuring tools for woodworking. It's used to measure long distances and is an indispensable tool for accurately sizing wood pieces before cutting, joining, or assembling.

- **Length and Flexibility:** A good tape measure should be long enough for the size of your typical projects, usually ranging from **16 to 25 feet**. This allows you to measure larger pieces of wood without needing to reposition the tape multiple times.
- **Ease of Use:** The tape should be easy to extend and retract. Look for a **spring-loaded mechanism** that smoothly pulls the tape back into the casing. Additionally, choose a tape with a **bold, clear scale** for easier reading.
- **Accuracy:** The tape measure should be graduated in both **inches** and **millimeters**. Some tapes also feature **fractions of an inch** (such as 1/16" or 1/32"), which is useful for fine woodworking projects requiring greater accuracy.
- **Features to Look For:**
    - **Locking Mechanism:** A locking mechanism holds the tape in place while measuring, allowing you to work hands-free.
    - **Durability:** The casing should be sturdy, especially if you plan to use it on rough surfaces. Look for a **metal or reinforced plastic** case for longevity.
    - **Wide Blade:** A wider blade (about 1" or more) will be more rigid and easier to use for precise measurements.

Use: A tape measure is used for measuring both **long and short distances**. It's crucial for determining lengths when cutting wood or assembling larger projects like cabinets or tables.

2. Combination Square:

The **combination square** is one of the most versatile measuring tools in a woodworking shop. It combines a ruler with a **90-degree square** and a **45-degree angle**, making it perfect for measuring, marking, and checking angles.

- **Components:** The tool consists of a **ruler** (usually 6 or 12 inches), a **movable head** that can slide along the ruler, and a **spirit level** embedded in the head for checking levels.
- **Key Features:**

- **90-Degree Square:** Used for measuring and marking perfect right angles, especially for checking corner joints and framing.
- **45-Degree Angle:** Ideal for marking or cutting miters.
- **Measuring Ruler:** The ruler allows you to measure and mark measurements along a straight edge. The head of the combination square can be locked in place for repeat measurements, ensuring consistency.
- **Spirit Level:** The small level built into the tool allows you to check the horizontality or verticality of pieces, which is especially useful for ensuring square cuts or assembly.

Use: The combination square is ideal for **marking straight lines**, **measuring angles**, and **checking square cuts**. It's particularly useful for woodworking projects that require precise joinery, such as **cabinet making** and **framing**.

3. Marking Gauge:

The **marking gauge** is a simple tool used to mark accurate, parallel lines along the wood grain. It consists of a metal body with an adjustable fence and a pin or blade that scores the wood.

- **Types of Marking Gauges:**
    - **Single Pin Marking Gauge:** Has a single pin that scores the wood to mark a line.
    - **Double Pin Marking Gauge:** Includes two pins, which can be adjusted to set the distance between the lines, making it useful for more precise markings, such as those needed for **mortise and tenon** joints.
- **Key Features:**
    - **Adjustable Fence:** The fence helps guide the pin to make consistent marks at the same distance from the edge of the wood.
    - **Fine Adjustment:** For accurate marking, look for a gauge that allows fine adjustments so you can mark lines at specific widths or distances.
    - **Durable Construction:** A quality marking gauge should have a solid construction, typically metal or hardwood, and a sharp pin that makes clear, precise marks without damaging the wood surface.

Use: A marking gauge is used to mark **straight, parallel lines** along the edge of a board, essential for tasks like creating dado cuts, marking mortise depths, or setting up precise measurements for joinery.

4. Calipers:

Calipers are used to measure internal and external dimensions with high precision. While they are often associated with metalworking, calipers are also useful in woodworking when measuring small parts or checking the thickness of materials.

- **Types of Calipers:**

- - **Vernier Calipers:** These offer the highest level of precision and can measure to thousandths of an inch (0.001").
  - **Digital Calipers:** A digital version makes it easier to read measurements as they are displayed on a digital screen.
  - **Dial Calipers:** These have a dial that displays the measurement, providing quick readings.
- **Key Features:**
  - **Precision:** Calipers are ideal for tasks that require **extremely fine measurements**, such as checking the thickness of wood, the width of a joint, or ensuring components fit together accurately.
  - **Versatility:** Calipers can measure **inside and outside dimensions** as well as **depth**, making them versatile for various woodworking tasks.

Use: Use calipers for **fine measurements**, particularly when working on precise joinery or checking the thickness of wood in furniture making and cabinetry.

5. Carpenter's Pencil:

A **carpenter's pencil** is specifically designed for marking wood. It's broader than a standard pencil, with a flat body to prevent it from rolling off work surfaces.

- **Key Features:**
  - **Flat Shape:** The flat shape allows for a larger marking area, which is ideal for marking thick wood and ensures the pencil doesn't roll away.
  - **Hardness:** Carpenter's pencils are typically softer than regular pencils, making them easier to see on rough wood surfaces.
  - **Sharpness:** The wide tip can be sharpened to create both broad and fine lines, depending on your needs.

Use: Carpenter's pencils are best for marking **cut lines**, **drill points**, and other measurements. They're especially useful for marking wood that will be cut or shaped.

6. Chalk Line:

A **chalk line** is used to mark long, straight lines on wood or other materials. It consists of a string coated with chalk powder that, when snapped, creates a straight, visible line.

- **Key Features:**
  - **Easy to Use:** Simply stretch the string along the surface, pull it taut, and snap it to create a sharp line.
  - **High Visibility:** The chalk marks are visible from a distance and can be cleaned off easily after use.
  - **Length:** The string length varies, but a **100-foot** chalk line is ideal for marking long cuts or aligning multiple pieces of wood.

Use: Use a chalk line for marking **long, straight cuts** across large pieces of wood or for alignment during larger projects like paneling, framing, or installing shelves.

How to Properly Maintain and Sharpen Hand Tools

Proper maintenance and sharpening of hand tools are essential to ensure they stay in optimal condition, perform efficiently, and have a long lifespan. Well-maintained tools not only make woodworking easier but also enhance safety and precision.

1. Cleaning Your Hand Tools:

Before any sharpening or maintenance, it's important to clean your tools thoroughly. Dirt, rust, and sap can all impair the performance of hand tools and potentially damage them over time.

- **Cleaning Techniques:**
    - **Remove Dust and Debris:** Use a **soft brush** or **compressed air** to clear any dust, dirt, or wood chips from the tool's surface, particularly the working edges.
    - **Remove Sap:** If the tool has sap residue (common with woodworking tools), soak a cloth in **mineral spirits** or a similar solvent and gently rub the surface. For stubborn sap, use a **plastic scraper** to avoid damaging the finish.
    - **Rust Removal:** If you notice any signs of rust on your tools, clean them using a **wire brush** or **sandpaper**. For light rust, a **rust eraser** can work wonders. If the rust is heavier, use **steel wool** or **abrasive pads** to scrub it away.
    - **Oiling:** After cleaning, apply a thin coat of **mineral oil** or **tool oil** to prevent rust from reforming and to keep the tools in top condition.

Maintenance Tip: Always store tools in a dry, cool place and keep them clean to prevent rust and corrosion. Tools that are frequently exposed to moisture should be cleaned and oiled after each use.

2. Sharpening Hand Tools:

A sharp tool is a safer and more efficient tool. Whether it's a chisel, plane, or saw, the right sharpening method ensures clean cuts, reduces fatigue, and prevents excessive wear on the tool.

Chisels and Plane Blades:

- **Sharpening Stones (Whetstones):** The most common method for sharpening chisels and plane blades is using a **whetstone** or **sharpening stone**. There are different types of stones:
    - **Coarse Stone (220-400 grit):** Used to remove large amounts of metal and restore a dull edge.
    - **Medium Stone (800-1000 grit):** Used for refining the edge and removing any roughness after using a coarse stone.
    - **Fine Stone (3000-8000 grit):** Used for polishing the edge to a razor-sharp finish.
    - **Process:**

1. **Soak the Stone:** If you're using a water stone, soak it in water for 10-15 minutes before use. Oil stones should be oiled as needed.
2. **Angle the Blade:** Hold the blade at an angle of approximately **25-30 degrees** to the surface of the stone for the bevel. A consistent angle is key to achieving a sharp edge.
3. **Use Long Strokes:** Move the blade in long, smooth strokes across the stone, alternating sides to maintain an even edge.
4. **Polish the Edge:** After sharpening with the coarse and medium stones, switch to a finer stone to polish the edge and remove any burrs (the tiny wire edge that forms on the opposite side of the blade).

- **Stropping:** After sharpening, **stropping** the blade on a leather or fabric strop (with or without polishing compound) removes any remaining burrs and gives the edge a final polish.

Tip: Sharpen blades regularly, especially after heavy use. A slight touch-up every few uses can save you from having to regrind a completely dull blade.

Saws (Handsaws and Panel Saws):

Saw blades also need to be sharpened, but their sharpening process differs slightly from chisels and plane blades.

- **Sharpening Method:**
  - **File:** Use a **saw file** (round or flat) to sharpen the teeth of the saw. Start by placing the saw on a **stable surface** or workbench, and make sure the teeth are facing upward.
  - **Proper Filing Angle:** Hold the file at the **correct angle** (usually around **60-70 degrees** to the surface) and move the file in one direction across the teeth. Ensure the file contacts the entire face of each tooth.
  - **Teeth Set:** Check the **set of the teeth** (the slight bend outward of the teeth on either side of the blade). If the set is uneven, use a **set tool** to adjust the teeth back to their proper position. This ensures smooth cutting action.
- **Steps for Sharpening:**

1. **File the Teeth:** Sharpen the teeth of the saw by filing in one direction only (usually toward the handle). Apply consistent pressure, but not too much force.
2. **Check the Tooth Shape:** Saw teeth come in different shapes (e.g., **pointed**, **raker**, or **crosscut** teeth). Make sure you match the correct file size and shape for your saw's tooth configuration.
3. **Check the Set:** After sharpening, test the saw's cut and adjust the set if needed for smooth cutting performance.

Tip: Hand saws should be sharpened more frequently than power saws, as they tend to dull faster. Make it a habit to check the sharpness of your saw blades regularly.

Screwdrivers and Other Edged Tools:

Although not as commonly sharpened as chisels and saws, **screwdrivers** and other hand tools that have edges (such as carving tools or knives) can also benefit from periodic sharpening.

- **Sharpening Method:**
  - **Honing the Edge:** Use a **fine sharpening stone** or a **diamond sharpening plate** to hone the edges of these tools, ensuring that the blades are smooth and free from nicks.
  - **File for Repairing Nicks:** If the edge has visible nicks or imperfections, use a **fine file** to smooth out the damaged area before honing.

3. Maintaining Wooden Handles:

Wooden-handled tools, such as hammers, chisels, and mallets, require attention to ensure they stay functional and safe.

- **Cleaning and Oiling:** Regularly clean the wooden handles with a soft cloth and wood cleaner. After cleaning, apply **linseed oil** or **mineral oil** to the handle to nourish the wood and prevent cracking or splintering.
- **Tightening Loose Handles:** Over time, handles can become loose. Check the tool for any movement, and if needed, tap the handle back into place or tighten the fastener. You can also re-seat the handle by soaking it in water for a few hours to expand the wood, which can help eliminate any looseness.

Tip: Always store wooden-handled tools in a dry, climate-controlled environment to avoid moisture damage or warping of the handles.

4. Storing Your Tools:

Proper storage extends the life of your hand tools. Here are some tips for keeping them in good condition:

- **Dry, Climate-Controlled Storage:** Store tools in a **dry** and **well-ventilated area** to prevent rusting and damage from excess moisture.
- **Tool Racks or Cabinets:** Keep tools organized on **wall-mounted racks** or in **tool chests** to prevent them from being knocked around or damaged.
- **Covering Tools:** For extra protection, cover tools with a cloth or **protective sheath** to shield them from dust and moisture.

2.2 Power Tools

Basic Power Tools: Drills, Sanders, and Circular Saws

Power tools are essential for speeding up projects, ensuring consistent results, and enabling more precise cuts and finishes. As a beginner woodworker, understanding the basic power tools – including **drills**, **sanders**, and **circular saws** – is key to efficiently tackling a variety of woodworking tasks. These tools help you work faster, with less effort, and with greater accuracy compared to their hand tool counterparts.

1. Drills:

A **drill** is one of the most versatile and essential power tools for any woodworking project. Drills are used for drilling holes and driving screws, making them crucial for everything from assembling furniture to creating precise dowel holes for joinery.

- **Key Features of a Drill:**
    - **Chuck Size:** The chuck is the part of the drill that holds the drill bit. Drills come with various chuck sizes, typically 3/8-inch or 1/2-inch. For most woodworking tasks, a **3/8-inch chuck** is sufficient, but larger chucks may be necessary for heavy-duty tasks.
    - **Variable Speed:** Many drills offer a **variable speed trigger**, allowing you to adjust the speed for different tasks, from slow drilling to high-speed driving.
    - **Cordless vs. Corded:** Cordless drills are more portable, powered by rechargeable batteries, while corded drills provide continuous power but require an electrical outlet. Cordless drills are often preferred for their convenience and mobility.
- **How to Use a Drill:**

1. **Choosing the Right Bit:** Select a drill bit that suits the material you're working with (wood, metal, plastic) and the size of the hole you need.
2. **Drilling Holes:** Secure your workpiece in place using a **clamp** or **vice**. Begin drilling at a low speed to create a pilot hole, then increase the speed for the final cut. Make sure to keep the drill perpendicular to the surface.
3. **Driving Screws:** Install a **screwdriver bit** into the chuck. Adjust the drill's torque settings to avoid overdriving screws and damaging the material. Use the drill to drive screws into pre-drilled holes for quick and accurate assembly.

- **Tips for Drilling:**
    - Always **drill pilot holes** for screws to avoid splitting wood.
    - **Lubricate drill bits** with wax to reduce friction and prevent overheating when drilling long or deep holes.
    - Use a **drill press** for highly precise, vertical drilling.

2. Sanders:

A **sander** is used for smoothing surfaces, removing material, and finishing wood projects. There are several types of sanders, but the most common for beginners are **orbital sanders**, **belt sanders**, and **detail sanders**.

- **Key Features of Sanders:**
    - **Orbital Sanders:** These are the most common and versatile sanders. They use a circular pad that moves in small orbital motions to produce a smooth finish. Orbital sanders are great for light to medium sanding tasks.

- o **Belt Sanders:** These sanders use a continuous belt of sandpaper and are ideal for heavy-duty sanding tasks, such as removing large amounts of material or smoothing rough surfaces.
- o **Detail Sanders:** Smaller and more maneuverable, detail sanders are designed to handle intricate sanding jobs, such as corners, edges, and tight spots.
- **How to Use a Sander:**

1. **Select the Right Sandpaper:** Choose sandpaper with the appropriate grit. Coarse grit (e.g., 40 to 80) is used for heavy material removal, while finer grits (e.g., 120 to 220) are used for finishing and smoothing.
2. **Sanding Technique:** Always move the sander in the direction of the grain to avoid scratching the surface. For orbital sanders, apply light, even pressure while sanding to avoid gouging the wood. With a belt sander, let the tool's weight do most of the work.
3. **Safety:** Wear a **dust mask** and **safety glasses** when sanding to protect your lungs and eyes from fine dust particles.

- **Tips for Sanding:**
  - o **Start with coarse grit** and gradually work your way to finer grits for a smooth finish.
  - o Make sure to **sand evenly** to avoid creating dips or flat spots.
  - o Always **clean the dust collection bag** or port regularly to maintain suction and reduce clogging.

3. Circular Saws:

A **circular saw** is one of the most powerful and versatile cutting tools in a woodworker's arsenal. It's primarily used for cutting straight lines through various materials, including plywood, MDF, and hardwoods. Circular saws come in both corded and cordless versions, and they are ideal for making long, accurate cuts with ease.

- **Key Features of Circular Saws:**
  - o **Blade Size:** The most common blade sizes for circular saws are **7 1/4 inches**, but you can also find blades as large as **10 inches** for cutting thicker materials. A smaller blade size is easier to maneuver but may be less powerful for tough cuts.
  - o **Depth Adjustment:** Circular saws allow you to adjust the **cutting depth** based on the thickness of the material. This feature helps when making cuts through different thicknesses of wood or other materials.
  - o **Bevel Adjustment:** Many circular saws allow for **bevel cuts** (angled cuts) by adjusting the base plate of the saw. This is useful for cutting angles, such as when creating joints for furniture or making trim pieces.
- **How to Use a Circular Saw:**

1. **Measure and Mark:** Before cutting, measure and mark your cut line carefully, using a **square** to ensure accuracy.
2. **Adjust the Blade Depth:** Set the blade depth just slightly deeper than the thickness of the material to avoid overcutting and causing unnecessary wear on the blade.
3. **Make the Cut:** Stand in a stable position, and guide the saw along the marked line, keeping the saw body and blade square with the material. Always move in a controlled, steady motion.
4. **Safety:** Always use both hands to grip the saw, wear **ear protection** for loud noise, and ensure the blade is free of debris before cutting.
    - **Tips for Using a Circular Saw:**
        - Use a **straight edge guide** or **clamp** a board to your workpiece to help guide the saw and ensure a straight cut.
        - Keep the blade sharp and well-maintained to avoid burn marks or jagged edges.
        - Consider using a **plunge-cut saw** for more advanced cuts, such as making cuts in the middle of a sheet of plywood.

4. **General Power Tool Safety:**
    - **Personal Protective Equipment (PPE):** Always wear appropriate safety gear, including **safety glasses, ear protection, dust masks**, and **work gloves** when using power tools.
    - **Tool Maintenance:** Keep your power tools clean and well-maintained. Regularly check for any damage or wear, such as frayed power cords or dull blades, and replace them as needed.
    - **Secure Workpieces:** Always ensure that your workpieces are secured properly with clamps or a vice before using power tools to avoid accidents.
    - **Know Your Tool:** Read the instruction manual for each power tool and understand how it operates before using it. Familiarize yourself with the different settings and functions to ensure proper and safe usage.

Choosing Cost-Effective Tools for Efficiency

When you're just starting out in woodworking, it's important to strike a balance between quality and affordability. Choosing cost-effective tools that still provide good performance is key to making your projects successful without breaking your budget.

1. Prioritize Essential Tools

For a beginner, it's easy to get excited about all the tools available, but it's essential to focus on the basics that are necessary to get started. The tools you choose should enable you to handle a variety of tasks while being versatile enough to be used for different types of projects.

- **Start with Must-Have Tools:**

- **Hand tools:** Chisels, hammers, mallets, clamps, and measuring tools are essential for most basic woodworking projects. These tools will allow you to build furniture, boxes, frames, and other simple projects.
- **Power tools:** A basic set of **drills**, **orbital sanders**, and a **circular saw** can cover a wide range of tasks from cutting, sanding, to assembly.

Investing in these must-have tools first ensures you have everything you need to start your woodworking journey without overspending on unnecessary gadgets.

2. Look for Tool Sets or Bundles

One of the most cost-effective ways to buy tools is by purchasing tool sets or bundles. Many manufacturers offer sets of tools, such as **drill/driver combos**, or **sander kits** that include all the essential attachments and accessories. These sets often come at a lower cost than buying each tool separately and provide everything you need to get started in one convenient package.

- **Toolkits for Beginners:** Look for starter kits designed for new woodworkers that offer a combination of hand tools and power tools. These kits often include a **drill**, **driver**, and a **circular saw** at a much lower price than buying them individually.
- **Versatility:** Bundled tools often provide multiple attachments or features, allowing you to use one tool for a variety of tasks. For instance, a drill/driver combo may include various drill bits and screw attachments, making it more versatile.

3. Consider Used or Refurbished Tools

Buying **used** or **refurbished tools** can significantly reduce your costs while still providing the quality you need. Many people sell their tools after only light use, so you can often find great deals on well-maintained equipment.

- **Used Tools:** Check local classified ads, pawn shops, online marketplaces, or tool auctions for used tools in good condition. Inspect the tools carefully before purchasing to ensure they are still functional and have no major defects.
- **Refurbished Tools:** Many manufacturers offer **refurbished** tools that have been repaired and tested to meet the original specifications. These tools often come with warranties, so you can feel confident in your purchase.

4. Choose Tools from Reliable, Affordable Brands

Some well-established brands offer tools that are reliable and affordable without compromising quality. While premium tools are tempting, it's often unnecessary for a beginner to invest in high-end models right away. Instead, focus on brands known for good performance at a reasonable price.

- **Good Value Brands:** Companies like **Makita**, **DeWalt**, **Ryobi**, and **Craftsman** are known for producing durable, reliable tools at competitive prices. These brands often offer a good balance of quality and cost-effectiveness, making them a great choice for beginners.

- **Research User Reviews:** Before making a purchase, check out online reviews and woodworking forums to see how other woodworkers rate these tools. Reviews will give you an idea of the tool's performance and durability at a specific price point.

5. Buy Quality Over Quantity

While it may be tempting to purchase a large number of tools all at once, focus on getting a few high-quality, versatile tools that you will use regularly rather than buying a bunch of tools that will just gather dust. **Quality over quantity** is the key to making smart investments.

- **Build Your Collection Gradually:** Start with the basic tools you need for your current projects and expand your collection as your skills progress. Instead of buying everything at once, save up for higher-end tools that will last longer and provide better performance.
- **Tools that Last:** Opt for tools that are well-constructed, even if they're a bit more expensive. These tools may cost more upfront but will save you money in the long run by lasting longer and reducing the need for frequent replacements.

6. Consider Multi-Use Tools

Another way to save money is by choosing **multi-use tools** that can serve more than one purpose. This reduces the need to buy separate tools for each task.

- **Cordless Drills with Attachments:** Many cordless drills come with interchangeable heads that can be used for different applications such as drilling, driving screws, or even sanding (with attachments). This can help reduce the need for separate tools like a sander or screwdriver.
- **Oscillating Multi-Tools:** These versatile tools can handle multiple jobs, including sanding, cutting, scraping, and polishing. While the initial investment may be higher than a single-purpose tool, it's often more cost-effective in the long run.

2.3 Machine Tools

Introduction to Machines (e.g., Planers, Jointers, Bandsaws) for Those Ready to Invest

As you progress in woodworking, the need for more advanced tools becomes apparent. While hand tools and basic power tools are essential for any beginner, machine tools offer increased precision, efficiency, and capability. These machines are designed for larger projects or tasks that require high accuracy and repeatability, enabling you to work faster and with better results.

In this section, we'll introduce some of the key **machine tools** that you can consider once you're ready to invest in more specialized equipment. These tools—**planers**, **jointers**, and **bandsaws**—are commonly used by woodworkers to achieve professional-level results. We'll discuss the benefits of each tool, how they can enhance your woodworking projects, and how to choose the right one for your needs.

1. Planers: Smoothing and Thicknessing Lumber

A **planer** (also called a thickness planer) is a machine used to smooth and level wood surfaces. It is particularly useful for dimensioning rough lumber and making sure that all pieces of wood in your project are of consistent thickness. If you purchase rough-cut lumber, planing is essential to prepare the wood for further use.

- **Functionality:** A planer shaves off thin layers of wood to ensure even thickness and smooth surfaces. It's ideal for turning rough, uneven lumber into material that's ready for joinery, finishing, and assembly.
- **Benefits:**
    - **Consistent Thickness:** Planers help you achieve uniform thickness across multiple pieces of wood, which is essential for creating a consistent, professional-looking project.
    - **Time Savings:** Instead of manually planing wood by hand, a planer significantly speeds up the process, especially when dealing with larger quantities of lumber.
    - **Surface Smoothing:** In addition to thicknessing, a planer can also improve the surface texture of the wood, which reduces sanding time later.
- **When to Invest:** If you're working with a lot of rough lumber or want to consistently produce smooth, evenly-sized wood pieces, investing in a planer will save you time and ensure a high-quality finish.

2. Jointers: Flattening and Edge-Squaring Wood

A **jointer** is a woodworking machine used to flatten one face of a board and square the edges. It's particularly useful when you're working with rough lumber and need to make one side flat and one edge straight to prepare for further processing.

- **Functionality:** The jointer works by passing wood across a set of rotating blades, which remove high spots and flatten the surface. The result is a smooth, straight edge and a flat surface on the opposite side, ready for jointing, gluing, or planing.
- **Benefits:**
    - **Precise Edges:** Jointers are essential for preparing the edges of wood for glue-ups, ensuring that the boards align perfectly when joined together.
    - **Surface Flatness:** They also flatten the surface of rough-sawn boards, making it easier to plane and finish the wood evenly.
    - **Accuracy:** A jointer ensures that both edges of a board are square, which is critical for precise joinery (e.g., edge jointing and making cabinets).
- **When to Invest:** If you frequently work with rough lumber and need accurate, flat surfaces for projects like furniture or cabinetry, a jointer is an essential investment. For smaller-scale projects, however, you might be able to get by with a hand plane or even a planer in some cases.

3. Bandsaws: Versatile Cutting for Curves and Resawing

A **bandsaw** is a powerful machine that utilizes a continuous loop of a toothed band (saw blade) to make straight or curved cuts. Bandsaws are incredibly versatile and can be used for cutting irregular shapes, curves, and even for resawing thick pieces of wood into thinner slices.

- **Functionality:** The bandsaw can handle a wide variety of cuts, including **straight cuts**, **curves**, and **resawing** (splitting thick boards into thinner planks). The blade is continuously driven by wheels, providing a smoother cut with less friction compared to other saws.
- **Benefits:**
    - **Curved Cuts:** Bandsaws excel at cutting curves, making them ideal for tasks like cutting out intricate designs for furniture or decorative items.
    - **Resawing:** They are excellent for resawing, which means cutting a piece of wood into thinner boards. This is useful for creating veneer or thin panels from thicker stock.
    - **Fine Cutting:** The continuous saw blade allows for finer, more controlled cuts with less effort, especially when cutting irregular shapes.
- **When to Invest:** If your woodworking involves intricate, curved cuts, or if you want to resaw larger boards into thinner stock, a bandsaw can be a great investment. It's also ideal for cutting irregular shapes and making precise cuts without wasting material.

Choosing the Right Machine Tool for Your Shop

When it comes to selecting the right **machine tools** for your woodworking shop, the key is to consider the types of projects you plan to tackle. Here's a quick guide to help you make the best choice:

- **Planers:** If you frequently work with rough lumber and need to dimension it to a consistent thickness, a planer is a worthwhile investment. It will save you considerable time and effort.
- **Jointers:** If your work involves a lot of edge jointing or needs perfectly flat surfaces for assembly, a jointer will be an essential tool for achieving high-quality results.
- **Bandsaws:** If you plan to do a lot of curve cutting, resawing, or intricate pattern work, a bandsaw is incredibly valuable and will offer unmatched versatility for such tasks.

For many woodworkers, having a combination of these three machines allows for a broader range of capabilities. However, for a **beginner** or those just starting to invest in larger tools, it's important to weigh the space, cost, and frequency of use for each machine. If you are limited in budget or space, consider purchasing one machine at a time as your needs evolve.

Safety Tips and Maintenance Basics

Working with machine tools can vastly improve your woodworking capabilities, but it also comes with a responsibility to ensure safety and longevity of your equipment. Machine tools like **planers**, **jointers**, and **bandsaws** are powerful and can be hazardous if used improperly.

---

1. Safety Tips for Using Machine Tools

General Machine Safety

- **Read the Manual:** Before using any machine, always read and understand the manufacturer's manual. This ensures you're aware of the machine's specific features, limitations, and safety guidelines.
- **Wear Safety Gear:** Always wear **safety glasses**, **ear protection**, and **dust masks** when operating any machine. Woodworking machines can produce flying debris, loud noise, and fine dust, all of which pose risks to your eyes, ears, and respiratory system.
- **Proper Clothing:** Avoid wearing loose-fitting clothing, jewelry, or anything that could get caught in the machine. Wear close-fitting clothing and tie back long hair to reduce the risk of entanglement in moving parts.
- **Keep the Work Area Clean:** A clean workspace is essential for safe operation. Make sure the area around your machines is free of clutter, dust, and debris that could cause accidents or interfere with the machine's operation.
- **Use the Right Tool for the Job:** Always use the correct tool for the task at hand. For example, don't attempt to cut curves with a planer or flatten boards with a bandsaw. Using the right machine for the task increases accuracy and safety.
- **Keep Hands at a Safe Distance:** Never place your hands or fingers too close to moving parts, such as the rotating blades of a bandsaw or the cutter head on a planer. Always use push sticks, clamps, or other tools to guide the wood.
- **Turn Off Power When Adjusting or Changing Blades:** Before making any adjustments or changing blades, make sure the machine is turned off and the power is completely disconnected. This prevents accidental starts that could cause injury.

Specific Safety Tips for Common Machines

- **Planer:**
  - Ensure the cutter head is properly shielded to avoid injury.
  - Use push blocks or sticks to feed wood through the planer, keeping hands clear of the moving rollers and blades.

- - Make sure the wood is straight and free of nails or screws before planing to avoid damaging the tool and creating dangerous flying debris.
- **Jointer:**
  - Always face the wood downwards when feeding it into the jointer to avoid the possibility of it lifting off the table.
  - Use push pads to ensure even pressure when passing wood through the machine.
  - Keep your hands at least six inches away from the cutting area to prevent injury.
- **Bandsaw:**
  - Set the blade guard so that it just clears the wood. This ensures that the blade is properly protected and reduces the risk of accidental contact.
  - Never try to remove cut-off pieces of wood while the saw is still running—wait for the machine to stop completely.
  - When cutting curves, feed the wood slowly to avoid the blade from binding or twisting.

---

2. Basic Machine Tool Maintenance

Proper maintenance ensures your tools perform at their best, stay safe, and last longer. Here are some basic **maintenance** steps for each of the major machine tools you'll encounter in woodworking.

Planer Maintenance

- **Cleaning the Dust and Debris:** After each use, clean the planer to remove sawdust and debris from the machine. Use a soft brush or compressed air to clear out the dust collection system and any vents to ensure smooth operation.
- **Blade Maintenance:** Keep an eye on the sharpness of the planer blades. Dull blades can cause uneven cuts and excessive strain on the machine. Sharpen or replace the blades as needed. Regularly inspect the blades for any signs of wear or damage.
- **Lubrication:** Periodically lubricate the moving parts, such as the feed rollers, to ensure smooth operation. Check the manual for the type of lubricant recommended for your machine.
- **Check Alignment:** Regularly check the alignment of the bed and the cutter head. Misalignment can lead to uneven cutting and inaccurate results.

Jointer Maintenance

- **Cleaning and Dusting:** Just like the planer, it's important to keep the jointer free of sawdust and debris. Dust buildup can impair its performance and lead to overheating. Use a vacuum or air compressor to remove dust from the machine.
- **Blade Sharpening:** The knives on a jointer can become dull with extended use. Sharpen them regularly to maintain smooth cuts. Dull blades increase the risk of splintering the wood and can cause more wear on the machine.

- **Table Maintenance:** Periodically check the jointer's table for flatness and smoothness. A warped or damaged table can affect the machine's ability to produce accurate cuts. Use a straight edge to check for any issues.
- **Lubrication:** Keep the table and fence parts lubricated to ensure smooth adjustments and prevent rust. A light coat of oil will help maintain the sliding mechanism.

Bandsaw Maintenance

- **Blade Tension and Tracking:** Regularly check the tension of the bandsaw blade and adjust it according to the manufacturer's instructions. Proper tension ensures smooth and precise cuts. Also, make sure the blade is tracking properly, meaning it runs straight and true along the wheels.
- **Blade Cleaning:** Clean the blade to prevent pitch buildup, which can cause the saw to bind or create excess friction. Use a blade-cleaning brush or a special blade cleaner to remove buildup.
- **Wheel Maintenance:** The bandsaw wheels should be kept clean and free of dust and resin. Over time, resin can accumulate and throw off the balance, leading to poor performance and premature wear.
- **Lubricate Bearings and Guides:** The blade guides and bearings should be lubricated to ensure smooth operation. This will reduce friction and wear on the moving parts.

Chapter 3: Project Design Essentials

3.1 Project Ideation and Conceptualization

Generating Ideas and Planning Out Your Project

The success of any woodworking project starts long before you pick up your tools. The **design phase** is crucial for determining what you want to create, how you will bring your vision to life, and what materials and tools you'll need to achieve it. This is the phase where you'll turn your initial ideas into something tangible, all while ensuring that the final piece aligns with your objectives, skills, and available resources.

The first step in any woodworking project is generating ideas that match your skills, space, and needs. Planning out your project thoughtfully is key to turning a vague concept into a reality.

1. Brainstorming Ideas

Before you begin your project, take some time to brainstorm. Look for inspiration in your home, the outdoors, or even in other woodworking projects. Ask yourself the following questions:

- **What do I need?** Think about practical needs. Do you need a new coffee table, bookshelf, or storage unit? Start with a functional idea that solves a problem or adds value to your space.
- **What am I passionate about?** If you are building something for enjoyment or personal satisfaction, consider projects that excite you. Whether it's a carving project, an intricate piece of furniture, or a decorative item, following your passion can make the process more enjoyable.
- **What skills do I have?** Match your project to your skill level. If you are a beginner, start small with simpler projects like shelves or picture frames. For advanced woodworkers, more complex pieces like furniture or intricate cabinetry might be the goal.

2. Sketching Your Idea

Once you have a clear idea in mind, sketch out your vision. You don't need to be a professional artist, but a simple drawing can help visualize the project and guide you in the next steps. This sketch can be as rough or detailed as you like, but it should outline the basic dimensions, features, and design elements. Consider:

- **Dimensions**: Measure the space where the project will go or the available wood you'll be using. Create a basic outline of the project to get a feel for its size.
- **Components**: Break the design into individual parts—such as legs, panels, or shelves—and think about how these pieces will fit together.
- **Materials**: Include any materials you'll need (e.g., hardwood, plywood, screws, hinges) and any tools that will be required to bring the idea to life.

3. Planning the Process

Once you've visualized your project, it's time to plan the work sequence. Consider the following:

- **Step-by-step timeline**: Break the project into manageable tasks. For example, if building a bookshelf, tasks might include measuring and cutting, assembling the frame, adding shelves, sanding, and finishing.
- **Tools and materials list**: Make a list of all the tools you'll need, from basic hand tools to power tools, and any materials like wood, screws, or finishing products.
- **Budget and time frame**: Estimate how long the project will take and how much it will cost. Be realistic about your budget, considering the cost of wood, tools, and finishing products.

By taking the time to plan your project, you'll have a clear roadmap that can help guide you through the process and avoid surprises along the way.

Choosing Design Styles: Traditional, Modern, Rustic, etc.

The style you choose for your project will influence not only the materials you use but also the methods and techniques you apply. Different design styles offer distinct aesthetics and functionalities, so it's important to select one that resonates with you and complements your space.

1. Traditional Design Style

The **traditional style** is often characterized by **classic details**, **symmetry**, and **elegance**. If you're aiming for a piece that feels timeless and refined, this style is a great choice. Traditional woodworking often involves ornate details, such as turned legs, dovetail joints, and decorative carvings. You'll also often find **rich wood finishes** like cherry, oak, or walnut in traditional designs.

- **Common Projects**: Coffee tables, cabinets, dressers, chairs.
- **Features**: Symmetrical shapes, ornate carving, dark wood finishes, brass hardware.
- **Techniques**: Mortise-and-tenon joints, dovetail joinery, hand carving, veneering.

2. Modern Design Style

Modern design is sleek, clean, and functional. It emphasizes **minimalism** and **geometric shapes** with a focus on simplicity and open spaces. Modern woodworking often uses **lighter woods**, such as maple, birch, or even plywood, with natural finishes or clear coats to highlight the grain. The goal is usually to create a piece that looks stylish but remains functional.

- **Common Projects**: End tables, desks, shelving units, media stands.
- **Features**: Clean lines, simple forms, smooth surfaces, minimalist details.
- **Techniques**: Butt joints, pocket-hole joinery, plywood construction, lacquer or matte finishes.

3. Rustic Design Style

Rustic woodworking emphasizes the **natural beauty** of the wood, often with a rough, unfinished look. The design is warm, cozy, and inviting, with imperfections embraced as part of the charm. Rustic pieces often use reclaimed wood, which brings a sense of history and character to each project. Expect visible wood grain, distressing, and unique textures in rustic furniture.

- **Common Projects**: Dining tables, benches, outdoor furniture, shelves.
- **Features**: Exposed wood grain, knots, weathered finishes, rough edges, sturdy construction.
- **Techniques**: Rough cutting, distressed finishes, simple joinery, and natural wood stains.

4. Industrial Design Style

Industrial design blends **raw materials** like metal and wood for a **contemporary yet rugged** aesthetic. It originated from the use of factory and warehouse materials and has grown to be very popular in urban and loft-style interiors. Industrial pieces often combine the warmth of wood with the coldness of metal, concrete, or glass.

- **Common Projects**: Loft furniture, shelving, stools, and desks.
- **Features**: Exposed metal, unfinished wood, neutral tones, open shelving.
- **Techniques**: Combination of wood and metal working, screw fastening, welding, and rustic finishes.

5. Shabby Chic and Cottage Style

This style incorporates a **soft, worn look** that evokes a sense of nostalgia and comfort. Shabby chic often uses **light, pastel colors** and weathered wood finishes to create a relaxed, vintage aesthetic. Furniture is often distressed or painted for a worn, timeworn look, perfect for a cozy, welcoming atmosphere.

- **Common Projects**: Side tables, chairs, cabinets, photo frames.
- **Features**: Soft colors, distressing, floral patterns, vintage hardware.
- **Techniques**: Distressed painting, sanding for a worn look, light staining.

Choosing Hardware: Hinges, Handles, Screws, and Brackets

electing the right hardware for your woodworking project is essential for both functionality and aesthetic appeal. The **hardware**—including **hinges**, **handles**, **screws**, and **brackets**—can influence how well the project performs, how durable it is, and how it looks once completed. Here's a breakdown of how to approach choosing the right hardware for various woodworking projects.

Hinges

Hinges are one of the most commonly used hardware items in woodworking, especially in projects like cabinets, doors, and boxes. The choice of hinge depends on several factors:

- **Type of Hinge**:
  - **Butt Hinges**: These are the most common type, used for doors and cabinets. They are typically hidden when the door is closed, offering a clean and traditional look.
  - **European Hinges**: These are popular for modern cabinets and are also known as concealed hinges. They offer a sleek appearance, and when installed, they remain hidden when the door is closed, making them a favorite for contemporary designs.

- o **Piano Hinges**: These long, continuous hinges are used for large doors or lids, such as in chests or storage boxes. They provide extra support and durability.
- o **Strap Hinges**: Commonly used for rustic or outdoor projects, these hinges are more decorative and often used for gates or barn doors.
- **Material**:
  - o **Steel**: Most commonly used and durable for general-purpose hinges.
  - o **Brass**: Offers a classic look and is often used for fine furniture and high-end cabinetry.
  - o **Stainless Steel**: Best for outdoor projects or environments where corrosion might be a concern (e.g., sheds, garden gates).
  - o **Bronze and Copper**: Often used in decorative applications, offering a rustic, vintage look.
- **Size and Weight**: When choosing a hinge, it is important to consider the weight and size of the door or lid that the hinge will support. Larger or heavier doors require larger, stronger hinges to ensure durability and proper function.

Handles and Pulls

Handles and pulls are essential not only for the functionality of cabinets, drawers, and doors but also for adding aesthetic appeal to your projects.

- **Types of Handles and Pulls**:
  - o **Knobs**: Typically used for smaller drawers or doors. They are available in various styles, from modern minimalist to ornate antique designs.
  - o **Pull Handles**: These are used for larger cabinets or drawers and offer a firm grip. Pull handles are available in many styles, such as bar pulls, arch pulls, and cup pulls, each providing a different look depending on the overall design.
  - o **T-Bar and L-Bar Pulls**: Popular in modern or industrial designs, these handles provide a sleek and minimal look.
- **Material and Finish**:
  - o **Brass**: Classic, warm, and elegant, brass pulls work well for traditional, antique, or country-style furniture.
  - o **Nickel or Stainless Steel**: These finishes give a sleek and modern appearance, ideal for contemporary designs.
  - o **Wooden Pulls**: Wood handles or pulls can blend seamlessly with wooden cabinetry, especially if you're aiming for a rustic or handmade aesthetic.
  - o **Antique Finishes**: Often chosen for vintage or farmhouse-style furniture, antique finishes, like aged bronze or oil-rubbed bronze, can give a timeless look to your project.

Screws

The choice of screws is a fundamental aspect of any woodworking project, as they provide the structural integrity of joints, fastenings, and assemblies. The wrong screws can weaken the wood or cause damage, so it's important to choose them carefully.

- **Types of Screws:**
    - **Wood Screws**: These screws are designed for use in wood and have threads that allow them to hold securely in the material. They often have a pointed tip to make them easier to drive into the wood.
    - **Deck Screws**: Used in outdoor projects, such as furniture for patios or decking, these screws are made of corrosion-resistant materials like stainless steel or coated steel.
    - **Drywall Screws**: Primarily used for attaching drywall to studs but can be useful in some wood applications, particularly for light framing or temporary projects.
- **Materials and Coatings**:
    - **Steel**: Standard screws made from steel are great for most indoor woodworking applications. They are relatively inexpensive and readily available.
    - **Stainless Steel**: For outdoor or high-moisture environments, stainless steel screws are essential as they are resistant to rust and corrosion.
    - **Brass**: Brass screws are often used for decorative purposes, especially in fine woodworking or antique restoration. They are softer than steel, which can sometimes be a drawback for strength.
    - **Coated Screws**: Some screws come with a protective coating (like zinc or ceramic) to prevent rust and improve their longevity, making them ideal for environments with high humidity or outdoor settings.
- **Size and Length**: It's essential to choose screws that are the correct size and length for your project. Too long a screw can split the wood, while a screw that's too short may not provide enough holding power. Always ensure that the screw length is appropriate for the material thickness and depth of the hole.

Brackets and Latches

Brackets and latches are commonly used for reinforcing structures or providing secure closures. Their selection depends largely on the type of project you're working on.

- **Types of Brackets:**
    - **Corner Brackets**: Used for reinforcing corners or joints in frames, cabinets, and furniture. These are often L-shaped and come in varying sizes.

- **Shelf Brackets**: These are used to support shelves and come in decorative and heavy-duty styles. A well-chosen shelf bracket can both reinforce the shelf and contribute to the overall design.
  - **Angle Brackets**: Similar to corner brackets, but typically used for reinforcing angles between larger pieces or structural components.
- **Latches**:
  - **Hasp and Staple**: These are commonly used on chests, gates, and cabinets, providing a secure but easily accessible closure.
  - **Slam Latches**: Often used in cabinets and doors where a more secure, self-locking latch mechanism is necessary.
  - **Spring Latches**: These are used when a fast, automatic closure is needed, often in applications where ease of use is a priority.
- **Materials**: Brackets and latches are commonly made from **steel**, **brass**, or **stainless steel** for durability. For heavy-duty applications, **galvanized steel** or **cast iron** may be necessary to ensure strength.

Choosing the Right Hardware for Your Project

- **Functionality**: Always choose hardware based on the primary function it will serve. For example, if you're building a large cabinet with heavy doors, make sure to choose strong, durable hinges and handles. A smaller drawer may only require lightweight screws or smaller handles.
- **Aesthetic Considerations**: Choose hardware that complements the style of your project. Modern projects tend to work well with sleek, minimalist hardware like brushed nickel or simple T-bar pulls. Traditional or rustic pieces might be better suited to antique-style brass handles or hand-forged hinges.
- **Quality**: Good quality hardware may cost more, but it's worth the investment. High-quality hinges, screws, and brackets will last longer and function better, ensuring the durability of your project.
- **Project Budget**: Consider your overall budget when selecting hardware. You don't have to purchase the most expensive options, but ensure the hardware you select is appropriate for the materials used and the weight/size of the project.

3.2 Creating Sketches and Plans

Translating Ideas into Sketches

The process of transforming your ideas into a tangible woodworking project begins with **sketching** and **planning**. This step is crucial because it helps you visualize your design, determine the materials and tools you will need, and anticipate any challenges before you begin the physical work. By **translating your ideas into sketches**, you lay a solid foundation for your project, ensuring you stay on track and avoid unnecessary errors.

1. The Importance of Sketching in Woodworking

Creating a sketch allows you to take your **mental concept** and bring it to life visually. It acts as a **blueprint** for your project, guiding you in terms of **dimensions**, **materials**, and **construction techniques**. Even for simpler projects, having a clear, visual representation can save time and help you avoid mistakes that could result from jumping straight into construction.

Sketching is the starting point for any project, whether it's a small DIY item like a bookshelf or a larger, more complex piece like a dining table or cabinet. It gives you the ability to:

- **Visualize proportions**: Ensure your piece fits in the space you have in mind, and that all elements are to scale.
- **Identify potential issues**: Spot any design flaws early, like how different parts of the project will come together, or whether components will fit within your material constraints.
- **Plan the build process**: Break down the project into manageable stages, such as assembly, finishing, or hardware installation.

2. Simple Sketching Techniques

You don't need to be an artist to create useful woodworking sketches. Basic sketches will be enough to communicate your design and construction needs. Here are some helpful sketching tips:

- **Start with basic shapes**: Use simple **rectangles**, **circles**, and **lines** to represent the major components of your design. This will help you focus on the overall structure and proportions before adding detail.
- **Use scale**: It's important that your sketches are to scale so you can visualize how the project will actually come together. Use graph paper, or divide your drawing into a grid to maintain proper proportions.
- **Label key dimensions**: Mark the **width**, **height**, **depth**, and other critical measurements on your sketch. This ensures that you know how large each part should be, and helps avoid mistakes during the build.
- **Include joinery details**: If your project involves any **joinery**, such as dovetails, mortise and tenon, or butt joints, make sure to represent those in your sketches. This will help you plan for tools and techniques ahead of time.

- **Add a material list**: Next to the sketch, note down the **materials** you'll need for each component (e.g., wood species, plywood, etc.) along with any additional materials like **screws**, **nails**, or **adhesives**.

3. Tools for Sketching

While a traditional pencil and paper are perfectly sufficient for most woodworking sketches, there are also some tools and resources that can help streamline the process:

- **Graph Paper**: Graph paper helps you draw to scale, making it easier to maintain accurate proportions. The grid also helps in creating symmetry and aligning different parts of your project.
- **Ruler or Scale**: For precise measurements and straight lines, use a **ruler** or a **scale ruler**. A scale ruler is particularly helpful for creating drawings to a specific scale (e.g., 1:10, where 1 inch on paper equals 10 inches in real life).
- **Digital Drawing Tools**: For more complex projects, you can use digital design software such as **SketchUp**, **AutoCAD**, or other **CAD (Computer-Aided Design)** programs. These tools can offer more precision, the ability to create 3D models, and options for printing full-scale plans.

4. Developing Your Sketch into a Full Plan

Once you have your initial sketch, the next step is to refine it into a **detailed plan**. This includes everything you'll need to successfully complete your project, from cutting lists to step-by-step instructions.

Here's how you can expand your basic sketch into a full project plan:

- **Break down the components**: For each piece in your project, draw out individual parts, such as legs, panels, and shelves. Show how they fit together in the overall design. For example, you may have a side view, top view, and front view to show the project from different angles.
- **Create a cutting list**: A cutting list specifies the exact dimensions of each piece you'll need. This can be helpful for organizing your materials and ensuring you have enough wood for the project. It also helps minimize waste, as you'll know exactly how to cut your materials to fit the design.
- **Assembly instructions**: Include any assembly steps, such as how the pieces are joined together, which screws or nails to use, and whether any wood glue is necessary. This will be your reference during construction, helping you keep the build process organized.
- **Hardware and Finishing Details**: Mark where hardware such as screws, nails, or hinges will go. If your design calls for **drawer slides** or **door hinges**, make sure to show where they are placed and how they will be installed. You should also include finishing instructions, such as sanding, staining, or applying any protective coatings.

5. Iterating on Your Sketch

Sometimes, the first sketch isn't perfect, and that's okay! As you work through the design process, you may come up with new ideas or discover aspects of your design that need tweaking. Don't hesitate to iterate and revise your sketches to ensure the final design works the way you want it to. Keep in mind that small changes in design can significantly impact the overall look, functionality, and ease of construction of your project.

Introduction to CAD and Digital Design for Woodworking

In today's woodworking world, traditional hand-drawing techniques are being complemented (and sometimes replaced) by **Computer-Aided Design (CAD)** and other **digital design tools**. These technologies allow woodworkers to create highly detailed, precise, and customizable designs for their projects. Digital design tools provide significant advantages, especially for more complex or large-scale woodworking projects, offering flexibility, accuracy, and the ability to make modifications quickly and easily.

What is CAD?

CAD stands for **Computer-Aided Design**. It is a type of software that enables users to create two-dimensional (2D) or three-dimensional (3D) models of physical objects. In woodworking, CAD software is used to design furniture, cabinets, doors, and other wood-based structures with precise dimensions and details that would be difficult to achieve by hand. CAD allows you to digitally visualize your project, make adjustments in real time, and create technical drawings that can be directly translated into physical construction.

Why Use CAD in Woodworking?

There are several key benefits to using CAD and digital design software in woodworking:

1. **Precision and Accuracy**: CAD software allows woodworkers to create designs with extremely precise measurements. This ensures that all parts fit together correctly, minimizing errors during construction and reducing material waste.
2. **Flexibility**: If you need to make changes to a design, CAD software makes it easy to adjust measurements, move elements around, and explore different design options. For example, if a project needs to be resized or altered to accommodate specific hardware, it's easy to update the digital plan and see how the changes impact the overall design.
3. **Visualization**: CAD tools, particularly those with 3D modeling capabilities, allow you to see your project in a fully realized, three-dimensional space. This helps you understand the proportions, aesthetic appeal, and functionality of the design before you start cutting wood.
4. **Efficiency**: With CAD, you can quickly generate accurate cutting lists, assembly instructions, and material estimations, which can save a lot of time compared to doing all of this manually. These features also help reduce the chance of mistakes, which can be costly in terms of both time and materials.

5. **Collaboration**: For those who work in teams or for larger projects, CAD files can be shared easily with colleagues, suppliers, or clients. This helps ensure that everyone is on the same page and that the design process is streamlined.
6. **Optimized Use of Materials**: With CAD, you can plan out your cuts more efficiently, ensuring you use your wood and materials in the most economical way possible. This helps reduce waste and can be especially valuable when working with expensive or rare wood species.

Popular CAD Software for Woodworkers

While there are many CAD programs available, some are particularly suited for woodworking and are widely used in the industry:

1. **SketchUp**: SketchUp is one of the most popular design tools for woodworkers. It's user-friendly and offers a wide range of features, including 3D modeling, 2D design, and an extensive library of pre-designed models. SketchUp allows you to create detailed models of furniture, cabinetry, and other wood projects, with easy-to-understand tools for dimensioning and material assignment.
2. **AutoCAD**: AutoCAD is a more professional and advanced CAD tool widely used by engineers, architects, and woodworkers alike. It allows for precise 2D and 3D modeling, detailed technical drawings, and the creation of complex designs. It's particularly useful for large-scale projects or when precise specifications and documentation are necessary.
3. **Fusion 360**: Fusion 360 is a powerful CAD software from Autodesk that combines 3D modeling, CAM (computer-aided manufacturing), and simulation. It's ideal for woodworkers who want to go beyond just design and also integrate aspects of digital fabrication, including CNC (computer numerical control) routing.
4. **SolidWorks**: SolidWorks is another advanced CAD software that's widely used in engineering and design, including woodworking. It's especially beneficial for woodworkers who want to create complex, interactive designs and run simulations on how the finished project will behave.
5. **FreeCAD**: For woodworkers on a budget, FreeCAD is an open-source alternative to paid CAD software. It offers many of the same capabilities, including 3D modeling and parametric design, though it might require more time to learn compared to some user-friendly options.
6. **TinkerCAD**: TinkerCAD is a beginner-friendly, web-based CAD tool that's great for simple designs and those new to CAD. It's an excellent starting point for beginners to learn the basics of 3D modeling and design. Although it may not have all the features of more advanced CAD tools, it's a great entry-level choice.

How CAD Translates to Woodworking

Once a design has been created in CAD, it can be exported in a variety of formats that can be used for both **manual woodworking** and **digital fabrication**. These include:

- **Cutting Lists**: Most CAD programs can automatically generate a detailed cutting list based on your design, showing the dimensions of each part and how many pieces of each you need. This can help you save time and ensure you purchase the right amount of material.
- **2D and 3D Views**: 2D technical drawings can be used for traditional hand-cutting methods, while 3D models give a more comprehensive understanding of the structure and assembly of your project.
- **CNC Integration**: For woodworkers with access to CNC machinery, CAD designs can be directly fed into the machine. The CNC then follows the digital plan to cut, carve, or route the wood to the exact specifications outlined in the software. This eliminates human error and can lead to faster and more accurate cuts.
- **Exportable Files**: CAD software can export files in formats like **DXF**, **SVG**, or **STL**, which are commonly used by CNC routers, laser cutters, and other digital fabrication tools.

Getting Started with CAD for Woodworking

If you're new to CAD, getting started may seem intimidating, but there are many resources to help you learn:

- **Tutorials and Online Courses**: There are countless online resources, including free tutorials, YouTube videos, and paid courses that walk you through using CAD software specifically for woodworking.
- **Practice**: The more you use CAD software, the more proficient you will become. Start with simple designs like shelves, tables, or boxes, and gradually progress to more complex projects as your skills improve.
- **Forums and Communities**: Many woodworking forums and online communities have dedicated sections for CAD and digital design. These are great places to ask questions, get advice, and share your designs.

3.3 Prototyping and Testing

Building Small-Scale Models

Prototyping is a crucial part of the woodworking process, especially for more complex or detailed projects. It allows you to test your design and make adjustments before committing to the final version. One effective way to begin the prototyping process is by **building small-scale models**. These scaled-down versions of your final project provide a hands-on way to explore design ideas, test functionality, and evaluate proportions. Here's a deeper look into the importance and approach of building small-scale models:

Why Build Small-Scale Models?

1. **Refine Your Design**:
   - Building a small-scale model gives you the opportunity to work out any design flaws before starting the full-scale project. It allows you to test different configurations, joinery techniques, and design elements that may be difficult to visualize on paper.

2. **Understand Proportions**:
   - A small-scale model can help you better understand the relationship between various parts of your project. For example, you can evaluate the scale of a chair's seat to its backrest, or the size of shelves relative to the cabinet frame. Proportions are key in woodworking, and creating a model ensures that your final piece will be visually balanced and functional.

3. **Test Functionality**:
   - Whether it's opening a cabinet door or fitting drawers into a frame, you can test how certain parts will function before committing to full-sized materials. This step helps identify potential issues with movement, alignment, and fit, which can be corrected in the model rather than the final build.

4. **Cost and Material Efficiency**:
   - By working on a smaller, less expensive version of your project, you can avoid costly mistakes with your main materials. In addition, experimenting with different ideas on a model prevents unnecessary waste of wood, hardware, and other supplies.

5. **Prototype Different Design Options**:
   - Prototypes allow you to try multiple designs or features without risking time and resources on an unsuccessful iteration. You can easily swap out different elements, such as different types of hinges, drawer layouts, or decorative features.

6. **Improved Problem Solving**:
   - Building a model can help identify unexpected challenges early in the design process. Whether it's a mechanical issue or a decorative detail that doesn't look as expected, a model allows you to address these problems before they arise in your larger project.

Steps to Build Small-Scale Models

1. **Select Appropriate Materials**:
   - For small-scale models, choose inexpensive and easy-to-work-with materials. **Plywood**, **masonite**, or **pine** are good choices, as they are affordable, easy to cut, and mimic the characteristics of larger woods without the high cost. If the final project will use hardwood, using softwood for the model is a practical and cost-effective choice.

2. **Scale the Design**:
   - When building a small-scale model, ensure the proportions are scaled down from the full-sized project. Use a consistent ratio for your scale (e.g., 1:2, 1:4, or 1:10). If your full project is 40 inches wide, then for a 1:10 scale model, the width would be 4 inches. Make sure all parts of the model are proportionately scaled.
3. **Create a Simple Plan**:
   - Like your final project, begin with clear plans for your small-scale model. This could be a detailed sketch, blueprint, or digital design, depending on your preference. Make sure to include key dimensions, and think about the scale of each component in the model.
4. **Cut the Pieces**:
   - Use basic hand tools (such as a **handsaw** or **jigsaw**) or **small-scale power tools** (like a **dremel** or **miter saw**) to cut out the pieces for your model. Focus on precision, as the goal is to replicate the proportions and design of the final product.
5. **Assembly**:
   - Assemble the pieces using appropriate adhesives for your model material. For a more realistic feel, you might use small nails or screws, but for prototyping purposes, wood glue is usually sufficient. Pay attention to joinery—this is where you can experiment with different techniques and see how well they hold up at a smaller scale.
6. **Testing and Evaluation**:
   - Once assembled, test the model by simulating the actions that will take place with the full-scale version (e.g., opening doors, drawers, or lids). Does the design work as expected? Are there any issues with stability or proportions? This step will highlight areas that need adjustment before you proceed to your main project.
7. **Refinement and Adjustments**:
   - If you encounter issues with the model, take notes on what needs to be changed. Perhaps a shelf is too narrow, or a drawer doesn't slide smoothly. Use this feedback to make adjustments to the final design, whether that's modifying the scale of certain parts or changing the joinery approach. Repeat the process if necessary, building a second or third model to refine your design further.

Tools and Equipment for Small-Scale Models

- **Measuring Tools**: A **caliper**, **ruler**, and **square** will help ensure precision when cutting and assembling your model.
- **Cutting Tools**: A **craft knife, small handsaw,** or **table saw** can be used to make clean cuts. A **scroll saw** is excellent for intricate cuts.

- **Adhesives**: **Wood glue**, **super glue**, or **hot glue** are commonly used for assembling small-scale models.
- **Clamps**: **Spring clamps** or **bar clamps** are helpful for holding pieces in place while the glue sets.
- **Sanding**: Use **sandpaper** or a **mini sander** to smooth the edges of the model and ensure a clean finish.

Design Considerations for Small-Scale Models
1. **Joinery Techniques**:
   - While small-scale models don't need the same level of strength as full-size projects, they provide an excellent opportunity to experiment with different joinery methods. Try using **dovetails, mortise-and-tenon joints**, or **butt joints** to see how they fit together and affect the structure.
2. **Proportional Accuracy**:
   - Small-scale models are all about proportion. Pay close attention to the thickness of materials, as even slight changes can affect the overall look. For example, a drawer front may look too bulky or too thin when scaled down incorrectly.
3. **Functional Testing**:
   - In addition to aesthetics, focus on the model's functionality. How well do the drawers slide? Do the doors swing open smoothly? Test each part of the design to ensure that the final build will perform as expected.
4. **Finish and Detail**:
   - If your project includes specific finishing elements, such as stain, paint, or varnish, consider applying them to the model as well. This will give you a preview of how the materials will look in the final version.

Chapter 4: Squaring, Marking, & Cutting Stock

4.1 Stock Preparation

Selecting and Preparing Wood for Accuracy and Stability

Before embarking on any woodworking project, one of the most important steps is to properly select and prepare your wood stock. Preparing wood correctly ensures that your final project is accurate, stable, and durable. In this section, we will cover how to choose the right wood and how to prepare it to guarantee that it meets the needs of your design and construction plans.

---

1. Selecting the Right Wood for Stability

When selecting wood for a project, especially if you're aiming for accuracy and stability, several factors need to be taken into consideration:

- **Wood Species**: The species of wood plays a significant role in how it behaves over time. Hardwoods like **oak, maple,** and **cherry** tend to be more stable than softwoods such as **pine** or **cedar**, which may warp more easily due to their lighter structure. For projects that require high precision, **hardwoods** are generally preferred.
- **Grain Orientation**: The orientation of the grain affects the wood's stability. **Quarter-sawn** wood, where the grain runs perpendicular to the surface, tends to be much more stable than **plain-sawn** or **flat-sawn** wood, which is more prone to cupping or twisting over time. Look for **straight grain patterns** to help ensure consistency and reduce the chances of distortion as the wood dries or ages.
- **Moisture Content**: Wood absorbs and loses moisture based on its environment, which causes it to expand or contract. Wood that has been **air-dried** or **kiln-dried** to a low moisture content (typically around 6-8%) is ideal for most woodworking projects. Wood with high moisture content can lead to instability during the project's lifecycle and cause the wood to warp or crack as it acclimates to a new environment.
- **Defects**: When selecting wood, check for **defects** such as cracks, knots, and warping. These imperfections can compromise the strength and stability of the wood. For instance, **knots** can weaken the structural integrity of the wood, while **cracks** may worsen over time. Choose wood that is relatively free from these flaws, or plan to cut around them during your project if necessary.

---

2. Preparing Wood for Accuracy

After selecting the right wood, the next step is to prepare it for your project. Proper preparation will ensure that your wood is straight, square, and flat, providing a solid foundation for accurate cuts and construction.

- **Acclimatization**: Allow your wood to **acclimate** to the working environment for several days before you begin working with it. This gives the wood time to adjust to the temperature and humidity levels of your workshop, minimizing the chances of moisture-related distortion during the project.
- **Surface Flattening**: The wood should be as flat and smooth as possible before you begin cutting or marking. Use a **planer** or a **joiner** to flatten one side of the board first. If you're working with rough-cut lumber, a planer is especially useful for removing high spots and smoothing the surface, creating a flat reference face.
- **Edge Jointing**: After flattening one side, use a **joiner** or **hand plane** to square one edge of the board. This edge will serve as your reference edge for the next steps. Squaring the edge ensures that subsequent cuts and measurements will be accurate. When jointing, take your time to ensure the edge is square to the face of the board and free from any noticeable curvature.
- **Truing the Board**: If your board has any warping, **cupping**, or bowing, it's essential to true the board before moving forward. You can do this by flattening the top surface, jointing one edge, and then running it through the planer until you achieve a flat and straight result. For severe warps, you may need to cut away the worst sections and then re-joint the remaining piece.

3. Ensuring Stability During Cutting

Once your wood has been properly selected and prepared, it's crucial to ensure stability during the cutting process. This will help prevent unwanted movement or imperfections in the final cuts.

- **Check for Bowing and Twisting**: Before cutting, lay the board on a flat surface and inspect for any noticeable bowing or twisting. If the wood is not completely flat, it could cause your cuts to be inaccurate or uneven. You can use clamps or the weight of other boards to keep the stock in place while cutting.
- **Use a Straight Edge**: When marking out cuts, use a **straight edge** or **t-square** to ensure your lines are accurate. For longer cuts, consider using a **track saw** or a **rail-guided circular saw** to ensure the cut follows the marked line and remains square to the board.
- **Measure and Mark Carefully**: Always double-check your measurements before cutting. A mistake in marking can lead to wasted wood and inaccurate joints. Use a **caliper** or **measuring tape** for precise measurements, and make sure all marking tools are clear and visible on the wood surface.
- **Cutting with a Stable Setup**: Set up your cutting area so the wood is supported on both sides. A **workbench**, **saw horses**, or a **cutting table** with appropriate supports ensures the board doesn't shift or flex during cutting, preventing inaccuracies.

4. Tips for Ensuring Wood Stability During Long-Term Use

While preparing the wood correctly for a project is essential, ensuring the wood remains stable over time is just as important. Here are some tips for maintaining wood stability during long-term use:

- **Store Wood Properly**: When storing your wood stock, ensure it is kept in a climate-controlled environment. Store wood flat, with spacers between the boards to allow for proper airflow, reducing the chance of warping, swelling, or cracking due to changes in humidity or temperature.
- **Use Proper Finish Techniques**: Applying a finish to your wood, such as **oil**, **wax**, or **varnish**, helps create a protective barrier that slows moisture absorption and loss. This ensures that the wood remains stable and protected over time, even in changing environmental conditions.
- **Avoid Direct Contact with Heat and Moisture**: Always avoid placing finished wood furniture or wood projects directly in contact with high heat sources (such as radiators or stoves) or areas with excessive moisture. This will help maintain the wood's dimensional stability and prevent damage.

Squaring and Flattening Lumber

When working with rough-cut lumber, the first essential steps before any cutting or assembly are **squaring** and **flattening** the boards. These processes ensure that your wood is true,stable, and accurate, which is crucial for creating well-fitting joints and a high-quality finished product. Here's a step-by-step guide on how to properly square and flatten lumber for your woodworking projects.

---

1. Flattening Lumber: Making One Face and Edge True

Before beginning any cuts or measurements, the first goal is to flatten one side of the board and square one edge. This creates a reference surface from which all other measurements and cuts can be made.

Flattening the First Face:

- **Inspection**: Start by inspecting the wood for visible defects like warps, twists, or bows. Lay the board flat on a surface to check if it is stable. The more stable and flat the board, the easier the flattening process will be.
- **Flattening with a Planer**: A **hand planer** or **power planer** is typically used to flatten the first side of the board. If using a power planer, start at one end of the board and work your way down, making multiple passes to gradually remove high spots.
    - If you're using a **hand planer**, start with long strokes along the length of the board, gradually moving from one end to the other. A **scrub plane** is ideal for removing rough spots, and once flat, switch to a **jack plane** for finer smoothing.
- **Checking for Flatness**: After planing, check for flatness by placing the board on a flat surface, such as a table or a **workbench**, and rocking the board back and forth. If the board rocks, more planing is necessary.

Creating a Flat Surface with a Jointer:

- If you have access to a **jointer**, this is an even more effective way to flatten one side of the wood. A jointer works by removing material from the high spots on the wood, creating a smooth, level surface.
    - After running the board through the jointer, inspect the flattened surface by placing a straight edge or ruler along it to confirm there are no high or low spots.
    - Keep the wood stable as you feed it through the jointer to avoid any twisting.

2. Squaring the Edge: Creating a True Reference Edge

Once one face is flat, the next step is to square one edge of the board. This reference edge will ensure all cuts are aligned properly and will serve as a guide for the rest of your cuts.

Using a Jointer or Hand Plane:

- **Jointing the Edge**: Use the **jointer** to flatten and square one edge of the board. The jointer's fence should be set at 90 degrees to the table to ensure the edge is perfectly perpendicular to the flattened surface.
    - Feed the board slowly through the jointer, applying even pressure. Once the edge is jointed, it should be square and smooth.
- **Hand Planing**: If you don't have a jointer, use a **hand plane** to square the edge. Place a **try square** or **combination square** against the edge of the board to check for squareness as you plane. Work slowly and evenly, checking frequently to ensure the edge remains square.

Checking for Squareness:

- **Using a Square**: To ensure the edge is perfectly square, use a **try square** or **combination square**. Place the square against the edge of the board and check for gaps between the square and the board. If there's any gap, continue to plane or joint the edge until it's perfectly square.
- **Using a Reference Board**: Another method to check squareness is to compare the edge of the board to a reference piece of lumber that you know is already square. Lay the reference board along the edge, ensuring both edges meet cleanly without any light showing through. If they match, your edge is square.

3. Flattening the Second Face:

Once the first face and edge are true, the next step is to flatten the opposite face, which should be parallel to the first. This step ensures that the board is consistently the same thickness across its length.

Using a Thickness Planer:

- A **thickness planer** is typically used to flatten the opposite face of the board. Once the first face is flattened and the edge is squared, you can pass the board through the thickness planer to reduce its thickness while maintaining parallelism.

- Ensure that the first flat face is facing down on the planer bed to maintain the correct thickness and parallelism.

Manual Flattening with a Hand Plane:
- If you do not have access to a thickness planer, you can continue using a hand plane to flatten the second face. This process can be labor-intensive and time-consuming but works effectively. Again, use a **scrub plane** for coarse removal and a **jack plane** or **smoothing plane** to finish the surface.
  - Regularly check for flatness by placing the board on a flat surface or using a straight edge.

---

4. Final Thickness and Consistency:

Once both faces are flattened and the edges are squared, the final step is to ensure the board is the correct thickness and that it remains consistent across its entire length.

Sanding and Smoothing:
- After flattening and jointing, some additional **sanding** may be needed to remove any planer marks or rough spots. Use progressively finer grits of sandpaper, starting with a **coarse grit** to remove any large imperfections, followed by **medium grit** and **fine grit** to achieve a smooth finish.
- Sand the board evenly across its entire length to ensure the thickness is consistent. Always sand with the grain to avoid damaging the wood surface.

---

5. Tips for Successful Squaring and Flattening
- **Take Your Time**: These initial preparation steps are crucial for the success of your project. Rushing through squaring and flattening may result in imprecise cuts and joinery later on.
- **Measure Frequently**: Constantly check your work with measuring tools like a **caliper**, **tape measure**, and **square** to ensure accuracy.
- **Use the Right Tools**: The process of squaring and flattening requires precision tools. A **jointer**, **planer**, and **hand plane** are invaluable, but for some beginners, starting with hand tools like a plane and a square is a great way to get used to the process.
- **Work on a Stable Surface**: Make sure your workbench or sawhorses are sturdy and level to avoid any unwanted movement or distortion as you work.

4.2 Measuring and Marking Techniques

Essential Techniques for Accurate Measurement and Layout

Whether you're cutting a single piece of wood or assembling an entire piece of furniture, the success of your project depends on how well you measure and mark your materials.

1. Essential Measuring Tools

Before diving into the techniques, it's crucial to understand the various measuring tools you'll need. These tools help establish accurate reference points, angles, and dimensions for your cuts and assembly.

Tape Measure:
- **Usage**: A **tape measure** is one of the most commonly used tools in woodworking. It's ideal for measuring long distances, such as the length of boards, or for finding the center of a piece of material.
- **Tip**: Always ensure the tape is not twisted, and avoid using the end hook of the tape to measure if it's worn out, as it can lead to inaccurate measurements.

Ruler/Steel Rule:
- **Usage**: A **steel rule** provides high accuracy and is perfect for smaller measurements. It is especially useful when you need to measure down to millimeters or inches.
- **Tip**: Use a rule with a finely marked graduation for more precision, and make sure the ruler is made of stainless steel to avoid warping over time.

Caliper:
- **Usage**: A **caliper** is ideal for measuring the thickness or diameter of objects and is especially useful when measuring the thickness of wood or checking for precise fits in joints.
- **Tip**: For more accurate measurements, use a digital caliper, but ensure it's calibrated before use.

Combination Square:
- **Usage**: The **combination square** is a versatile tool that can be used to measure and mark 90-degree and 45-degree angles. It is also useful for checking the squareness of edges and marking lines.
- **Tip**: Make sure the blade of the combination square is free of debris and properly tightened to avoid inaccurate readings.

Measuring Jig or Story Stick:
- **Usage**: A **story stick** or **measuring jig** is a custom-made tool to transfer measurements directly to your workpiece. It's especially useful for complex or repeated measurements, such as those for rail and stile joints or when building furniture pieces with multiple parts.
- **Tip**: When using a story stick, always mark the dimensions on the same edge consistently for uniformity.

---

2. Marking Techniques for Accuracy

Marking your wood accurately is just as important as measuring it. Clear, precise markings ensure that your cuts align perfectly with your plans and that joints fit as intended.

Pencil Marks:

- **Usage**: A **pencil** is the most common marking tool in woodworking. It's perfect for making lines and marks on wood, especially on rough surfaces.
- **Tip**: Use a sharp pencil for fine, clear marks, and always use a light touch. Dark, heavy lines can make it difficult to cut accurately.

Carpenter's Square (Speed Square):
- **Usage**: A **carpenter's square**, also known as a **speed square**, is a right-angled tool used to mark and measure 90-degree and 45-degree angles. It's particularly useful when marking cuts for framing or any straight-line cuts.
- **Tip**: To mark accurately, hold the square firmly against the edge of the wood and use a pencil to trace along its edge.

Marking Gauge:
- **Usage**: A **marking gauge** is used for making parallel lines on wood, typically along the length of a board. It consists of a fence and a blade that can be adjusted to measure different distances from the edge of the board.
- **Tip**: Ensure the blade is sharp, and the gauge is set to the correct measurement before starting. A dull blade can lead to uneven marks.

Knife Marks (for Precision):
- **Usage**: For more precise marks, use a **marking knife** instead of a pencil. This tool creates a small, sharp incision along the wood grain, which is ideal for marking cutting lines.
- **Tip**: Marking with a knife will give you a more exact reference than a pencil, especially when using a saw to cut along the line.

---

3. Layout Techniques for Precise Cuts

Once your measurements and marks are in place, it's time to start laying out your cuts. The layout process ensures that all the cuts are made in the correct locations and at the proper angles.

Using a Straight Edge:
- **Usage**: A **straight edge** or **ruler** is used to connect two points for drawing a straight line across your material. This is essential for ensuring that cuts are aligned along the desired path.
- **Tip**: When using a straight edge, make sure it's longer than the length of the cut you intend to make to avoid any curvature or bowing, which can lead to inaccurate cuts.

Crosscut and Rip Cut Layout:
- **Usage**: When marking for a **crosscut** (cutting across the grain) or **rip cut** (cutting with the grain), use a **speed square** to make 90-degree marks at the end of the wood for crosscuts and parallel lines for rip cuts.

- **Tip**: Use a **miter gauge** for crosscuts to ensure the board is held at a consistent angle to the saw blade.

Transfer Marks Accurately:
- **Usage**: When transferring measurements from a plan to your material, be sure to double-check the distance before marking it on the board. Using a **story stick** is a great way to transfer multiple measurements with precision.
- **Tip**: Use a **tape measure** to measure, but transfer those measurements with a **pencil** or **marking knife** to avoid any mistakes from tape measure inaccuracies.

---

4. Tips for Accurate Measuring and Marking

1. Double-Check Measurements:
- It's easy to make mistakes, especially when measuring long pieces of wood. Always double-check measurements before making any cuts to ensure accuracy.

2. Keep Tools Clean:
- Dirt, dust, and debris can affect the accuracy of your measurements and markings. Make sure your measuring tools are clean and free of any obstructions that could cause inaccuracies.

3. Work on a Stable Surface:
- Always ensure your workpiece is secure and resting on a stable surface. A wobbly workbench or unstable material can lead to inaccurate measurements and poor cuts.

4. Mark Both Sides:
- When marking cuts or measurements, mark both sides of the wood whenever possible. This ensures that you can work from either side, providing more flexibility and accuracy.

5. Use the Right Method for the Job:
- Choose the appropriate marking tool for your needs. For example, a marking knife provides more precision for cutting than a pencil. Similarly, a marking gauge is great for creating consistent, parallel lines.

4.3 Cutting Techniques

Using Handsaws vs. Power Saws

When it comes to cutting wood, the choice between **handsaws** and **power saws** depends on the project type, the level of precision needed, and your available tools and experience. Both types of saws have their advantages, and understanding when to use each can significantly impact the outcome of your project.

---

1. Handsaws: Precision and Control

Advantages:
- **Manual Control**: Handsaws give you complete control over the cutting process. This allows for fine adjustments and more detailed work, especially when cutting small or intricate pieces.
- **Portability**: Handsaws are lightweight and easy to carry around. They don't require electricity or batteries, making them ideal for small projects or work in places where access to power tools is limited.
- **Precision in Tight Spaces**: Because handsaws are manually operated, they offer a greater degree of finesse in tight or hard-to-reach spaces, where larger power tools might not fit or be effective.

When to Use:
- **Fine Cuts**: Handsaws are ideal for making precise cuts, such as when trimming joints, cutting dovetails, or fine-tuning angles in smaller, more detailed projects.
- **Small Projects**: For DIY projects or smaller furniture pieces, a handsaw can provide the necessary control for accurate cuts without the need for a power saw.
- **Quiet Work**: If you're working in a small or shared space, handsaws are quieter than power saws, which makes them a better choice when working indoors or in a confined area.

Disadvantages:
- **More Physical Effort**: Cutting with a handsaw can be physically demanding, particularly when working with large pieces of wood or hardwood.
- **Slower Cutting Speed**: Handsaws are slower than power saws, and for large-scale cuts, they can be less efficient.

Examples of Handsaws:
- **Backsaw**: Ideal for fine, straight cuts and detailed joinery work.
- **Coping Saw**: Perfect for intricate curves and detailed cuts in smaller wood pieces.
- **Crosscut Saw**: Used for cutting across the grain of wood, especially for rough cuts.

---

2. Power Saws: Speed and Efficiency

Advantages:
- **Speed**: Power saws cut through wood much faster than handsaws. This makes them ideal for large projects, such as building furniture, framing, or cutting down large pieces of lumber.
- **Consistency**: With power saws, you can achieve more consistent cuts, especially in straight lines, without the effort of manually guiding the saw.
- **Less Physical Effort**: Power saws require far less physical exertion, allowing you to work for longer periods without tiring.

When to Use:

- **Large Projects**: For bigger, more complex woodworking projects such as cabinetry, framing, or large furniture pieces, power saws save time and energy.
- **Straight Cuts and Ripping**: Power saws excel at making long, straight cuts, such as ripping plywood or cutting through thick lumber.
- **Repetitive Cuts**: If you need to make many identical cuts (like cutting multiple pieces of wood to the same length), a power saw will be much faster and more efficient than a handsaw.

Disadvantages:
- **Less Precision**: While power saws are great for straight cuts, they can lack the fine control you get with a handsaw, making them less ideal for detailed or intricate cuts.
- **Noise and Dust**: Power saws are noisy and can create a lot of dust, which might not be ideal in certain environments or workspaces.
- **Power Source Requirement**: Power saws require electricity or batteries, which may not always be available in certain work environments.

Examples of Power Saws:
- **Circular Saw**: A versatile saw that can make both straight cuts and bevel cuts in lumber, plywood, and other materials. Perfect for ripping boards or cutting sheets of plywood.
- **Jigsaw**: A great tool for making curved cuts or cutting irregular shapes, typically used in cutting softer woods or laminated materials.
- **Table Saw**: A stationary saw with a spinning blade used for precise, straight cuts. Ideal for ripping large sheets of plywood or crosscutting long boards.
- **Miter Saw**: A saw with a fixed blade used to make precise crosscuts and angle cuts, often used for trimming and framing.

---

3. Handsaws vs. Power Saws: When to Choose Which

The decision to use a handsaw or a power saw depends on the nature of the cut, the materials you're working with, and the speed at which you need to work.

- **For Small, Detailed Cuts**: Handsaws are ideal for precise, intricate work. If you need to make a detailed cut or work with small pieces where you need control over each stroke, a handsaw is your best option.
- **For Large, Straight Cuts**: Power saws, such as circular saws or table saws, are perfect when you need to make fast, straight cuts across large pieces of wood or plywood. They save time and provide more consistent cuts, especially for larger-scale work.
- **For Finishing Touches and Joinery**: When working on fine joinery or finishing cuts, a handsaw can provide the precision and control necessary for perfect fitments. For example, dovetailing or trimming edges for a smooth finish is often best done with handsaws.

- **For Repetitive Cuts**: Power saws shine when you need to make multiple cuts of the same length or size. A miter saw or table saw can help you cut consistently and accurately without excessive setup.

4. Combining Handsaws and Power Saws

In many woodworking projects, using both handsaws and power saws can be the most effective approach. Power saws can handle the bulk of the cutting—speeding up your workflow—while handsaws can be used for more delicate or precise tasks, such as trimming joints, cutting curves, or working in tight spaces.

- **Example**: When building a bookcase, a circular saw can quickly cut the main panels and shelves to size, while a handsaw might be used to fine-tune the edges or trim the pieces for perfect fits in the frame.
- **Example**: When installing door hardware or making detailed cuts around intricate parts of a project, a handsaw provides the accuracy needed for a professional finish.

Techniques for Rip Cuts, Crosscuts, and Angled Cuts

Understanding the different types of cuts and how to execute them accurately is essential for achieving clean, precise results in your woodworking projects. Rip cuts, crosscuts, and angled cuts each serve different purposes and require distinct techniques and tools. Let's break down the best practices for making each of these cuts.

1. Rip Cuts: Cutting Along the Grain

Definition: A **rip cut** is a cut made **parallel** to the wood's grain. This type of cut is often used when you need to reduce the width of a board, such as when cutting down a large piece of plywood to size.

Tools to Use:
- **Circular Saw**: A circular saw is the most common power tool used for rip cuts. It's versatile and portable, making it ideal for cutting through thick pieces of lumber or plywood.
- **Table Saw**: A table saw is one of the most precise tools for making rip cuts. It allows for consistent width cuts, especially when paired with a rip fence.
- **Handsaw**: For smaller, controlled cuts or if you're working with thinner stock, a handsaw can also be used for rip cuts.

Techniques:
- **Measure and Mark**: Use a measuring tape and a carpenter's square or marking gauge to mark a straight line along the length of the board.

- **Use a Guide**: When using a circular saw, attach a straightedge or guide to the wood to help keep the cut straight. This ensures that the saw follows the correct path, even for long rip cuts.
- **Set the Blade Depth**: For power saws, ensure the blade is set to a depth just slightly greater than the thickness of the wood. This reduces the strain on the saw and helps to prevent kickback.
- **Steady Your Hands**: Always maintain a steady grip on the saw to avoid uneven cutting. For longer cuts, feed the wood through the saw slowly and steadily.
- **Use the Right Fence**: On a table saw, the rip fence should be set parallel to the blade at the desired width of the cut. Keep the wood pressed firmly against the fence for a smooth, straight cut.

Safety Tips:
- Always use a push stick when working with narrow pieces on a table saw to keep your hands at a safe distance from the blade.
- For power saws, wear safety glasses and hearing protection to safeguard yourself from debris and loud noise.

---

2. Crosscuts: Cutting Across the Grain

Definition: A **crosscut** is a cut made **perpendicular** to the wood's grain. This is typically used when cutting wood to length, such as when cutting boards for frame components, shelving, or furniture parts.

Tools to Use:
- **Miter Saw**: A miter saw is the go-to tool for making crosscuts, as it provides the most accurate and consistent cuts, especially for angles.
- **Circular Saw**: If a miter saw isn't available, a circular saw can be used with a guide to make crosscuts.
- **Handsaw**: For smaller projects or when working in confined spaces, a handsaw can also be used for crosscuts.

Techniques:
- **Mark the Cut**: Measure and mark the length you need, then use a carpenter's square or framing square to draw a perpendicular line across the board.
- **Support the Wood**: Make sure the board is supported properly at both ends to prevent it from binding or snapping as you cut through it.
- **Use a Stop Block**: On a miter saw, using a stop block can help you make multiple identical crosscuts at the same length. Simply clamp the stop block at the desired position on your workpiece.
- **Slow, Steady Cuts**: Crosscuts typically produce more dust and require more power, so feed the wood slowly through the saw to maintain control and ensure a clean cut.

Safety Tips:

- Always ensure that the wood is secured before making a crosscut. This prevents the wood from shifting during the cut.
- Use clamps to hold the wood firmly in place on a miter saw or a circular saw to reduce the chance of kickback.

---

3. Angled Cuts: Cutting at an Angle (Bevel and Miter Cuts)

Definition: **Angled cuts** include both **bevel cuts** (cuts at an angle to the surface of the wood) and **miter cuts** (cuts at an angle across the face of the wood). These cuts are essential when making frame corners, angled joints, or decorative edges.

- **Bevel Cut**: A bevel cut is made at an angle to the surface of the wood, usually to change the angle of the edge, such as when making a slanted edge or chamfer.
- **Miter Cut**: A miter cut is made at an angle across the face of the wood, typically at 45 degrees, often used in picture frames or cabinet trim.

Tools to Use:

- **Miter Saw**: This tool is the best option for making accurate miter cuts at preset angles. It's ideal for cutting angles in trim work and framing.
- **Table Saw**: A table saw can also be used for angled cuts by adjusting the blade to the desired angle and using the miter gauge.
- **Circular Saw**: For bevel cuts, a circular saw can be adjusted to the desired angle, although it may be less precise than a miter saw.
- **Handsaw**: A handsaw with an adjustable miter box can be used for cutting at angles, but it's best for smaller projects or less precise cuts.

Techniques:

- **For Miter Cuts**:
    - Use a **miter saw** with the angle set to the desired degree (commonly 45° for trim work).
    - If using a table saw, set the blade to the desired angle using the miter gauge, and carefully feed the wood through the saw.
    - Always double-check the angle with a protractor or miter gauge before cutting to ensure the cut is accurate.
- **For Bevel Cuts**:
    - Set the blade of your circular saw or table saw to the desired bevel angle. Typically, this is a 45° angle for trimming edges, but the angle may vary based on your design.
    - For precise bevel cuts, use a bevel gauge to set the angle of the cut before starting.
    - Support the board firmly to avoid shifting while cutting, especially when making deep bevel cuts.

- **Test Cuts**: Before committing to the final piece, make a test cut on scrap wood to check the angle. This helps you ensure that the cut is smooth and accurate.

Safety Tips:
- Be cautious when making angled cuts, especially when using a circular saw or table saw, as the material may shift or bind. Always use a clamp or proper support to stabilize the wood.
- Wear safety glasses and ear protection when cutting, as angled cuts can produce a significant amount of dust and debris.
- Use a proper saw guide or miter box when making cuts by hand to maintain accuracy.

Avoiding Common Cutting Mistakes

Whether you're using a hand saw, power saw, or table saw, even small errors can result in poor-quality cuts, wasted wood, or safety hazards. Here are some of the most common cutting mistakes and how to avoid them:

---

1. Not Measuring Properly

Mistake: One of the most common cutting mistakes is inaccurate measurements. If your measurements are off, your cuts will be too, and this can ruin the fit of your joints or result in misaligned pieces.

How to Avoid It:
- **Double-Check Your Measurements**: Always measure twice before cutting. Ensure that your measuring tape or ruler is straight and level before taking measurements.
- **Use the Right Tools**: Use a **carpenter's square** or **speed square** to ensure your measurements are accurate and squared.
- **Mark Your Cut Line Clearly**: Use a pencil or marking tool to draw a precise and visible cut line, especially for important cuts. Make sure the line is straight and bold enough to see clearly.

---

2. Using Dull Blades

Mistake: Trying to cut with a dull blade can lead to jagged, uneven cuts, and it can also put unnecessary strain on your saw, potentially damaging the tool or causing dangerous kickbacks.

How to Avoid It:
- **Sharpen Blades Regularly**: Keep your saw blades sharp to ensure clean, smooth cuts. For handsaws, periodically file the teeth to maintain cutting efficiency.
- **Change Saw Blades When Necessary**: If you're using power tools, replace the blades or saw blades when they become dull or damaged. It's worth investing in a high-quality blade for better precision and longer-lasting performance.

- **Test the Cut**: Before making your final cut, test on a piece of scrap wood to ensure the blade is cutting efficiently and smoothly.

3. Not Securing the Wood Properly

Mistake: Failing to secure the wood properly before cutting can lead to shifting, binding, or uneven cuts. It can also cause kickback or dangerous wood movement during cutting.

How to Avoid It:

- **Use Clamps**: Always use clamps to secure your workpiece firmly on a workbench or sawhorse before cutting. This ensures stability and prevents any movement during the cut.
- **Use a Sacrificial Board**: When cutting through thick stock, use a sacrificial piece of scrap wood underneath your project to help support it and prevent any splintering or kickback on the cut side.
- **Check for Movement**: Before starting to cut, give the wood a gentle push to make sure it doesn't shift. If it does, adjust the clamps or supports.

4. Incorrect Blade Depth

Mistake: Setting the blade depth too shallow or too deep can result in rough cuts or even kickback, especially with power tools like circular saws.

How to Avoid It:

- **Set Blade Depth Just Right**: The ideal depth is to set the blade just slightly deeper than the thickness of the material you're cutting. This ensures that the saw cuts through the material without overexposing the blade.
- **Check Blade Alignment**: Ensure that the blade is aligned properly with your cutting line and that it remains at the correct depth throughout the cut.

5. Not Using a Guide for Straight Cuts

Mistake: Attempting to make straight cuts without using a guide can lead to crooked, uneven cuts, especially with power saws.

How to Avoid It:

- **Use a Saw Guide**: For **circular saws**, use a straightedge, or clamp a scrap piece of wood as a guide to keep your cut straight.
- **Track Your Cut Line**: Use a carpenter's square or cutting guide to keep your saw on track and ensure the cut stays aligned with your marked line.
- **Use a Fence for Power Saws**: If you're using a **table saw**, always set the fence parallel to the blade to keep the piece of wood steady as you cut.

6. Not Accounting for Blade Kerf

Mistake: The **kerf** is the width of the cut made by the blade. If you don't take this into account, your measurements can end up too short, and your pieces won't fit together properly.

How to Avoid It:
- **Measure from the Cut Side**: When marking your cut, account for the kerf by measuring from the outside edge of the blade (if cutting on the waste side). This ensures the final piece is the correct size.
- **Use the Right Blade**: Choose a blade with the appropriate kerf width for the precision you need, especially for projects requiring tight joints.

7. Cutting Too Fast

Mistake: Rushing through cuts, especially with power tools, can result in uneven or jagged edges, reduced accuracy, and even the risk of injury.

How to Avoid It:
- **Take Your Time**: Always feed the wood slowly through the saw, allowing the tool to cut without forcing it. This ensures a smoother cut and helps avoid mistakes.
- **Maintain Control**: Hold your saw firmly and guide it steadily. For power saws, don't push the tool too hard — let the blade do the work.

8. Incorrect Cutting Angle

Mistake: Making angled cuts (like bevel or miter cuts) without adjusting the saw or measuring the angle correctly can result in slanted edges that don't fit properly, affecting the project's final quality.

How to Avoid It:
- **Double-Check the Angle**: Before making angled cuts, measure the angle with a protractor or adjustable square to make sure it's accurate.
- **Use a Guide for Angled Cuts**: A **miter saw** is ideal for making accurate angled cuts. If using a **table saw**, adjust the blade and use a miter gauge to maintain the correct angle.

Chapter 5: Joinery Techniques and Essential Joints

5.1 Introduction to Joinery

Overview of Joinery Principles

that maximizes both strength and design. Several fundamental principles guide the process of choosing and executing woodworking joints:

1. **Strength and Stability**: The primary purpose of joinery is to create a bond that can hold up over time and withstand stress. Different types of joints offer varying levels of strength, and selecting the right one for your project ensures that it will stand the test of time.
2. **Precision and Fit**: A tight, precise fit is essential for joints to hold securely. Gaps between pieces can weaken the bond and detract from the overall appearance. Achieving a perfect fit involves careful measuring, cutting, and planing.
3. **Durability**: The strength of a joint is not only about the wood and the tools but also about the technique. Properly executed joints can add significant durability to a project, particularly those exposed to pressure or movement.
4. **Aesthetics**: The style and design of a joint can also contribute to the final look of your project. Some joints, like dovetails or mortise and tenon, are decorative in addition to being functional. Choosing the right joint also involves considering how it will contribute to the overall appearance of your work.
5. **Ease of Execution**: Different joints require different levels of skill, time, and equipment. For beginners, simpler joints such as butt joints or lap joints might be ideal, while more experienced woodworkers can experiment with more complex joints like dovetails or box joints.

Choosing Joints Based on Project Type and Durability

When deciding which joinery technique to use, it's important to consider the project's purpose, aesthetic requirements, and the environmental factors it will face. Not all joints are suited to every project. Here's a breakdown of how to choose the right joints based on project type and durability needs:

---

1. For Structural Strength:

- **Mortise and Tenon**: This is one of the oldest and most reliable joints used for making strong, permanent connections. The mortise (a hole in one piece) and the tenon (a protruding tongue on the other piece) fit together to form a secure bond. It's ideal for furniture and cabinetry, particularly when strength is essential, such as in table frames and chairs.

- **Dovetail**: Known for both its strength and its decorative appearance, the dovetail joint is frequently used in drawers and boxes. It resists pulling forces better than many other joints, making it ideal for parts that will experience tension and compression.
- **Box Joint**: A strong alternative to dovetails, box joints are simple to cut and can be used for boxes, drawers, and frames. They offer a high level of strength for their simplicity and can be quite aesthetically pleasing when well-executed.

2. For Simpler Projects or Temporary Joints:
- **Butt Joint**: A basic joint where two pieces of wood are simply butted together at a right angle. While easy to make, it lacks strength and durability on its own. It's best used for decorative pieces where the joint will not be under a lot of stress. Adding screws, nails, or wood glue can improve its holding power.
- **Lap Joint**: This involves overlapping two pieces of wood by cutting away part of each piece so they can fit together. It's a stronger version of the butt joint and is often used in frame constructions. It's not as strong as the mortise and tenon but is easier to make and suitable for projects like basic shelving and smaller boxes.
- **Pocket Hole Joint**: Pocket holes are drilled at an angle and are typically joined with screws. This is a quick and easy method, often used in cabinetry and furniture construction. While strong, pocket hole joints are usually hidden within the project, as the screws are visible on the surface.

3. For Aesthetic Considerations:
- **Dovetail Joint**: As mentioned earlier, dovetail joints are not only strong but also a beautiful addition to furniture. Their interlocking design creates a pleasing, symmetrical appearance, making them a popular choice for high-quality drawer construction.
- **Biscuit Joint**: Used mainly for edge-to-edge joints, biscuit joints involve a small, oval-shaped piece of wood (a biscuit) that fits into corresponding slots in the two pieces being joined. This method is fast and effective for joining flat panels, making it ideal for table tops and large panels where appearance matters.
- **Miter Joint**: A miter joint involves two pieces of wood being cut at angles (usually 45 degrees) to meet at a corner. This is typically used in frames and trim work where a clean, sharp corner is desired without exposed end grain.

4. For Outdoor or Heavy-Duty Applications:
- **Dowels**: Dowels are small, cylindrical rods that fit into holes drilled in both pieces of wood. Dowels create strong joints, especially when reinforced with glue, making them suitable for furniture,

cabinetry, and other load-bearing items. For outdoor projects, it's essential to use a durable wood species and exterior-grade glue.
- **Through Dovetail**: Often used in furniture where both strength and beauty are important, through dovetail joints allow for a visible dovetail on both the front and back sides of the workpiece. It's great for drawers or cabinets that are exposed to high loads and frequent handling.
- **Tongue and Groove**: This joint is commonly used in flooring, paneling, and wallboards, as well as some types of cabinetry. It allows for strong connections, especially when the wood will expand and contract with changes in humidity.

---

5. For Specialized Applications:
- **Spline Joint**: Used in the joining of edges of panels (such as cabinet sides), the spline joint involves inserting a thin piece of wood (the spline) into slots cut along the edges of two pieces. It adds strength and alignment and is a great choice for larger panels or for situations where edge alignment is crucial.
- **Scarf Joint**: A long, slanted joint used for joining two pieces of wood end-to-end, the scarf joint is great for extending wood pieces that are not long enough. This is often used in boat building or in long beams.

5.2 Essential Joints for Beginners

Butt Joint

A **butt joint** is one of the most basic and commonly used types of woodworking joints. It involves connecting two pieces of wood by simply butting the ends of the pieces together, either edge-to-edge or end-to-edge. The simplicity of the butt joint makes it an easy choice for many woodworking projects. However, the butt joint is not as strong as other more advanced joints, but when properly reinforced, it can be used effectively for many applications like frame construction, shelves, and boxes.

Here's how to make one:

1. **Measure and Cut the Wood:** Measure and mark the lengths of the pieces to be joined. Cut the wood to size using a saw, ensuring straight, clean cuts.
2. **Mark the Joint:** Place the pieces together, aligning them as they will be joined. Use a square to ensure the pieces are aligned at a 90-degree angle.
3. **Apply Wood Glue:** Apply a thin, even layer of wood glue to the edge of one piece. Press the two pieces together.
4. **Clamp the Pieces:** Clamp the pieces together, ensuring they are flush at the edges. Wipe away any excess glue with a damp cloth. Let the glue dry as per the manufacturer's instructions.

5. **Reinforce (Optional):** If desired, drill pilot holes and drive screws into the joint for added strength. Alternatively, you can use nails.
6. **Smooth the Joint:** Once the glue is dry, remove the clamps and sand the joint smooth to eliminate any rough spots.
7. **Finish the Joint (Optional):** Apply wood finish, such as stain or varnish, to protect the joint and enhance the appearance.

Miter Joint

A **miter joint** is a joint where two pieces of wood are cut at an angle, typically 45 degrees, to form a corner. It's commonly used in frame construction and for creating neat, angled edges.

Here's how to make one:
1. **Measure and Cut the Wood:** Measure and mark the lengths of the pieces to be joined. Use a miter saw or a hand saw with a miter box to cut each piece at a 45-degree angle. Ensure the cuts are clean and accurate for a tight fit.
2. **Mark the Joint:** Place the two pieces together to form the desired corner. Use a square or protractor to verify that the angle is exactly 90 degrees.
3. **Apply Wood Glue:** Apply a thin, even layer of wood glue along the angled edges of both pieces. Press the pieces together to form the joint.
4. **Clamp the Pieces:** Clamp the pieces together firmly, ensuring the edges meet flush and the angle is precise. Wipe away any excess glue with a damp cloth. Let the glue dry according to the manufacturer's instructions.
5. **Reinforce (Optional):** For added strength, you can drill pilot holes and drive screws into the joint. Alternatively, you can use nails or dowels to reinforce the joint.
6. **Smooth the Joint:** Once the glue is fully dry, remove the clamps and sand the joint smooth to eliminate any rough edges or glue residue.
7. **Finish the Joint (Optional):** Apply wood finish (such as stain or varnish) to the joint to protect it and enhance its appearance.

Tips:
- Use a miter saw for the most accurate cuts, but a hand saw with a miter box can also do the job well.
- For precise angle cuts, double-check your measurements before cutting, as small errors can affect the joint's fit.

- Consider reinforcing the miter joint with a splint or dowel for additional durability, especially for larger pieces.

Dado Joint

A **dado joint** is a type of woodworking joint where a groove is cut across the grain of one piece of wood to fit another piece snugly. This joint is ideal for shelf construction, cabinet making, and other furniture projects.

Here's how to create a dado joint:

1. **Measure and Mark the Dado:** Measure the width and depth of the dado groove you want to cut on the piece that will receive the other board. Mark the position of the dado across the wood using a pencil, square, and measuring tape.
2. **Set Up the Saw:** If using a table saw, install a dado blade or dado stack to create the groove. Adjust the blade to the desired width and depth for the dado, and make sure it is properly aligned with the fence.
3. **Cut the Dado Groove:** With the wood securely positioned, make the first cut by running the piece through the saw, ensuring it stays aligned with the fence. Make additional passes if necessary to achieve the desired width or depth.
4. **Test the Fit:** After cutting, test the fit of the board that will fit into the dado groove. It should fit snugly, without being too tight or too loose. If needed, trim the groove or the fitting board slightly for a better fit.
5. **Apply Wood Glue:** Once the dado is cut, apply a thin, even layer of wood glue inside the groove and along the edge of the fitting board.
6. **Fit the Joint:** Insert the fitting board into the dado groove, ensuring the edges are flush and properly aligned. Press it in gently but firmly.
7. **Clamp the Pieces:** Clamp the pieces together to ensure a tight bond. Wipe away any excess glue with a damp cloth. Let the glue dry according to the manufacturer's instructions.
8. **Reinforce (Optional):** For added strength, drill pilot holes and drive screws through the sides of the dado groove into the fitting board. Alternatively, you can use nails, dowels, or wooden splints.
9. **Smooth the Joint:** Once the glue is dry, remove the clamps and sand the joint smooth, removing any rough edges or excess glue.
10. **Finish the Joint (Optional):** Apply wood finish (such as stain or varnish) to the joint to protect it and improve its appearance.

Tips:
- If you don't have a dado blade, you can create a dado joint by making multiple passes with a standard table saw blade or use a router with a dado bit.
- Ensure the dado groove is cut across the grain of the wood, not along it, to ensure maximum strength.
- For precise and consistent results, consider using a dado jig for your router or saw.

Mortise and Tenon Joint

The **mortise and tenon joint** is one of the strongest and most traditional woodworking joints, commonly used in furniture making, cabinetry, and frame construction. It consists of a "tenon" (a projection at the end of one piece) that fits into a corresponding "mortise" (a hole or slot) in the other piece, creating a strong, interlocking bond.

Step-by-Step Instructions:
1. **Mark the Mortise and Tenon:** Measure and mark the location of the mortise on the piece that will have the hole (usually the frame piece). Mark the tenon dimensions on the end of the piece that will fit into the mortise (typically the rail or horizontal member). Use a square to ensure your marks are at a 90-degree angle.
2. **Cut the Tenon:**
    - Use a saw to cut along the lines for the tenon. The tenon should fit snugly into the mortise, so ensure your cuts are precise.
    - The tenon typically has two shoulders (the outer edges) and a neck (the projection that fits into the mortise).
    - Use a hand saw, table saw, or miter saw to cut the tenon's length and width. Ensure it is slightly thinner than the mortise to allow a good fit.
3. **Create the Mortise:**
    - The mortise is the hole that will accept the tenon. Use a drill with a bit wide enough for the mortise, drilling multiple holes along the line of the mortise.
    - Once the holes are drilled, use a chisel to clean out the remaining wood and shape the sides of the mortise to fit the tenon snugly.
    - You can also use a router to hollow out the mortise if you prefer a faster method.
4. **Test the Fit:** After cutting the mortise and tenon, test the fit by inserting the tenon into the mortise. The fit should be snug but not forced. If it's too tight, slightly adjust the tenon or mortise to achieve a better fit.

5. **Apply Wood Glue:** Once the fit is correct, apply a thin layer of wood glue to the tenon and inside the mortise.
6. **Assemble the Joint:** Insert the tenon into the mortise, ensuring it fits tightly. The tenon should sit flush with the edge of the mortised piece.
7. **Clamp the Joint:** Use clamps to hold the pieces together while the glue dries. Make sure the pieces are square and aligned properly. Wipe away any excess glue with a damp cloth.
8. **Reinforce the Joint (Optional):** For added strength, especially in large or load-bearing joints, you can reinforce the mortise and tenon joint by adding dowels, wooden pegs, or screws. Drive the pegs into the tenon at a slight angle to secure it in place.
9. **Finish the Joint:**
    - Once the glue has dried, remove the clamps and use a chisel to smooth out any excess glue or rough spots around the joint.
    - Sand the joint and the surrounding area for a clean, smooth finish.
10. **Apply Finish (Optional):** Apply your preferred wood finish, such as stain, varnish, or oil, to protect and enhance the wood's appearance.

Tips:
- Make sure your cuts for both the tenon and mortise are square to ensure the joint will be tight and strong.
- Use a mortise chisel with a mallet for cleaner cuts and better control.
- For very precise mortise and tenon joints, you might want to use a tenon jig on a table saw or a dedicated mortiser.

Dovetail Joint

The **dovetail joint** is a classic and highly durable woodworking joint, often used in fine woodworking, especially in drawer construction, cabinets, and furniture. Its interlocking "tails" and "pins" make it strong and resistant to pulling apart. This joint is known for its aesthetic appeal as well as its strength.

Step-by-Step Instructions:
1. **Mark the Pins (on the Drawer Side):**
    - Begin by marking the dimensions of the drawer side (or whatever piece is receiving the pins) on the edge of the wood. Use a pencil, square, and ruler to mark evenly spaced vertical lines for the tails (or pins).
    - The number of pins depends on the size of the joint; typically, 3-5 pins per side are used.
    - The pin area should be slightly smaller than the thickness of the other piece (the tails).

2. **Mark the Tails (on the Drawer Front or Connecting Piece):**
   - Next, mark the tail shape on the piece that will receive the tails (the front of the drawer, for instance). To do this, use the drawer side as a template, transferring the exact measurements of the pins onto the edge of the front piece.
   - The tails should be wider than the pins to create the interlocking pattern, with a slight taper for an angled cut (around 7–10 degrees, depending on style preference).
3. **Cut the Pins:**
   - With the pins marked on the drawer side piece, use a dovetail saw or fine-toothed saw to cut along the lines. Make sure to keep the saw perpendicular to the wood for clean, straight cuts.
   - Use a chisel to remove the waste wood between the pins, carefully following the line to create clean, precise cuts. A mallet can be used to tap the chisel, allowing it to make deeper cuts as needed.
4. **Cut the Tails:**
   - Use the drawer side (with the marked pins) as a guide to mark the corresponding tail cuts on the front piece.
   - Carefully saw along the tail lines, cutting the angled portions with a dovetail saw. If you're cutting tight corners, you can use a coping saw or fine saw to reach them.
   - Remove the waste wood between the tails with a chisel, ensuring the cuts are clean and precise.
5. **Test the Fit:**
   - Once the tails and pins are cut, test the fit by dry-fitting the two pieces together. The tails should fit snugly into the pins, and the two pieces should align flush with each other.
   - If necessary, adjust the cuts by trimming or sanding until the fit is perfect. The joint should be tight, but not forced.
6. **Apply Wood Glue:** Once the fit is correct, apply a thin layer of wood glue to the surfaces of the pins and tails. Be sure not to use too much glue, as it may squeeze out when the joint is clamped.
7. **Assemble the Joint:** Carefully fit the tails into the pins. The interlocking nature of the dovetail joint should ensure a strong bond. Tap the joint lightly with a mallet to ensure the pieces fit together tightly.
8. **Clamp the Joint:**
   - Use clamps to hold the joint firmly in place while the glue dries. Make sure the joint is flush on all sides and that the pieces remain square and aligned.
   - Wipe away any excess glue that may squeeze out from the joint using a damp cloth.
9. **Finish the Joint:**

- Once the glue has dried, remove the clamps and use a chisel to clean up any excess glue or rough spots around the joint.
- Sand the joint and the surrounding area for a smooth, professional finish.
10. **Apply Finish (Optional):** Once the joint is smooth and clean, apply your desired finish, such as wood stain, varnish, or oil, to enhance the appearance and protect the wood.

Tips:

- For perfectly straight and accurate cuts, use a dovetail jig, especially if you're new to the process.
- Use a marking gauge or caliper to ensure your measurements are exact and consistent.
- For a tighter, more refined joint, make sure your cuts are as clean as possible, avoiding tear-out or rough edges.
- The angle of the tails can vary, but a 7–10 degree slope is a common and strong option.
- When using a dovetail saw, ensure you're cutting on the correct side of the line to maintain precision.

Finger Joint

The **finger joint** (also known as a box joint) is a strong and versatile woodworking joint, commonly used in box and drawer construction. The interlocking "fingers" create a large gluing surface, which results in a very durable joint. Finger joints are often used for joining end pieces, especially when strength and resistance to pulling forces are important.

Step-by-Step Instructions:

1. **Measure and Mark the Pieces:**
    - Begin by measuring and marking the dimensions of the pieces to be joined. You will need to determine how many "fingers" you want on the joint. Typically, 3 to 5 fingers per side work well, depending on the width of the wood.
    - Mark the wood with a pencil and square, making sure your measurements are exact for consistent finger cuts.
2. **Set Up the Finger Joint Jig:**
    - If you're using a finger joint jig (often attached to a table saw or router), set it up according to the manufacturer's instructions. The jig should be adjusted to the size of the fingers, based on the thickness of the wood you are working with.
    - Ensure the blades or router bit are set to the correct depth for cutting the fingers. Typically, the cuts should be slightly deeper than half the thickness of the wood to ensure a solid joint.
3. **Cut the Fingers on the First Piece:**

- With the jig set up, cut the fingers (or slots) on one edge of the first piece. The saw blade will make a series of vertical cuts, leaving the "fingers" between the slots.
- Carefully move the piece through the jig, ensuring that each cut is straight and consistent. Continue cutting until all fingers are formed on this piece.

4. **Cut the Matching Slots on the Second Piece:**
   - Now, mark the second piece in the same manner as the first, ensuring the corresponding finger slots are aligned.
   - Use the jig again to cut the matching fingers on the second piece. This time, the cuts should line up with the slots on the first piece, ensuring a tight fit.
   - Double-check that your cuts are aligned before proceeding.
5. **Test the Fit:**
   - Once the pieces are cut, test the fit of the joint by dry-fitting the two pieces together. The fingers should interlock tightly with the corresponding slots.
   - If necessary, adjust the cuts by trimming or sanding lightly to achieve a snug fit. The pieces should be flush when assembled, with no gaps.
6. **Apply Wood Glue:** Once the fit is correct, apply a thin layer of wood glue to the fingers and slots on both pieces. Be sure to coat the entire joint surface evenly to ensure a strong bond.
7. **Assemble the Joint:** Fit the pieces together, interlocking the fingers with the corresponding slots. The joint should slide together smoothly, with the fingers forming a solid connection.
8. **Clamp the Pieces:**
   - Clamp the pieces tightly together to hold the joint in place while the glue dries. Make sure the joint remains square and flush on all sides. If necessary, wipe away any excess glue with a damp cloth.
   - Allow the glue to set according to the manufacturer's instructions, usually for at least 30 minutes to an hour.
9. **Smooth the Joint:**
   - After the glue has dried, remove the clamps and inspect the joint. Use a chisel to clean up any excess glue or rough spots around the joint.
   - Sand the joint and surrounding area to smooth out any rough edges and ensure a clean finish.
10. **Finish the Joint (Optional):** Once the joint is smooth and clean, you can apply your preferred wood finish, such as wood stain, varnish, or oil, to protect and enhance the appearance of the wood.

Tips:

- If you don't have a finger joint jig, you can make one yourself or use a router with a box joint bit.
- The width of the fingers can be varied to fit the design and aesthetic you want. Wider fingers provide more surface area for glue and add strength.
- Always measure and double-check your cuts before assembling the joint to avoid mistakes.
- For a more professional finish, consider using a dado blade set on the table saw, or a router with a box joint bit, to achieve cleaner cuts.

Rabbet Joint

A rabbet joint is a simple but effective joint where one piece of wood has a notch (rabbet) cut along its edge to fit another piece. It is commonly used for joining edges of plywood, backing panels, and creating box or cabinet frames. The rabbet provides a strong joint and increases the gluing surface area. The rabbet joint is a useful, easy-to-make joint, ideal for cabinets, frames, and many other woodworking projects where a strong edge connection is needed.

Step-by-Step Instructions:

1. **Measure and Mark**: Measure and mark the depth and length of the rabbet on the edge of the wood that will be cut. Use a square to ensure accuracy.
2. **Set Up the Saw**: If using a table saw, adjust the blade height to the depth of the rabbet. If using a router, install a rabbet bit with the appropriate depth.
3. **Cut the Rabbet**: Using a table saw, make the cut along the marked line, ensuring the piece is securely clamped. If using a router, follow the marked line to rout the rabbet.
4. **Clean Up the Cut**: After cutting, check for any rough edges or imperfections. Use a chisel or sandpaper to smooth the rabbet and ensure it fits the joining piece well.
5. **Dry Fit**: Test the joint by inserting the rabbeted edge into the mating piece to ensure a tight, flush fit.
6. **Apply Wood Glue**: Apply a thin layer of glue to the rabbet joint surfaces and press the pieces together.
7. **Clamp and Dry**: Clamp the pieces together, ensuring they are aligned properly. Wipe away any excess glue and let the joint dry for the recommended time.
8. **Finish**: Once dry, remove the clamps, smooth the joint with sandpaper, and finish with your choice of stain, paint, or varnish.

When to Use Glued Joints vs. Mechanical Fasteners

When deciding whether to use **glued joints** or **mechanical fasteners** in woodworking, it's important to consider the project type, material, strength needs, and desired appearance. Both methods have their advantages, and understanding when to use each can improve your results.

Glued Joints

Gluing is ideal for fine woodworking where aesthetics and strong, invisible joints are required.

Advantages:
- **Strength and Durability**: Glued joints can be stronger than the wood itself, especially with high-quality adhesives like PVA or epoxy.
- **Clean Appearance**: Glued joints are seamless with no visible hardware, perfect for fine furniture or cabinetry.
- **Versatility**: Works with various joint types, such as butt, dovetail, and finger joints, and provides long-term strength.
- **No Rust or Corrosion**: Unlike fasteners, glue won't rust over time.

Disadvantages:
- **Time-Consuming**: Requires drying and curing time, slowing down the project.
- **Requires Clamps**: Clamping is necessary while the glue sets, adding time and effort.
- **Non-Reversible**: Once set, the joint is permanent and hard to undo.

When to Use:
- **Furniture Making**: For fine, detailed projects where clean, strong, and invisible joints are important.
- **Strength**: When strength is a priority, such as in **frame-and-panel** construction or **dovetail joints**.
- **Aesthetic Appeal**: When you want a seamless, professional look with no visible hardware.

Mechanical Fasteners

Mechanical fasteners (like screws, nails, and bolts) are useful for quick assembly and projects that require added strength or ease of disassembly.

Advantages:
- **Quick Assembly**: Fasteners allow for immediate assembly without waiting for drying time.
- **Immediate Holding Power**: Provides immediate strength for quick, functional builds.
- **Reversibility**: Fasteners can be removed or adjusted if needed, which is useful for projects requiring flexibility.
- **Durability Under Stress**: Especially in outdoor or load-bearing projects, fasteners provide strong holding power.

Disadvantages:
- **Visible Joints**: Fasteners can be unsightly, especially for projects where a clean finish is desired.
- **Risk of Wood Damage**: Poorly placed fasteners can split the wood or cause other damage.
- **Corrosion**: Metal fasteners may rust or corrode, weakening the joint over time.

When to Use:
- **Quick Construction**: When you need fast assembly, like in **rough frames** or **plywood boxes**.
- **Outdoor Projects**: Ideal for **decks**, **sheds**, and other projects exposed to the elements where fasteners hold up well under stress.
- **Modular Designs**: When you need to adjust or disassemble the project later, fasteners allow for easy changes.

Criteria	Glued Joints	Mechanical Fasteners
Strength	Strong, durable when done correctly	Immediate holding power, good under stress
Speed of Assembly	Slower, requires curing time	Fast, no waiting for glue to set
Aesthetics	Invisible, seamless finish	Visible fasteners, unless hidden
Durability Over Time	Long-lasting, no rust or corrosion	May corrode or weaken, especially outdoors
Reversibility	Non-reversible once set	Can be adjusted or removed easily
Project Types	Fine furniture, cabinetry, delicate joints	Quick builds, outdoor structures, modular designs

5.3 Advanced Joinery Techniques

Dowel Joint

A **dowel joint** is a method of joining two pieces of wood using small cylindrical rods, known as dowels, to create a strong and precise connection. This joint is often used for edge-to-edge or edge-to-face connections in furniture making, cabinet construction, and other woodworking projects. It offers increased strength compared to basic butt joints and is an excellent option when screws or nails are not ideal.

Step-by-Step Instructions:

1. **Prepare the Wood**: Cut your pieces of wood to the required lengths for the joint. Ensure that the edges are square and smooth.
2. **Mark the Dowel Placement**: Use a doweling jig or a marking tool to precisely mark where the dowels will go. Typically, dowels are placed 1-2 inches from the edge of the wood, depending on the size of the pieces and the joint's purpose. Use a ruler and square to ensure the dowels are aligned correctly on both pieces.
3. **Drill Holes for the Dowels**: Using a drill and a dowel drill bit, carefully drill holes in the marked locations. Drill straight, consistent holes to ensure the dowels fit snugly. If you're using a doweling jig, it will help you maintain the correct alignment and depth for the holes.
4. **Apply Wood Glue**: Apply a thin layer of wood glue inside the holes on both pieces of wood. It's important to avoid over-applying the glue, as it can squeeze out when the dowels are inserted.
5. **Insert the Dowels**: Insert dowels into the holes of one piece of wood. Ensure the dowels are centered and fit snugly in the holes. Then align the second piece of wood and press it onto the dowels.
6. **Clamp the Pieces Together**: Once the dowels are inserted, use clamps to hold the pieces together while the glue dries. Make sure the pieces are flush and aligned properly.
7. **Wipe Off Excess Glue**: Before the glue dries, use a damp cloth to wipe off any excess glue that may have squeezed out of the joint.
8. **Let the Glue Dry**: Allow the glue to fully dry according to the manufacturer's instructions (usually 30 minutes to 1 hour for initial set and 24 hours for full curing).
9. **Trim and Sand the Dowels**: After the glue has dried, trim any excess dowel length that may be sticking out of the joint. Use a flush-cut saw or a saw to cut the dowels, then sand the area smooth to ensure the joint is clean and flush.
10. **Finish the Joint**: Once the joint is dry and smooth, you can proceed with sanding the entire project and applying your desired finish.

Biscuits Joint

Biscuit joinery involves cutting matching slots in two pieces of wood, inserting a biscuit (an oval-shaped wooden piece) with glue, and then clamping the pieces together. This method is used for edge-to-edge or panel glue-ups. This method provides strong alignment and is fast, making it ideal for cabinet-making and panel assembly.

Step-by-Step Instructions:
1. **Measure and Mark**: Mark the positions of the biscuit slots on both pieces of wood to be joined.
2. **Cut the Slots**: Use a biscuit joiner to cut slots at the marked locations.

3. **Apply Glue**: Apply wood glue to the slots and on the biscuits.
4. **Insert Biscuits**: Insert a biscuit into the slot on one of the pieces.
5. **Align and Clamp**: Join the two pieces, aligning the biscuits, and clamp them tightly.
6. **Wipe Excess Glue**: Remove any excess glue and let the joint dry according to the manufacturer's instructions.
7. **Sand and Finish**: Once dry, remove the clamps, sand the joint smooth, and finish as desired.

Pocket-Hole Joint

A pocket-hole joint involves drilling angled holes into one piece of wood and driving screws through them into another piece, creating a strong, durable joint. It's often used for furniture assembly and woodworking projects where a visible joint is not an issue. Pocket-hole joinery is ideal for fast assembly and provides a strong, hidden joint when screws are used properly.

Step-by-Step Instructions:

1. **Measure and Mark**: Mark the position of the pocket holes on the workpiece, ensuring they are evenly spaced.
2. **Drill Pocket Holes**: Use a pocket hole jig and drill bit to create angled holes at the marked positions.
3. **Apply Wood Glue**: Apply glue to the edge of the piece where the joint will be made.
4. **Align and Clamp**: Align the two pieces, ensuring the holes are properly positioned, and clamp them securely.
5. **Drive Screws**: Insert screws into the pocket holes and tighten them to join the pieces together.
6. **Wipe Excess Glue**: Clean any excess glue and let it dry.
7. **Finish**: Once the glue is dry, sand the joint smooth and finish as desired.

Bridle Joint

A bridle joint is a type of woodworking joint where one piece of wood is notched to fit into the end of another piece, typically used for framing and door construction. It's a strong and simple joint that doesn't require additional fasteners. The bridle joint is often used in the construction of frames, offering a durable connection without the need for screws or nails.

Step-by-Step Instructions:

1. **Measure and Mark**: Mark the location and dimensions of the notch on the end of the piece that will receive the joint.
2. **Cut the Notch**: Using a saw or router, cut the notch to the desired depth and width.

3. **Prepare the Second Piece**: Measure and mark the area on the second piece where the notched end will fit.
4. **Fit the Pieces Together**: Slide the notched piece into the second piece, ensuring a snug, flush fit.
5. **Apply Wood Glue**: Apply a thin layer of wood glue to the joint surfaces for added strength.
6. **Clamp and Dry**: Clamp the pieces together tightly to ensure a strong bond, wiping away any excess glue. Let the glue dry as per the manufacturer's instructions.
7. **Finish**: Once dry, remove the clamps, sand the joint smooth, and apply your finish.

Half Lap Joint

A half lap joint is a woodworking joint where two pieces of wood overlap, with each piece having half of its thickness removed at the joint. This joint is ideal for framing and provides a strong, stable connection. The half lap joint is a strong, simple joint often used in framing and for creating strong connections without additional fasteners.

Step-by-Step Instructions:
1. **Measure and Mark**: Mark the centerline and thickness on both pieces of wood where the joint will be made.
2. **Cut the Lap**: On each piece, use a saw or a router to remove half of the thickness along the marked area, ensuring both cuts are even and meet at the center.
3. **Test the Fit**: Place the two pieces together to check the fit. Adjust the cuts if necessary for a snug fit.
4. **Apply Wood Glue**: Apply glue to the joint surfaces on both pieces.
5. **Clamp the Joint**: Press the pieces together and clamp tightly to hold the joint while the glue sets. Wipe away any excess glue.
6. **Allow Glue to Dry**: Let the joint dry completely as per the glue manufacturer's instructions.
7. **Finish**: Sand the joint for smoothness and apply a finish to the project.

Box Joint

A box joint is a type of interlocking joint commonly used for creating strong corners in boxes or drawers. It consists of alternating notches (or "fingers") that fit together like a puzzle, providing a large surface area for glue to bond and adding strength and visual appeal. Box joints are particularly useful for creating strong, durable corners in projects like boxes and drawer fronts, where both strength and aesthetics are important.

Step-by-Step Instructions:

1. **Measure and Mark**: Mark the exact locations for the fingers on the ends of your workpieces. The fingers should be evenly spaced, typically around 1/4" to 1/2" wide, depending on your project.
2. **Set Up a Dado Blade or Router**: If using a table saw, set up a dado blade with a spacer to match the width of the fingers. If using a router, use a finger-jointing bit.
3. **Cut the Notches**: Carefully cut the notches on each end of the wood. Make sure to cut the same depth and width on both pieces for a consistent fit.
4. **Test the Fit**: Dry fit the two pieces to check if the fingers interlock correctly. Adjust as needed for a snug, but not too tight, fit.
5. **Apply Wood Glue**: Apply glue to the notches of the joint and on the mating surfaces.
6. **Clamp the Joint**: Assemble the pieces, interlocking the fingers, and clamp them tightly to ensure a secure bond.
7. **Allow Glue to Dry**: Let the glue set according to the manufacturer's instructions, typically for at least 30 minutes to 1 hour.
8. **Finish**: Once the glue is dry, remove the clamps and sand the joint smooth. Finish as desired.

Tongue and Groove Joint

A tongue and groove joint is a type of interlocking joint commonly used to join two pieces of wood edge-to-edge, providing both strength and alignment. This joint consists of a "tongue" (a protruding ridge) on one piece and a "groove" (a corresponding slot) on the other. When the two pieces are joined, the tongue fits snugly into the groove, creating a strong and precise connection. Tongue and groove joints are often used in flooring, paneling, and cabinetry, where a seamless, secure bond is needed.

Step-by-Step Instructions:
1. **Measure and Mark:** Measure and mark the exact location for the tongue and groove on the edges of your workpieces. The tongue should typically be around 1/4" to 1/2" wide, and the groove should match the width and depth of the tongue for a snug fit.
2. **Set Up the Router or Table Saw:** Set up a router with a tongue-and-groove bit or a table saw with a dado blade. The tongue bit should be set to create the correct width and depth of the tongue, while the groove bit should match the tongue's dimensions.
3. **Cut the Tongue:** On the first piece of wood, carefully cut the tongue along the edge, ensuring it is straight and of the correct size for the groove on the other piece.
4. **Cut the Groove:** On the second piece of wood, cut the groove along the edge to match the dimensions of the tongue. Ensure the groove is centered and of equal depth on both pieces.
5. **Test the Fit:** Dry fit the two pieces to check if the tongue fits snugly into the groove. If the fit is too tight or too loose, adjust the cuts as needed for a proper, but not overly tight, fit.

6. **Apply Wood Glue:** Apply glue to the groove of the second piece and the tongue of the first piece. Be sure not to apply too much glue, as it can cause squeezing out when the pieces are joined.
7. **Assemble and Clamp:** Insert the tongue into the groove, ensuring a tight fit. Clamp the pieces together firmly to allow the glue to bond the joint securely.
8. **Allow Glue to Dry:** Let the glue set according to the manufacturer's instructions, typically for 30 minutes to 1 hour, to ensure a strong bond.
9. **Finish:** Once the glue is dry, remove the clamps and sand the joint smooth. Finish the joint with your desired wood finish to enhance the look and protect the wood.

Chapter 6: Finishing Techniques

6.1 Surface Preparation

Sanding Techniques and Tools

The quality of your wood finish depends greatly on how well you prepare the surface before applying any stains, oils, or varnishes. Proper surface preparation is essential for achieving a smooth, even finish that enhances the natural beauty of the wood.

Sanding is one of the most important steps in surface preparation. It smooths rough surfaces, removes imperfections, and opens up the wood's pores, allowing finishes to better adhere. The right technique and tools are crucial for achieving the best results.

1. Choosing the Right Sandpaper
- Sandpaper comes in a variety of grits, which indicate how coarse or fine the abrasive material is. The lower the grit number, the coarser the paper.
- **Coarse grit (60-80):** Used for initial sanding or removing deep scratches and imperfections.
- **Medium grit (120-150):** Used for smoothing out the surface after coarse sanding.
- **Fine grit (180-220):** Used for final sanding to create a smooth, refined surface.
- **Extra fine grit (320-400):** Used for polishing the surface before applying the finish.

2. Sanding by Hand vs. Power Sander
- **Hand Sanding:** For smaller projects or when more control is needed, hand sanding allows you to focus on particular areas. Use a sanding block to ensure an even pressure distribution across the surface.
- **Power Sanding:** For larger surfaces or when you need to sand quickly, an orbital sander or a belt sander can speed up the process. Start with a coarse grit and gradually move to finer grits. An orbital sander provides a more consistent finish, while a belt sander is more aggressive and better for rough surfaces.

3. Sanding Direction
- Always sand with the grain of the wood, not against it. Sanding against the grain can create unsightly scratches that are difficult to remove.
- For the final sanding stages, switch to a fine grit paper and apply less pressure to avoid sanding away too much material.

4. Dust Removal
- After each sanding stage, make sure to thoroughly clean the surface of any dust. Use a vacuum with a brush attachment, or wipe the wood down with a damp cloth. Dust left on the surface can ruin the finish and create uneven spots.

Filling, Planing, and Preparing Wood for a Smooth Finish

Once the surface is sanded, it's important to address any imperfections, such as cracks, dents, or knots, to ensure the wood is perfectly smooth and even for finishing. This section will explain how to fill, plane, and prepare wood to achieve a flawless surface.

1. Filling Imperfections

- **Wood Filler:** For minor cracks, dents, or holes, use a high-quality wood filler that matches the wood type or color. Choose a filler with a similar texture to the wood to ensure a smooth and consistent finish.
    - Apply the filler with a putty knife, pressing it into the cracks or holes. Smooth it out with the knife, and allow it to dry according to the manufacturer's instructions.
    - Once dry, sand the filled areas with fine-grit sandpaper until the surface is smooth and level with the surrounding wood.
- **Wood Putty vs. Epoxy:** For deeper or larger imperfections, use a more durable product like epoxy. Epoxy is more flexible and can handle larger voids or cracks in the wood, while wood putty is more suited for smaller repairs.

2. Planing the Surface

- **Hand Planing:** For slight unevenness in the wood or when you need to reduce the thickness of a board, a hand plane can be a useful tool. A smoothing plane is used to flatten the surface, and a jack plane is used for removing thicker material. Always plane with the grain to avoid gouging the wood.
- **Power Planing:** For larger or more uneven surfaces, a power planer can be used to remove material more quickly. Use a light touch, and always work in the direction of the grain to avoid causing tear-out or rough surfaces.
- **Edge Planing:** When working with edges, ensure they are smooth and free from rough spots by using a block plane. This is especially important for edges that will be visible in the final piece.

3. Preparing for a Smooth Finish

- **Final Sanding:** After filling and planing, give the surface a final sanding with fine-grit sandpaper (220-grit or higher). This smooths out any imperfections left by the filling and planing process.
- **Checking the Surface:** Run your hand over the surface to feel for any rough spots. If any areas still feel uneven, go back and lightly sand them with fine-grit sandpaper. You should be able to feel a smooth, consistent texture across the entire piece before applying the finish.

4. Sealing the Wood (Optional)

- If the wood is particularly porous or contains open grain, you might want to apply a **wood conditioner** or **pre-stain wood sealer**. This helps to minimize blotchiness when applying stains or varnishes. Follow the product's instructions for application, and allow it to dry thoroughly before proceeding with staining or finishing.

6.2 Choosing Finishes for Different Wood Types

Understanding Various Finishes

The most common finishes for wood are **oil**, **wax**, **stain**, **varnish**, and **lacquer**. Each has distinct properties, making them suitable for different uses and wood types.

1. Oil Finishes

- **Description:** Oil finishes penetrate deep into the wood, providing a natural, rich look while enhancing the wood's grain. They offer moderate protection against water and wear but require periodic reapplication for maintenance.
- **Types:**
    - **Tung Oil:** A popular choice for its water-resistant properties and matte finish. It enhances the wood's color and grain without leaving a surface film.
    - **Linseed Oil:** Common in furniture-making, linseed oil provides a warm, amber tone and is often mixed with other finishes like beeswax.
    - **Teak Oil:** Ideal for exotic woods like teak and mahogany, this oil provides water resistance and maintains the wood's natural beauty.
- **Pros:** Penetrates the wood, gives a natural finish, easy to apply and maintain.
- **Cons:** Offers minimal protection compared to varnishes or lacquers and needs frequent reapplication.
- **Best For:** Wood furniture, countertops, and cutting boards where the wood's texture and natural beauty are the focal point.

2. Wax Finishes

- **Description:** Wax finishes provide a smooth, satin-like finish with a soft glow. They add a layer of protection, though it's less durable than oils or varnishes. Wax works well in conjunction with other finishes, such as oil or stain, to create a soft, hand-rubbed look.
- **Types:**
    - **Beeswax:** Used for polishing and protecting wood, beeswax gives a soft, lustrous finish, especially on fine furniture.
    - **Carnauba Wax:** A harder, more durable wax, often used on wood floors or in combination with other waxes for a high-gloss finish.
- **Pros:** Enhances the natural look of the wood, adds a soft, glossy finish, easy to apply, and provides a low-maintenance protective layer.
- **Cons:** Less durable, wears off with use, and provides minimal water resistance.
- **Best For:** Decorative wood pieces, fine furniture, or pieces that won't face heavy wear and tear.

3. Stain Finishes

- **Description:** Stains are primarily used to change the color of the wood while enhancing its grain. They don't provide as much protection as other finishes, so they're usually followed by a topcoat like varnish or lacquer.
- **Types:**
    - **Oil-Based Stains:** These penetrate the wood deeply, providing a richer, more vibrant color. They also offer a bit of protection against moisture.
    - **Water-Based Stains:** They dry faster, have a lower odor, and offer a more even finish. However, they don't penetrate as deeply as oil-based stains.
    - **Gel Stains:** Thicker than traditional stains, gel stains provide more control over the application and are ideal for vertical surfaces or intricate wood pieces.
- **Pros:** Allows you to change the color of the wood while preserving the grain. Can create a range of shades, from light to dark.
- **Cons:** Requires additional finishing (such as varnish or lacquer) for protection, as stains alone don't offer enough durability.
- **Best For:** Customizing the color of hardwoods and softwoods or achieving uniform color on less attractive wood grain.

4. Varnish Finishes

- **Description:** Varnish creates a hard, durable surface finish that provides excellent protection against moisture, scratches, and wear. Varnishes contain a blend of resin, oil, and solvent, and they come in various sheens, from matte to high gloss.
- **Types:**
    - **Polyurethane Varnish:** Known for its durability and water resistance, polyurethane is a common choice for high-traffic areas and furniture.
    - **Spar Varnish:** Specifically formulated for outdoor use, spar varnish offers superior UV protection and flexibility.
    - **Alkyd Varnish:** Often used for furniture and cabinetry, providing a durable, glossy finish.
- **Pros:** Offers superior durability and protection, especially for high-use surfaces. Available in a range of finishes from matte to high gloss.
- **Cons:** Takes longer to dry, and can be difficult to apply evenly without leaving brush marks.
- **Best For:** High-traffic furniture, floors, doors, windows, and outdoor furniture.

5. Lacquer Finishes

- **Description:** Lacquer is a fast-drying, high-gloss finish that creates a tough, protective surface. It is typically sprayed onto the wood and produces a very smooth, hard finish. While it's highly durable, lacquer can be prone to scratches and requires special application techniques.

- **Pros:** Fast drying time, high gloss, and excellent protection. It is commonly used in fine furniture making for a smooth, glass-like finish.
- **Cons:** Requires professional application for the best results (especially when sprayed). Can be sensitive to heat and moisture.
- **Best For:** Fine furniture, musical instruments, and high-end cabinetry where a glossy, smooth finish is desired.

How to Match Finishes with Wood Types

Choosing the right finish for a specific wood type is essential to enhance the wood's natural beauty while providing the appropriate level of protection. Different woods have unique characteristics that interact differently with various finishes. Below is a guide to help you match finishes with wood types:

1. Hardwoods (e.g., Oak, Maple, Cherry, Mahogany)
- **Finish Match:** Hardwoods are dense, and their smooth surfaces make them ideal candidates for varnishes, lacquers, and oils. These finishes enhance the natural grain of the wood and provide long-lasting protection.
- **Oil Finishes (Tung or Linseed Oil):** Enhance the grain and provide a natural matte to satin finish, especially on walnut or oak.
- **Varnish or Lacquer:** Best for cherry, maple, and mahogany, as these finishes can highlight the richness of the grain while providing durability for high-traffic furniture.
- **Stain:** Can be used to deepen the color of oak, cherry, or maple but be sure to follow with a protective topcoat like varnish.

2. Softwoods (e.g., Pine, Cedar, Fir)
- **Finish Match:** Softwoods are generally more porous and can absorb finishes quickly. These woods often benefit from stains to create a more uniform color, along with an oil-based or wax finish to enhance their appearance.
- **Oil Finishes (Linseed or Teak Oil):** These work well on pine and cedar, offering a warm, natural glow while providing a moderate level of protection.
- **Wax Finishes:** Ideal for softer woods like pine, as wax can protect the surface while maintaining a rustic, natural look.
- **Stain:** Cedar and pine often require staining to reduce blotchiness and provide a more even tone, particularly when used in cabinetry or furniture.

3. Exotic Woods (e.g., Teak, Mahogany, Ebony)
- **Finish Match:** Exotic woods have distinctive grains and rich colors that can be highlighted with minimal staining. These woods generally benefit from oils and varnishes that enhance their natural beauty.

- **Tung Oil or Teak Oil:** Perfect for exotic woods like teak and mahogany. These oils penetrate deeply to bring out the natural richness of the wood without altering its color.
- **Varnish:** Spar varnish is great for outdoor use on exotic woods, offering UV protection and enhancing the wood's appearance.
- **Lacquer:** If you want a high-gloss finish, lacquer is perfect for highlighting the fine grain of exotic woods.

4. Wood with Open Grain (e.g., Oak, Ash, Walnut)
- **Finish Match:** Woods with open grain patterns may require filling to create a smoother surface before finishing. Once filled, they look great with varnishes or oils that highlight their unique grain structure.
- **Filling:** Before applying finishes, use grain fillers to fill the open pores in woods like oak and ash.
- **Oil and Varnish:** Oil finishes work well on these woods, allowing the grain to stand out while providing protection. Varnish can be used afterward for a durable, high-gloss finish.

Enhancing Wood Grain and Color with Different Finishes

The natural beauty of wood lies in its grain and color, which can be dramatically enhanced or altered using various finishes. Whether you want to accentuate the intricate grain patterns of oak, the deep hues of walnut, or give a uniform tone to a more porous wood like pine, the right finish can elevate the wood's appearance and bring out its best features.

Understanding how different finishes interact with the wood's surface and color is essential for achieving the desired result. Below, we explore how oil, stain, varnish, and other finishes can be used to enhance the grain and color of wood.

---

1. Oil Finishes

Oil finishes, such as **tung oil, linseed oil**, and **teak oil**, are excellent for enhancing the natural color and grain of wood. These finishes penetrate deeply into the wood fibers, enriching its color while highlighting the grain patterns. Oil finishes are known for providing a natural, matte to satin sheen, giving the wood a soft, hand-rubbed appearance.

How Oil Enhances Wood Grain and Color:
- **Grain Highlighting:** Oil finishes bring out the wood's grain by penetrating the surface, making the natural patterns more visible. The oils soak into the porous areas, creating a slight contrast between the denser and softer parts of the grain.
- **Deepening Color:** Oils like linseed or tung oil deepen the wood's natural color, giving it a warm, rich tone. This is particularly effective on woods like walnut, oak, and teak, which darken over time with oil treatments.

- **Warmth:** The oil adds warmth to the wood, especially when applied to lighter woods like pine or maple, enriching their light hues without drastically changing their appearance.

Best For:
- **Hardwoods** like walnut, cherry, and oak.
- **Softwoods** like pine, cedar, and fir.
- Projects where you want to enhance the wood's natural look without creating a glossy, reflective finish.

---

2. Staining

Staining is a popular technique for altering the color of wood, allowing you to enhance or completely change its hue. Stains are available in a wide range of colors and can be used to create a more uniform tone or to highlight specific aspects of the wood's grain. Stains can be oil-based, water-based, or gel-based, each with distinct properties and applications.

How Stains Enhance Wood Grain and Color:
- **Grain Accentuation:** Stains can enhance the natural grain pattern of wood by contrasting with the darker and lighter areas of the grain. A dark stain, for example, can make the grain of oak or ash stand out, while a lighter stain can preserve the natural appearance of the wood.
- **Color Depth and Uniformity:** Stains can be used to deepen the color of a wood piece, making it appear richer and more uniform. For instance, pine, which often has an uneven color tone, can be stained to create a more consistent look that mimics higher-end woods like cherry or mahogany.
- **Highlighting Wood Features:** Different types of stains can bring out specific features of the wood. For example, a **mahogany stain** can enhance the reddish-brown hues in woods like oak or maple, while **walnut stain** can give lighter woods a deep, dark tone.

Best For:
- **Pine** and **poplar** when you want to reduce blotchiness and create a uniform finish.
- **Oak** and **ash** to accentuate the open grain patterns.
- Projects where you need to change the wood color significantly while still showcasing the natural grain.

---

3. Varnish and Lacquer

Varnishes and lacquers provide a durable, glossy finish that can help accentuate both the color and the grain of the wood. Unlike oils and stains, these finishes sit on top of the wood, forming a protective layer that enhances the overall appearance of the wood.

How Varnish and Lacquer Enhance Wood Grain and Color:

- **Glossy Sheen:** Varnish and lacquer finishes provide a high-gloss or satin sheen that can make the wood appear vibrant and polished. This enhances the wood's color by reflecting light, giving the finish a depth that oil finishes cannot achieve.
- **Grain Depth:** The build-up of varnish or lacquer can deepen the perception of the wood grain by creating a smooth, even surface that allows the light to reflect off the wood more evenly. This makes the grain more defined and visible, especially on fine-grained woods like cherry and walnut.
- **Color Preservation:** These finishes provide excellent protection to the wood's color, especially when used on light-colored woods like maple or oak, preventing them from yellowing or fading over time.

Best For:
- **Fine furniture** and **cabinetry** where a glossy, high-end finish is desired.
- **Wood floors** and high-traffic areas requiring a durable finish.
- **Exotic woods** like mahogany and teak, which benefit from a deep, protective finish.

---

4. Wax Finishes

Wax finishes, typically used as a topcoat over oil or stain, add a soft sheen to the wood, offering a natural, hand-rubbed finish. While wax does not dramatically alter the color of the wood, it enhances its richness and provides a subtle glow.

How Wax Enhances Wood Grain and Color:
- **Soft Glow:** Wax gives wood a warm, soft finish that enhances the natural texture and color without being too shiny. It is particularly effective at enhancing the warmth of woods like cherry or mahogany.
- **Smooth Finish:** Wax finishes help smooth out the surface, which can bring out the wood's grain and highlight the natural color without changing it drastically.
- **Minimal Alteration:** While wax does not darken or lighten the wood significantly, it can enrich the appearance by adding a deeper, more refined tone.

Best For:
- **Fine furniture** and **woodwork** where a subtle finish is desired.
- **Small wooden items** like picture frames or carvings, where you want to showcase the natural beauty of the wood without a high-gloss finish.
- Projects that will not be exposed to heavy wear and tear, as wax finishes require periodic reapplication.

---

5. Blending Finishes for Maximum Effect

In many cases, combining finishes can offer even greater enhancement of the wood's grain and color. For example:

- **Layering oil with lacquer:** Applying an oil finish followed by a lacquer topcoat can provide the depth of oil while also offering the durable, glossy finish of lacquer.
- **Using stain and wax together:** Staining the wood first and then applying a wax finish can add both color depth and a smooth, satin sheen, without a heavy gloss.
- **Wax over varnish:** A light coat of wax over varnish adds a softer sheen and more tactile texture, making the wood feel more natural while retaining the protective properties of the varnish.

6.3 Application Techniques

Best Practices for Brushing, Spraying, and Wiping Finishes

Applying finishes to wood requires precision and care to achieve a smooth, professional-quality result. The method you choose—whether brushing, spraying, or wiping—affects the final appearance and durability of the finish.

1. Brushing Finishes

Brushing is one of the most common methods for applying wood finishes, especially for oils, varnishes, and latex-based paints. This method works well for both large and small projects, allowing you to control the finish and ensure an even application.

Best Practices for Brushing:

- **Choose the Right Brush:** The type of brush you use is critical for achieving a smooth finish. For oil-based finishes, use a **natural bristle brush** (e.g., hog bristle), as it holds the finish better and leaves fewer brush marks. For water-based finishes, use a **synthetic brush** (e.g., nylon or polyester), as it resists the water and provides a smoother finish.
- **Apply Thin Coats:** Always apply thin, even coats of finish to prevent drips, streaks, and heavy buildup. Thin layers will allow the finish to dry more evenly and prevent issues such as pooling or uneven gloss.
- **Brush with the Grain:** To achieve a smooth, professional finish, always brush in the direction of the wood grain. Brushing across the grain can create visible streaks and disrupt the wood's natural appearance.
- **Work in Small Sections:** When brushing, work in manageable sections of the wood. This allows you to apply the finish quickly and maintain control over the application, ensuring even coverage.

- **Avoid Overworking the Finish:** Once the finish has been applied, avoid going back over it too many times. Brushing too much can cause the finish to become streaky or create unwanted bubbles. Apply a coat, then leave it to dry before assessing if another layer is needed.
- **Clean the Brush Properly:** After finishing, clean the brush thoroughly with the appropriate solvent (water for water-based finishes or mineral spirits for oil-based finishes). This ensures the brush remains in good condition for future use.

Best For:
- **Large surfaces** such as furniture, cabinetry, and doors.
- **Oil-based and water-based finishes** like varnish, polyurethane, and stains.

---

2. Spraying Finishes

Spraying finishes is ideal for achieving a smooth, even coating over large, flat surfaces without visible brush strokes. Spraying works well for finishes that need to be applied in multiple thin layers, such as lacquers, varnishes, or spray paints.

Best Practices for Spraying:
- **Use the Right Equipment:** Choose the right spray system depending on your project. A **spray gun** (either HVLP, conventional, or airless) is suitable for large projects, while a **spray can** is better for smaller items. Make sure the equipment is clean and in good working order to ensure an even spray pattern.
- **Thin the Finish if Necessary:** Some finishes (like lacquer or polyurethane) may need to be thinned to spray effectively. Follow the manufacturer's recommendations on how much to thin the finish to achieve the correct consistency.
- **Maintain the Proper Distance:** Keep the spray nozzle around 6 to 8 inches from the wood surface. Too close, and you risk overspray or dripping; too far, and the finish may dry before it hits the surface, leading to a rough texture.
- **Spray in Even Passes:** Begin spraying at one edge of the piece, and make overlapping passes from side to side, moving continuously to avoid applying too much finish in one area. Hold the spray gun at a consistent angle and speed to ensure an even coat.
- **Work in a Well-Ventilated Area:** Spraying finishes can release fumes, especially from solvent-based products. Ensure you work in a well-ventilated space or, ideally, use a spray booth with proper ventilation to protect your health.
- **Allow Proper Drying Time Between Coats:** To avoid the finish becoming too thick or uneven, allow adequate drying time between coats. This helps to prevent drips and ensures that each layer bonds effectively with the previous one.

Best For:

- **Large or intricate projects** where brush strokes would be visible, like tables, cabinetry, and doors.
- **Clear finishes** like lacquer, shellac, and polyurethane, as well as **painted surfaces**.

3. Wiping Finishes

Wiping finishes, such as oils and stains, are applied by rubbing the finish onto the wood surface with a cloth and then wiping off the excess. This method is particularly useful for wood types that are prone to blotching, such as pine, or when you want to enhance the wood's natural color without adding a heavy coating.

Best Practices for Wiping:

- **Apply Generously, Then Wipe Off Excess:** Start by applying a generous amount of finish with a soft, lint-free cloth. Allow the finish to sit on the wood for a few minutes to penetrate, then use a clean cloth to wipe off the excess. This prevents a sticky, uneven buildup of finish on the surface.
- **Work in Small Sections:** Wiping finishes are best applied in small sections to ensure even coverage and to avoid the finish drying prematurely on the surface. This is especially important when working with stain or oil finishes.
- **Use Circular or Back-and-Forth Motions:** When applying wiping finishes, use circular or back-and-forth motions to ensure the finish is applied evenly and works into the grain of the wood.
- **Buff to Desired Sheen:** For some finishes, like wax or oil, after wiping off excess and allowing it to dry, you can buff the surface with a clean, soft cloth to bring out a satin or semi-gloss sheen. Buffing enhances the depth of the color and can leave a smooth, tactile surface.
- **Be Mindful of Drying Times:** Wiping finishes tend to dry quickly, so work swiftly, especially when applying oil-based products. Some finishes may require a second or third application to build up depth and enhance the wood's appearance.

Best For:

- **Small projects** like picture frames, furniture, or small wooden objects.
- **Oils and stains** where a natural look is desired without the heavy build-up of lacquer or varnish.

Tips for Layering and Polishing Finishes

Layering and polishing finishes are essential for creating a smooth, durable, and aesthetically pleasing wood surface. Here are some concise tips to help you achieve professional-quality results:

1. Layering Finishes

- **Apply Thin Coats:** Use thin, even layers for better adhesion and durability.
- **Allow Drying Time:** Let each coat dry completely before applying the next, usually 2-24 hours.
- **Sand Between Coats:** Lightly sand with fine-grit sandpaper (320-grit) to ensure smooth adhesion.

- **Build Gradually:** Multiple thin coats are more effective than one thick coat.
- **Compatible Finishes:** Ensure finishes are compatible before layering (e.g., oil first, then polyurethane).

2. Polishing Finishes
- **Wait for Full Cure:** Let the finish cure fully before polishing, which may take a few days.
- **Polish with the Grain:** Always polish in the direction of the wood grain to avoid scratches.
- **Use Proper Tools:** Buff with a soft cloth or polishing pad for best results.
- **Polish in Stages:** Start with a coarser compound and finish with a fine compound for a smooth, glossy surface.
- **Maintain Sheen:** Reapply wax or polishing compound as needed to restore shine.

3. Final Touches
- **Final Sanding:** Lightly sand with ultra-fine sandpaper (600-grit) before buffing for an ultra-smooth finish.
- **Use a Tack Cloth:** Remove dust with a tack cloth before each coat or polishing.
- **Protect the Surface:** Let the piece cure in a dust-free environment for the best finish.

6.4 Maintenance of Finished Woodwork
Protecting and Maintaining Finished Projects
Once your wood project is finished and polished, it's important to protect and maintain the finish to ensure it lasts and remains visually appealing. Proper care and protection can prevent damage from environmental factors, wear, and tear. Here's how to keep your finished projects looking great for years to come.

1. General Protection Tips
- **Use Coasters and Mats:** Place coasters under glasses and mats under objects to prevent scratches and stains, especially on furniture like tables and cabinets.
- **Avoid Direct Sunlight:** Prolonged exposure to sunlight can cause finishes to fade or discolor. Keep your projects out of direct sunlight or use UV-protective finishes.
- **Control Humidity and Temperature:** Wood is sensitive to moisture and temperature changes. Try to maintain stable humidity levels (between 40-60%) and avoid extreme temperatures, as they can cause the wood to warp or crack.

2. Regular Cleaning
- **Dust Frequently:** Use a soft, dry cloth to dust your finished projects regularly. Dust buildup can scratch the finish over time if left unchecked.
- **Clean with Mild Soap:** For deeper cleaning, use a soft cloth dampened with mild soap and water. Avoid harsh chemicals or abrasive cleaners that can damage the finish.
- **Avoid Excess Water:** When cleaning, use only a damp cloth, not a soaking wet one. Excess water can seep into the wood, damaging the finish and the wood itself.

---

3. Touching Up the Finish
- **Repair Scratches:** For minor scratches, use a matching wax, touch-up pen, or wood filler to fill in the damage. Always test in an inconspicuous area first.
- **Reapply Finish:** Over time, finishes can wear down. Reapply a thin layer of the original finish (e.g., polyurethane, lacquer, or wax) to restore shine and protection. Sand lightly between coats to ensure proper adhesion.

---

4. Long-Term Maintenance
- **Refinishing When Necessary:** If the finish becomes heavily damaged or worn, consider sanding the piece down and applying a fresh coat of finish. This is particularly useful for furniture or high-traffic items like tabletops.
- **Rewaxing:** For wax finishes, periodic reapplication is necessary to maintain both protection and sheen. Use a clean cloth to apply a thin layer of wax and buff it to a shine.
- **Protective Covers:** For items like chairs or tables that experience frequent use, consider using protective covers when not in use to preserve the finish.

Repairing Damaged Finishes Over Time

Even with the best care, wood finishes can get damaged over time due to scratches, wear, moisture, or accidents. Repairing these damages properly will restore the beauty of your project and extend its lifespan. Here's a guide to repairing damaged finishes effectively.

---

1. Assess the Damage
- **Minor Scratches and Scuffs:** Small, surface-level scratches can be repaired easily with minimal effort.
- **Deep Scratches or Gouges:** Deeper damage that affects the wood beneath the finish will require more intensive repair.

- **Water or Heat Marks:** Stains or discoloration caused by spills, heat, or moisture often need specialized attention.

2. Repairing Minor Scratches and Scuffs

- **Use a Touch-Up Pen or Marker:** For small scratches, use a matching wood touch-up pen or marker to conceal the damage. Apply the pen directly to the scratch, then wipe away excess with a soft cloth.
- **Rub With Wax:** For light surface scuffs, rubbing with a wax stick or furniture wax can help to blend the damage into the surrounding finish.
- **Buff the Area:** After using a touch-up product, buff the area with a soft cloth to restore a uniform finish.

3. Fixing Deep Scratches and Gouges

- **Wood Filler or Putty:** For deeper gouges, apply wood filler or putty that matches the color of your wood. Use a putty knife to fill the gouge, then sand the area smooth once it dries.
- **Refinish the Area:** After filling, sand the repaired area with fine-grit sandpaper (220-320 grit) until smooth. Apply the same finish (stain, lacquer, or polyurethane) to the patched area to match the surrounding surface.
- **Blend the Finish:** Use a polishing compound to blend the new finish with the existing one for a seamless look.

4. Repairing Water or Heat Marks

- **For Water Rings:** Apply a small amount of mayonnaise or petroleum jelly to the water stain and let it sit for several hours. Wipe away gently with a soft cloth. The oil helps to lift the stain from the finish.
- **For Heat Marks:** Use a mixture of equal parts baking soda and water to gently scrub the affected area. Alternatively, rubbing a small amount of furniture polish on the mark can help reduce its visibility.
- **Refinish if Necessary:** If the damage is severe, sanding the affected area lightly and reapplying the finish may be necessary.

5. Repairing Cracks and Peeling Finish

- **Reapply Finish:** If the finish has cracked or peeled, sand the affected area lightly, remove dust, and reapply the finish. Be sure to apply thin, even layers for the best results.

- **Seal the Edges:** For peeling or lifting finishes, carefully apply a thin coat of clear finish along the edges where the finish has lifted to seal it.

6. Prevent Future Damage

- **Regular Maintenance:** Regular cleaning and waxing help to prevent scratches and maintain the integrity of the finish.
- **Use Furniture Pads:** For items subject to heavy use, place protective pads under objects to avoid abrasion.
- **Keep Humidity Stable:** To prevent cracking or warping, maintain a consistent humidity level in the room where your wood project is kept.

Chapter 7: DIY Projects

DIY Headphone Stand

5"Wx6"Dx11"H

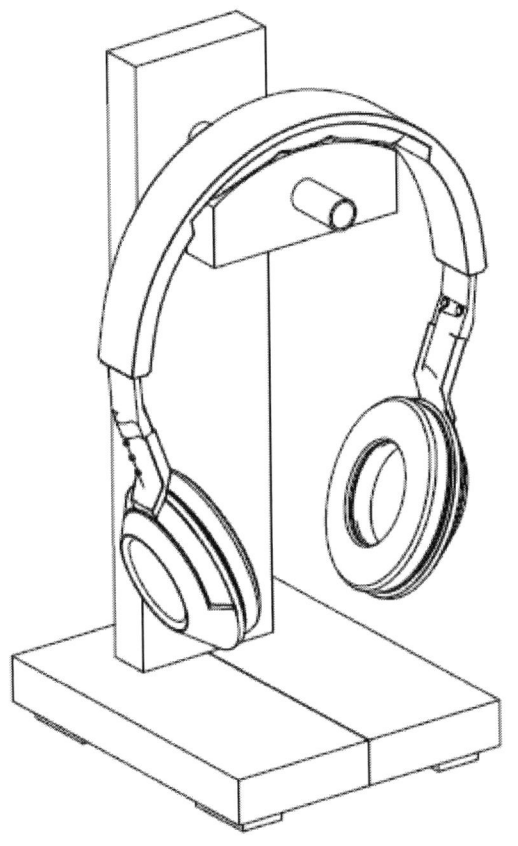

Materials

x1 Board, 1x3", 4' Length - (use the wood of your choice)

x1 ½" Diameter Aluminum Tube, 5-½" Length

Hardware

x2 1-¼" Coarse thread pocket-hole screws

Tools

Jigsaw

Electric drill

Miter Saw

Pocket-hole jig

Clamps

Tape measure

Sandpaper

Cut List and Parts

x2 Foot, ¾" x 2-½", ¼" Length

x2 Base, ¾" x 2-½", 6" Length

x1 Upright, ¾" x 2-½",, 10" Length

x1 Holder, ¾" x 1-½", 2-½" Length

x1 Aluminum Tube, ½" Diameter, 5-½" Length

x1 1x3", 4' Length

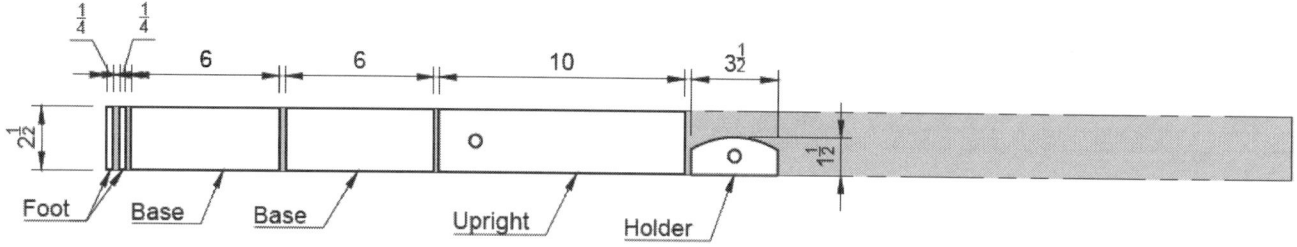

x1 ½" Aluminum Tube

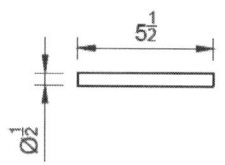

Exploded Diagram

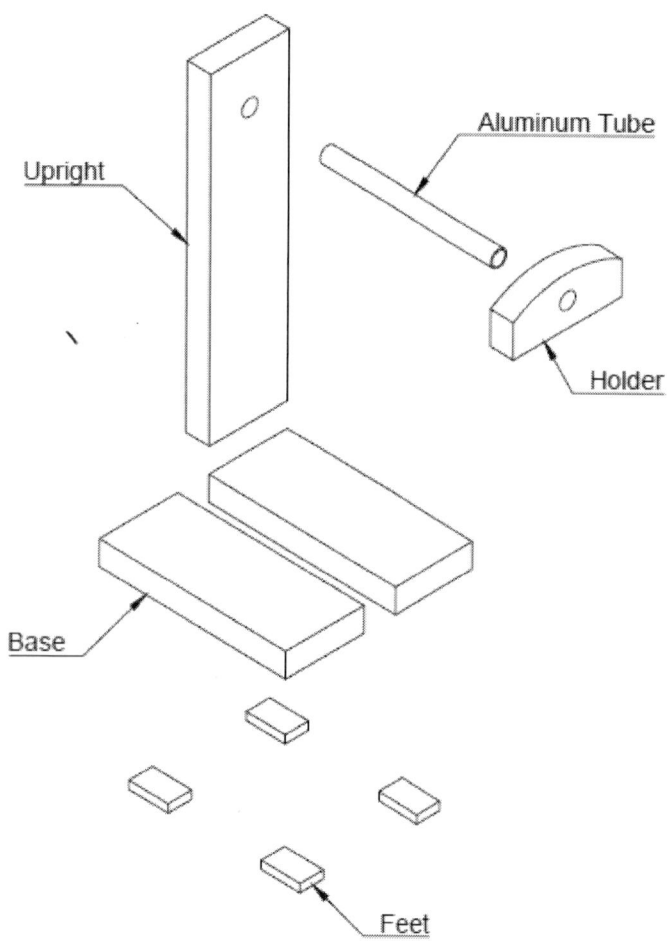

Step 1 - Cut the Parts

1. Use a miter saw to cut all the wooden pieces in the order shown on the Cut List diagram. When cutting smaller components, be sure to keep your fingers a safe distance from the blade.
2. Sand smooth any cut edges using sandpaper.

Step 2 - Assemble the Base

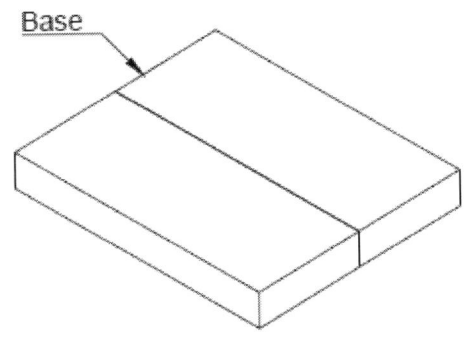

1. Lay the two Base pieces on a level surface and apply a thin line of wood glue on the long edge between the two pieces.
2. Align the edges and clamp them together.
3. Allow them to dry completely. Once dry, remove any excess glue with fine-grit sandpaper

Step 3 - Prepare the Feet

1. Cut the two Foot pieces in half to make 4 smaller feet as shown below.
2. Sand smooth any cut edges using sandpaper.

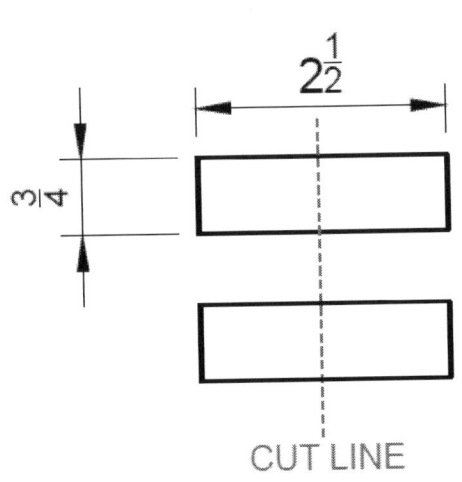

Feet as initially cut from the board

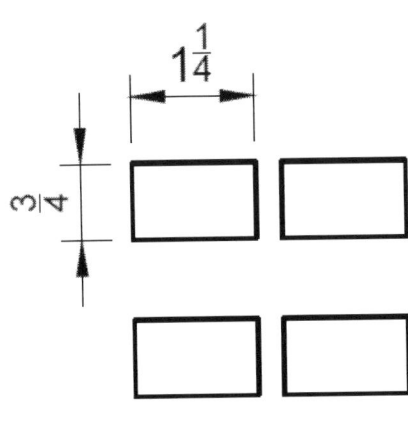

Final Feet

Step 4 - Secure the Feet to the Base

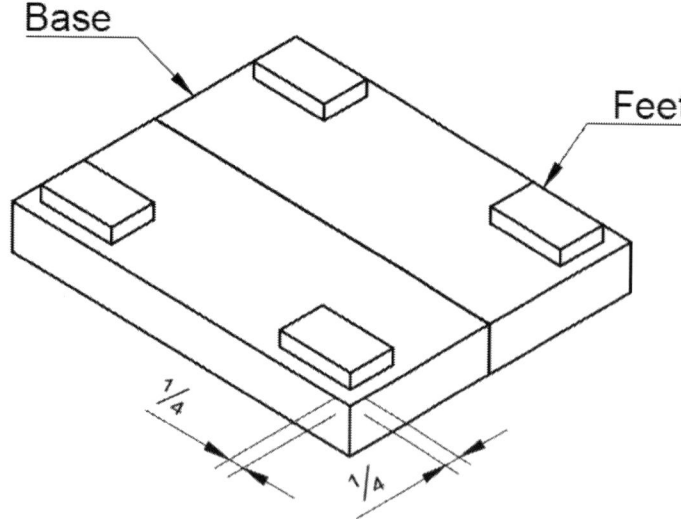

1. Turn the base upside down and apply a small about of glue to the first foot you mean to attach.

2. Position the foot on the base ¼" from the sides, clamp the base and the foot together.

3. After allowing it to dry completely, repeat this process with the other 3 feet.

Step 5 - Prepare the Upright

1. Drill a ½" through hole at the location shown below.

2. Drill x2 pocket holes at the indicated locations using a pocket-hole jig.

3. Sand smooth using sandpaper.

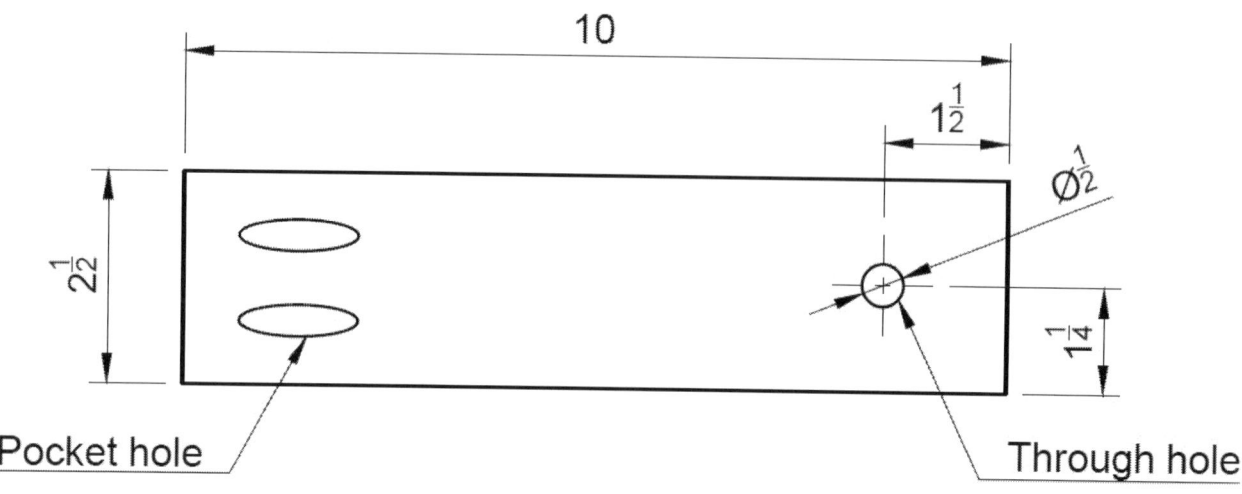

Step 6 - Join Upright and Base

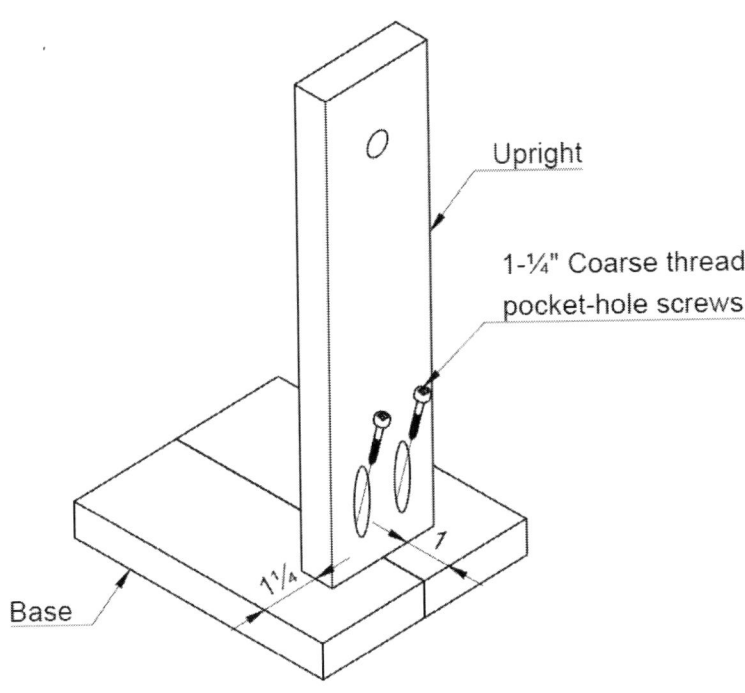

1. Align the Upright on the Base as shown below. Esure the pocket holes are facing the back.
2. Secure the Upright to the Base using 1-¼" Coarse thread pocket-hole screws.

Step 7 - Prepare the Holder

1. Mark out the holder's size, arch and hole location as shown below.
2. Drill a ½" through hole at the marked location.
3. Cut to size using a jigsaw.
4. Sand smooth any cut edges using sandpaper.

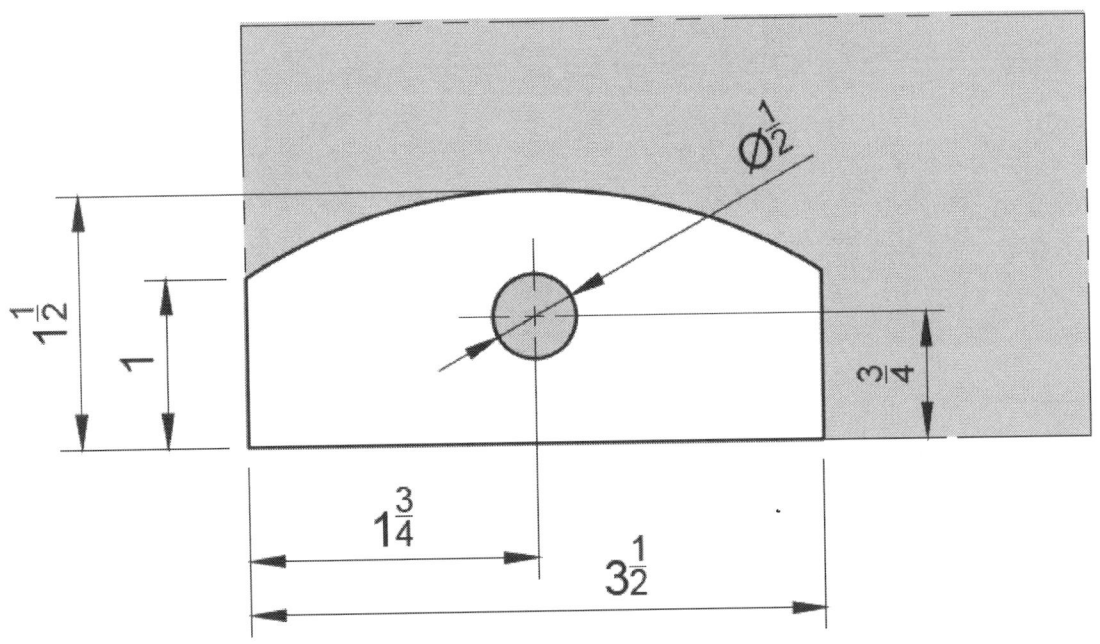

Step 8 - Apply Finishes

1. Double check that all the wooden components are sanded smooth and clean.

2. Apply the paint or stain of your choice and leave to dry.

Step 9 – Assemble

1. Push the Aluminum Tube through the Holder and then through the Upright to complete the assembly.

2. Enjoy!

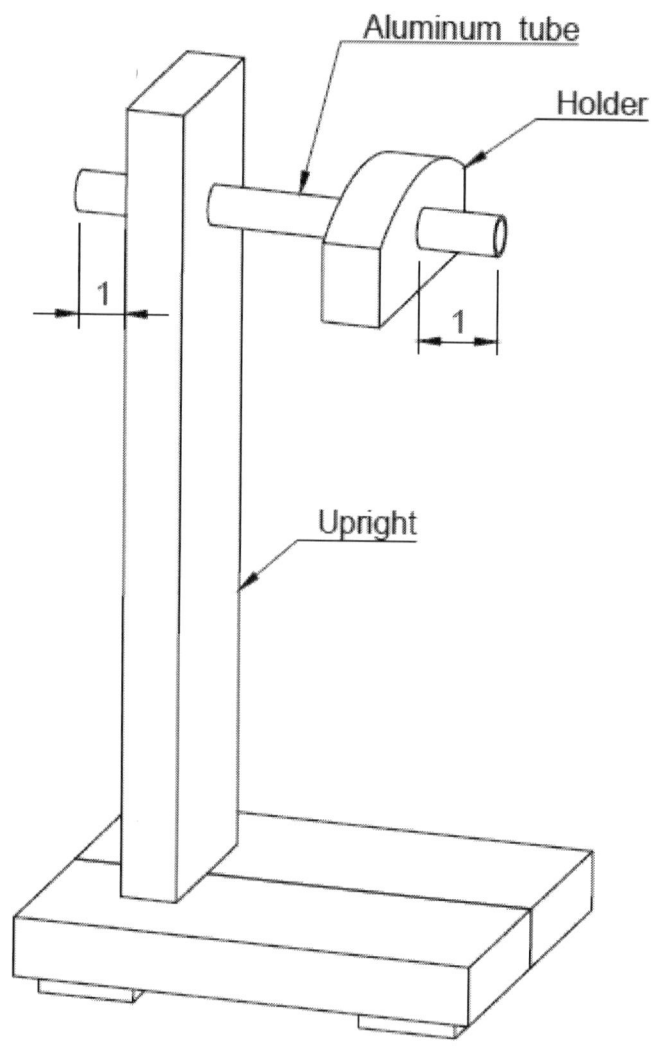

DIY Coffee Table

33"Wx33"Dx19.25"H

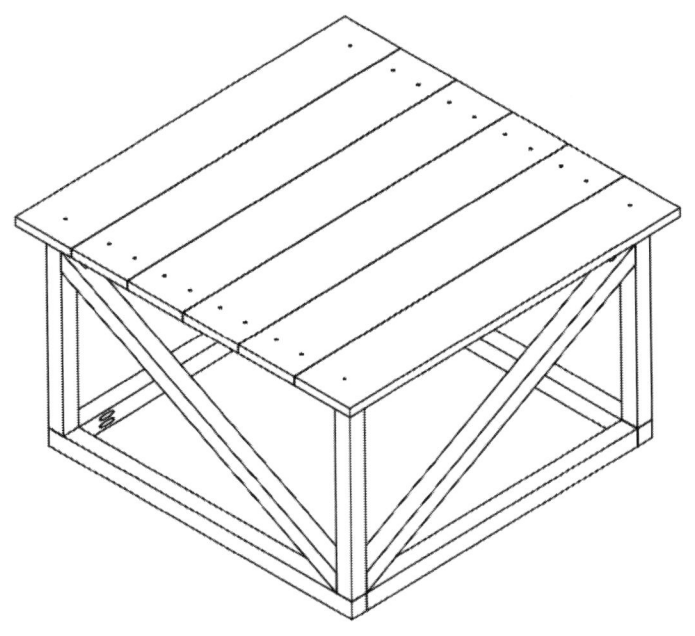

Materials

x5 Pine Board, 2x2", 8' Length

x3 Pine Board, 1x6", 6' Length

Hardware

x32 2-½" Coarse thread pocket-hole screws

x8 2" Coarse thread pocket-hole screws

x20 1-½" Finishing nails

Tools

Miter saw

Electric drill

Pocket-hole jig

Hammer

Tape measure

Sandpaper

Cut List and Parts

x4 No.1, 1-½" x 1-½", 30" Length

x4 No.2, 1-½" x 1-½", 15-½" Length

x4 No.3, 1-½" x 1-½", 27" Length

x4 No.4, 1-½" x 1-½", 32" Length

x6 No.5, ¾" x 5-½", 33" Length

x2 2x2", 8' Length

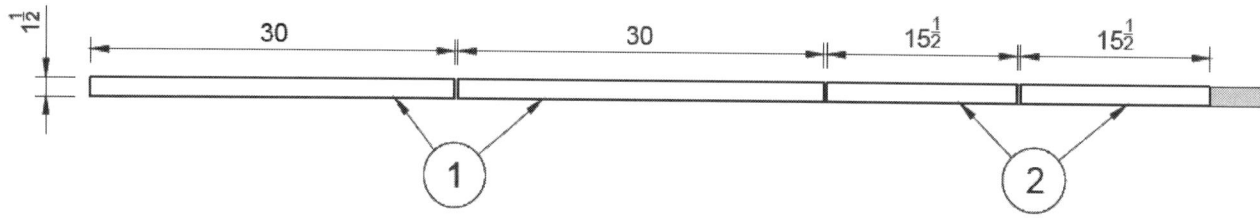

x1 2x2", 8' Length

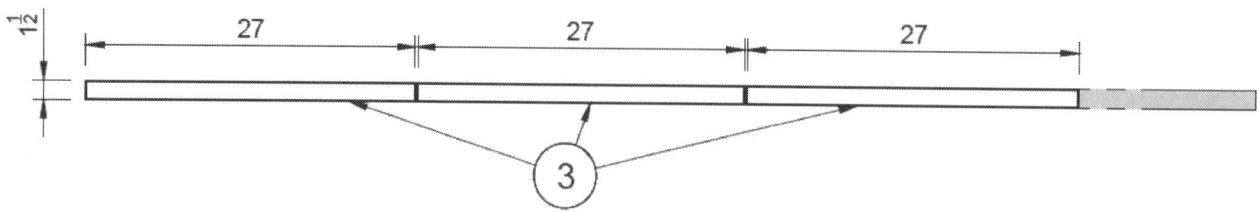

x1 2x2", 8' Length

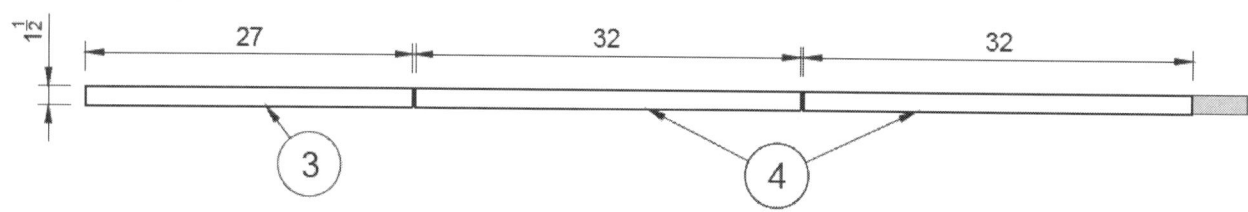

x1 2x2", 8' Length

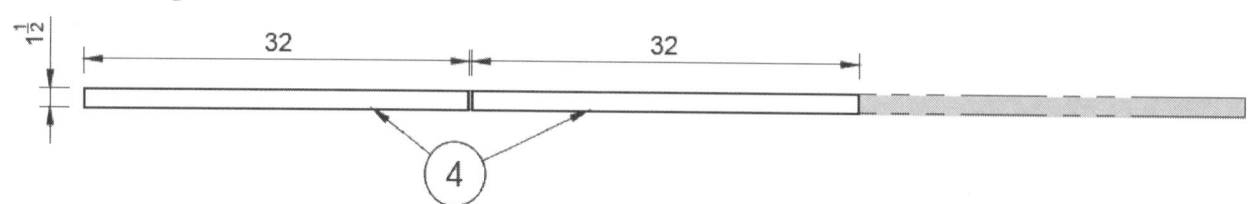

x3 1x6", 6' Length

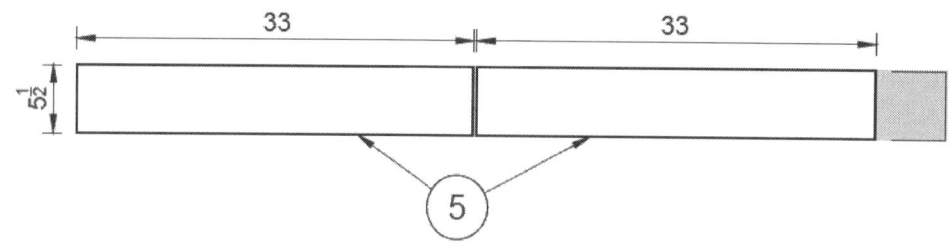

Exploded Diagram

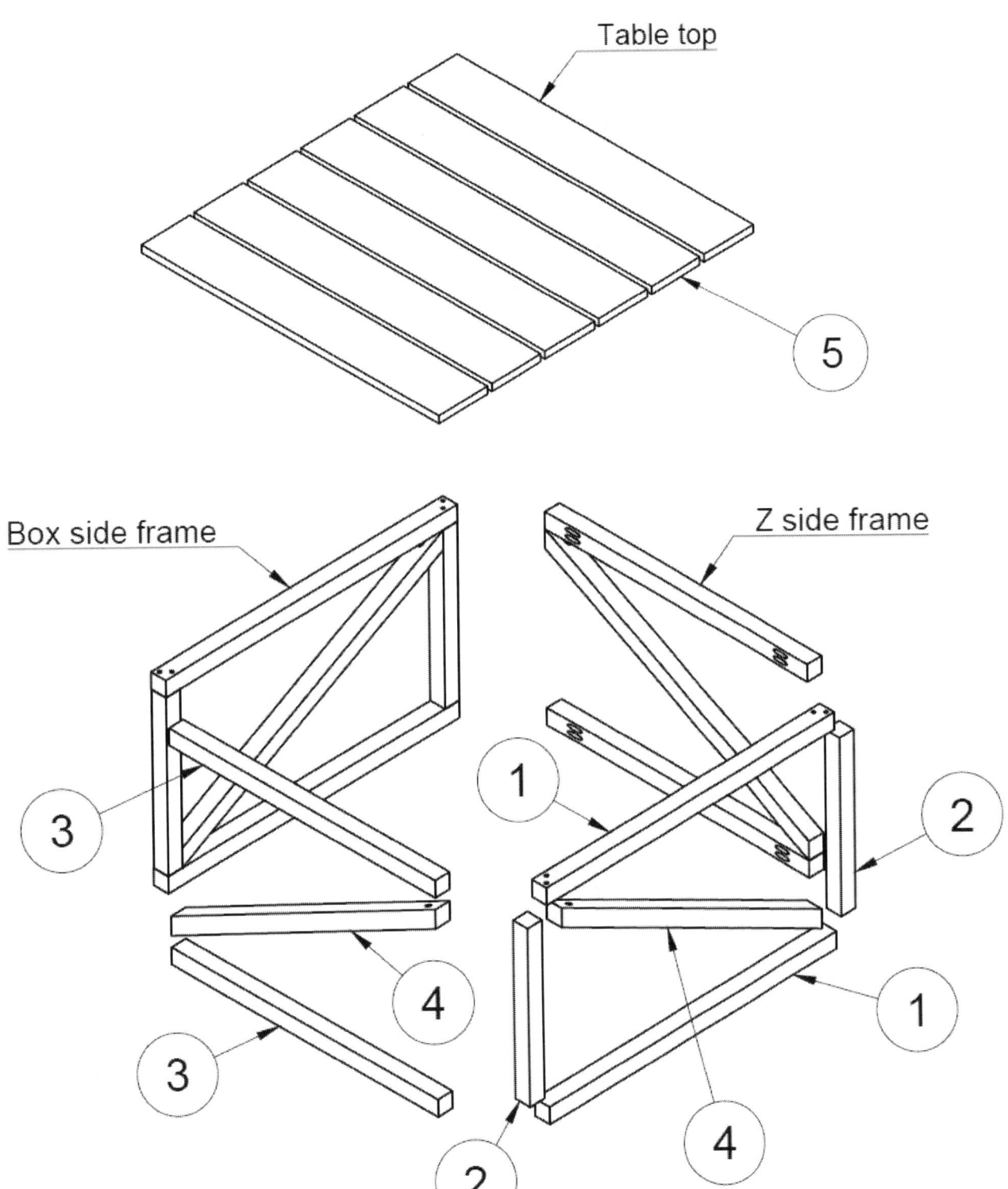

Step 1 - Assemble the Box Side Frames

1. Lay on a level surface x2 No.1 pieces and x2 No.2 pieces to make 1 Box Side Frame.

2. Secure each end of the No.2 pieces to the No.1's with x2 2-½" pocket-hole screws in the indicated locations. Ensure that the tops of the screws are either flush with or slightly below the surface of the wood.

3. Repeat and assemble the second Box Side Frame.

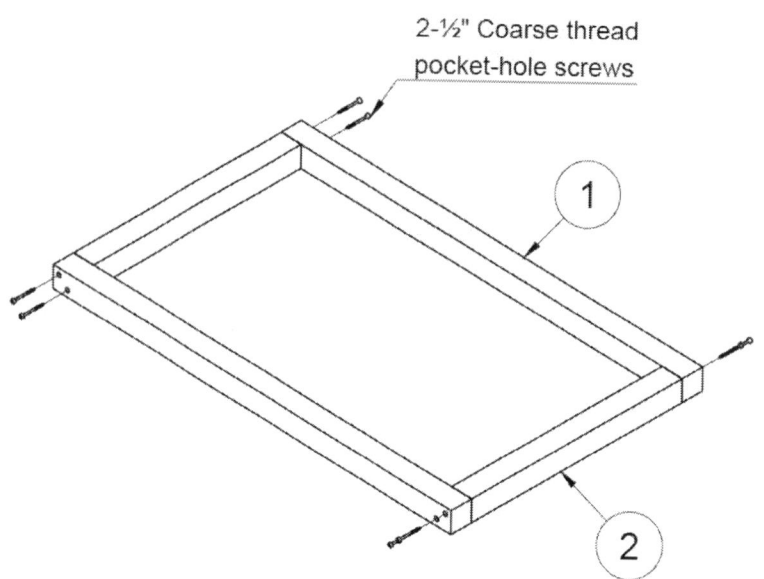

NOTE: Instead of pocket-hole screws, self tapping wood screws are fine to use as long as the tops of the screws are flush with the wood.

Step 2 - Prepare No.3 Pieces

1. Using a pocket-hole jig, drill 4 pocket holes in the locations shown below on each of the four No. 3 pieces.

2. Sand smooth using sandpaper.

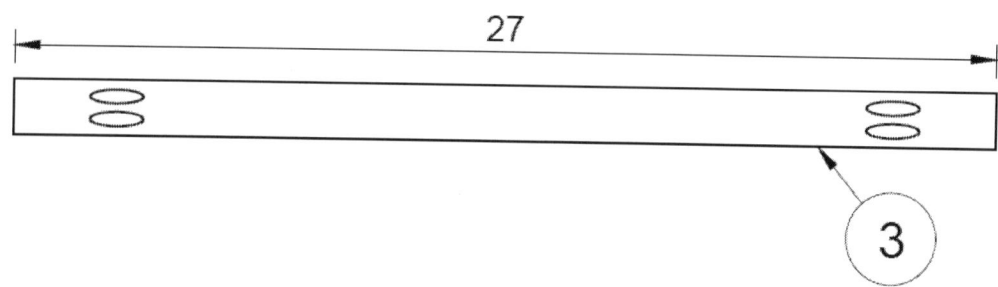

Step 3 - Secure No.3 Pieces to the Box Side Frames

1. Lay the 1 Box Side Frame on a flat surface and align the No.3 pieces as shown below.

2. Secure the No.3 pieces to the Frame using 2-½" pocket-hole screws.

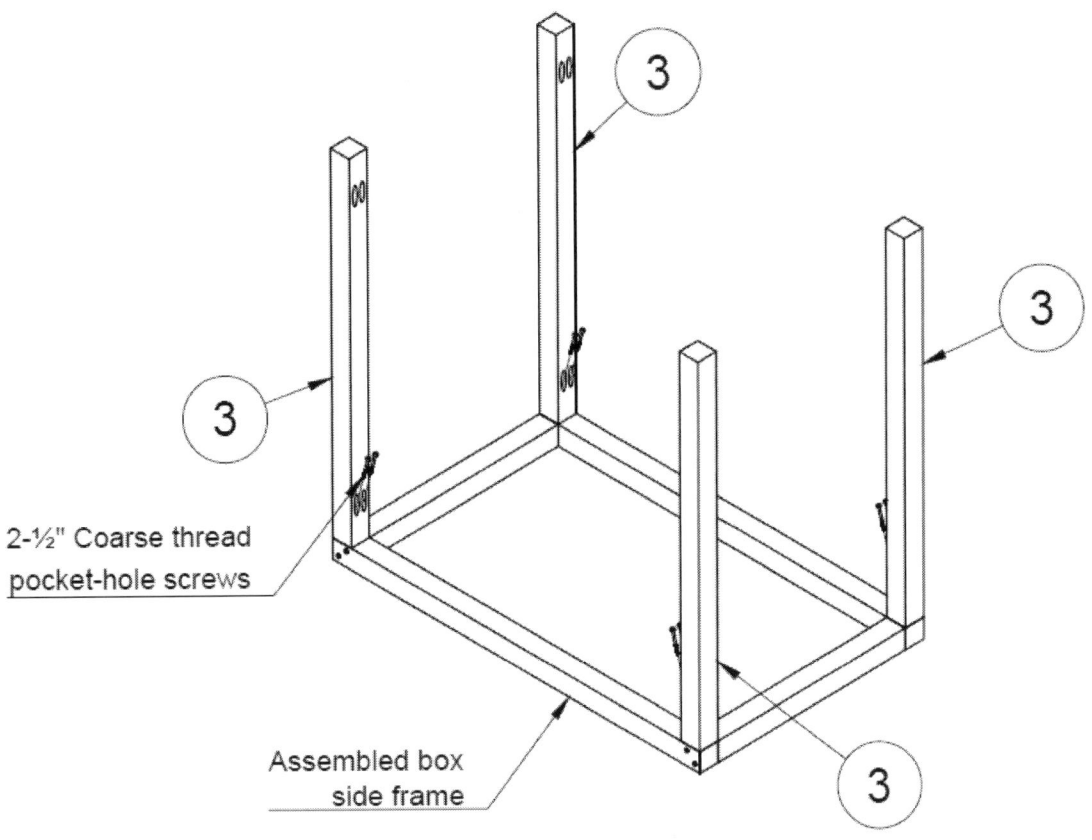

Step 4 - Repeat

1. Repeat the same pAroscseesms absle Sdte bpo 3x to join the frame on the opposite side.

side frame.

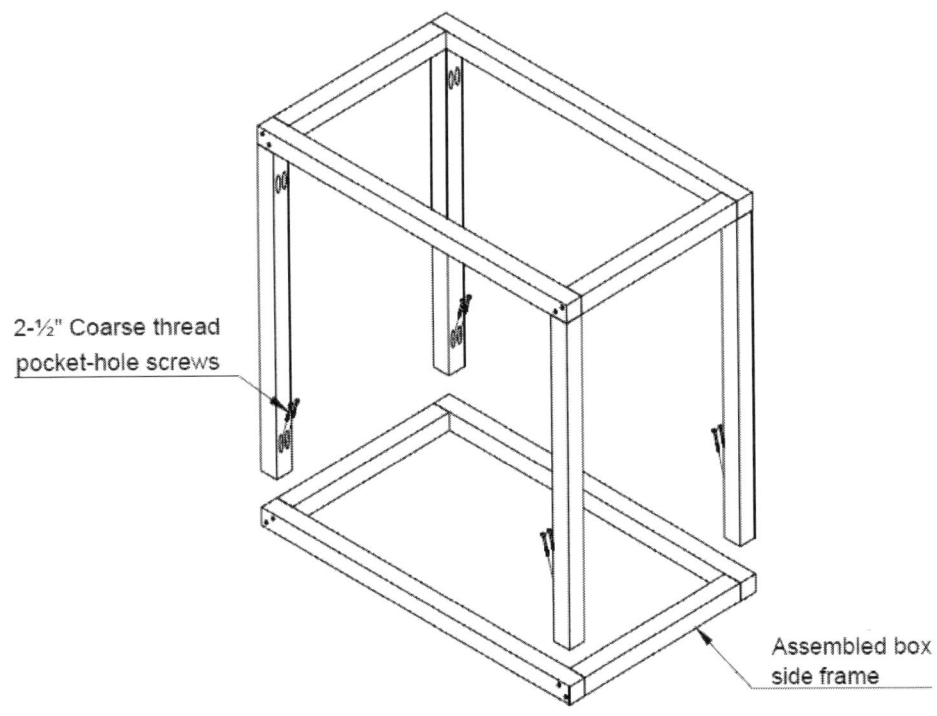

Step 5 - Prepare No.4 Pieces

1. In order to get the correct angle and length, lay each No.4 piece over the frame and mark the angle that needs to be cut.

2. Cut to size using a Miter saw.

3. Repeat for all No.4 pieces.

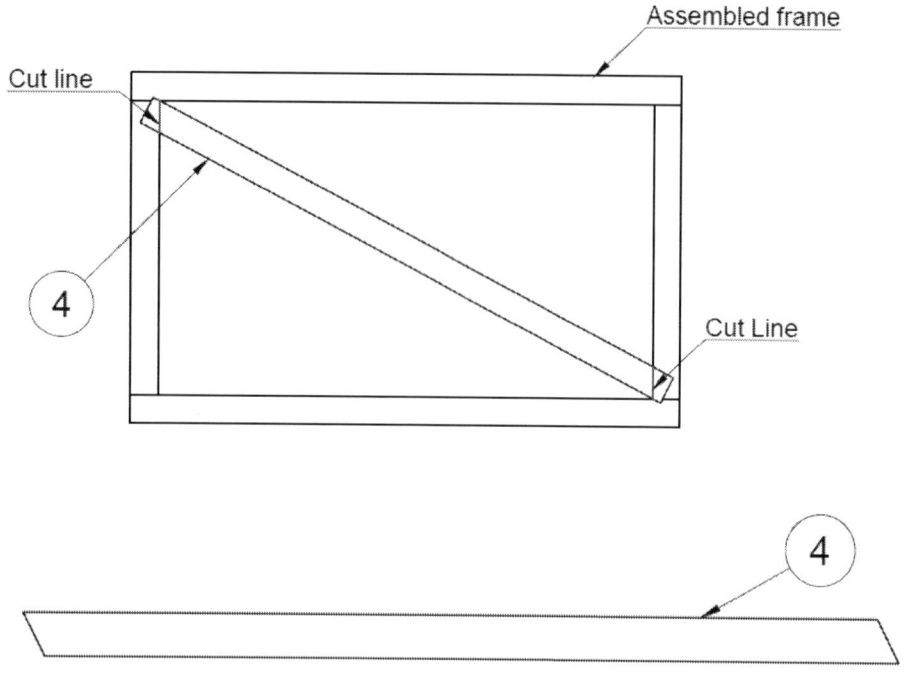

No. 4 cross piece cut to size

Step 6 - Secure No.4 Pieces to the Frame

110

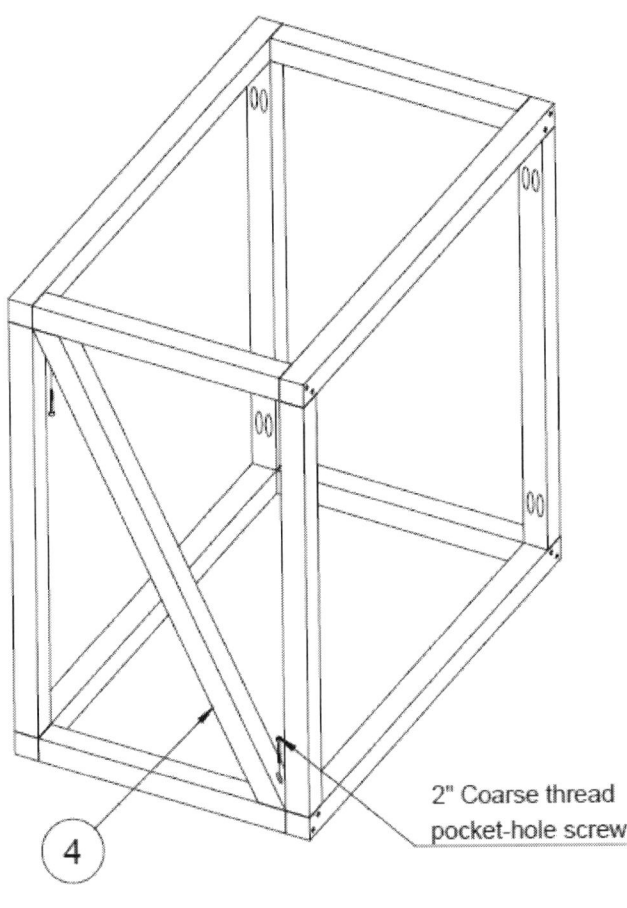

1. Stand the assembled frame on one side and put your No.4 piece in the correct position.
2. Secure using x1 2" pocket-hole screw in each end. These cross pieces are not structural so this is sufficient.

NOTE: Instead of pocket-hole screws, self-tapping wood screws are fine to use

2" Coarse thread pocket-hole screw

Step 7 - Repeat

1. Repeat Step 6 for all No.4 cross pieces, assembling them in the pattern shown below.

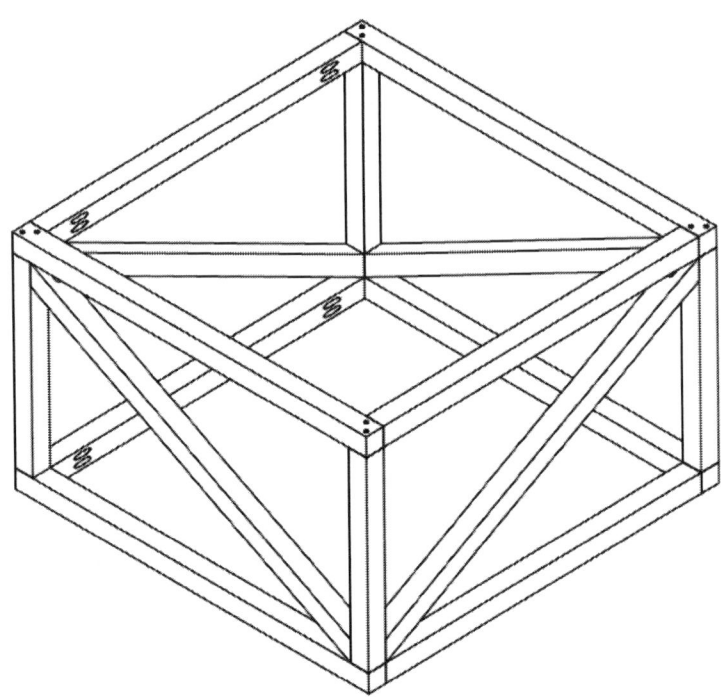

Step 8 - Finish

1. Take the time to smooth any rough areas and even out the joints using sandpaper. For a more professional look you can also fill the pocket-holes with wood filler and sand them down afterwards.

2. Finish the assembled frame and No. 5 tabletop pieces with your chosen paint or stain, and allow them to dry.

Step 9 - Secure Table Top to Frame

1. Lay the 6x No.5 table top pieces on top of the frame, leaving a 1-½" overhang on all sides.

2. Using 1-½" finishing nails and a hammer, secure each piece to the frame to finish the project.

3. Enjoy!

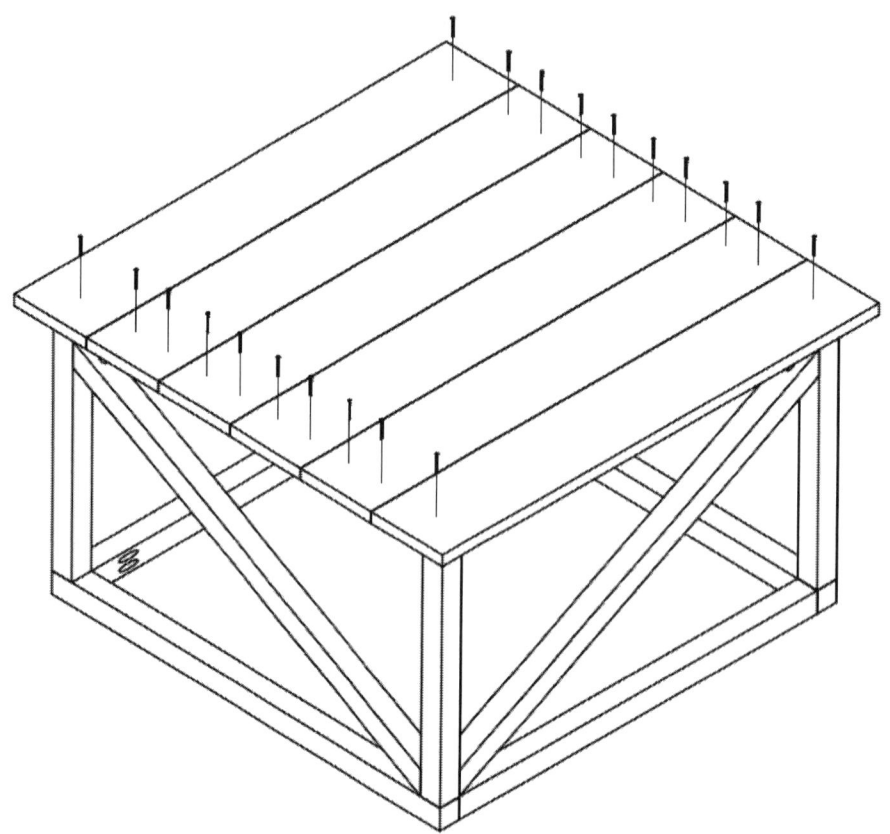

DIY Plant Stand
18"Wx18"Dx24"H

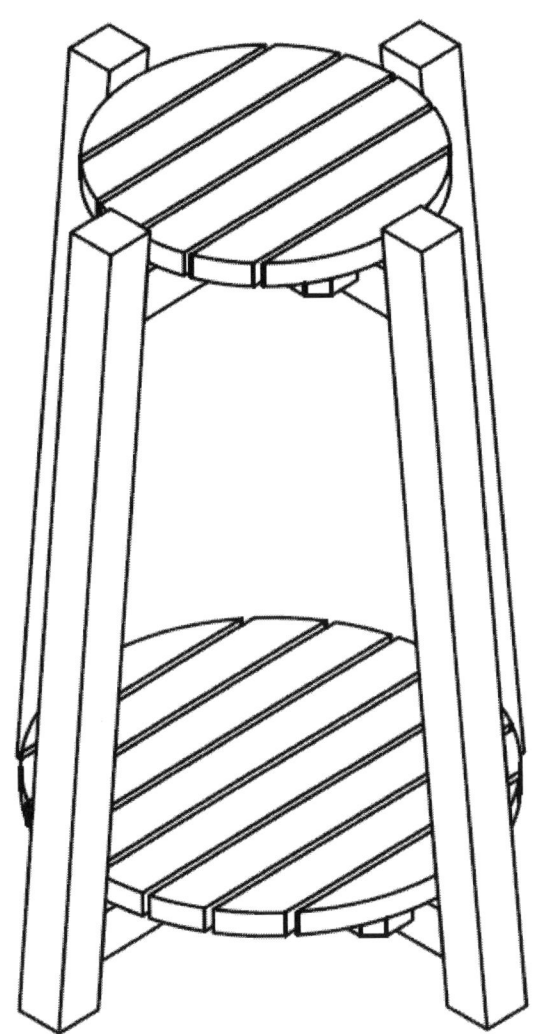

Materials

x1 Pine Board, 2x2", 6' Length

x1 Pine Board, 2x2", 8' Length

x3 Pine Board, 1x2", 6' Length

Hardware

x24 2-½" Coarse thread pocket-hole screws

x28 1" Wood Screws

Tools

Miter saw

Jigsaw

Electric drill

Pocket-hole jig

Chisel

Tape measure

Sandpaper

Cut List and Parts

x4 No.1, 1-½" x 1-½", 24-½" Length	x6 No.6, ¾" x 1-½", 10" Length
x1 No.2, 1-½" x 1-½", 11-¼" Length	x2 No.7, ¾" x 1-½", 9" Length
x2 No.3, 1-½" x 1-½", 5" Length	x8 No.8, ¾" x 1-½", 13-½" Length
x1 No.4, 1-½" x 1-½", 15" Length	x2 No.9, ¾" x 1-½", 12-½" Length
x2 No.5, 1-½" x 1-½", 6-¾" Length	

x1 2x2", 6' Length

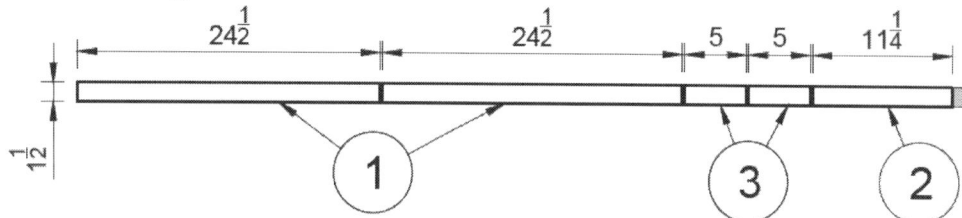

x1 2x2", 8' Length

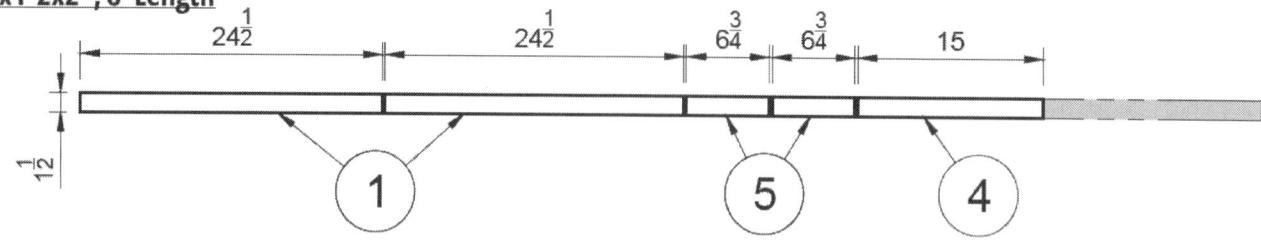

x1 1x2", 6' Length

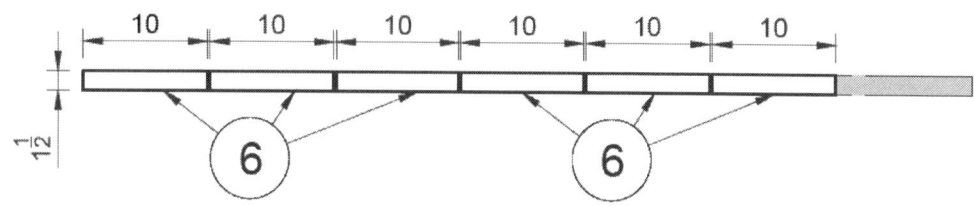

x1 1x2", 6' Length

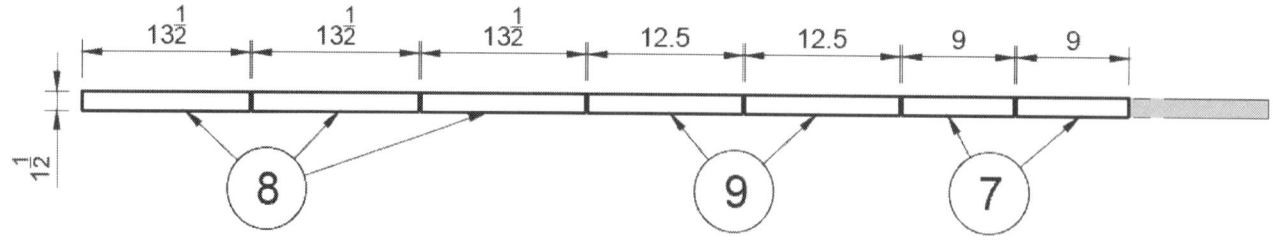

x1 1x2", 6' Length

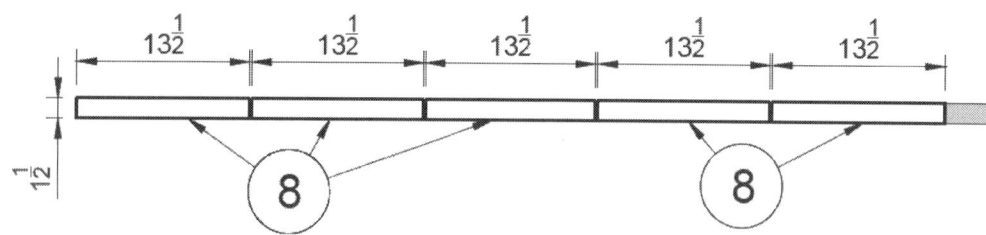

Exploded Diagram

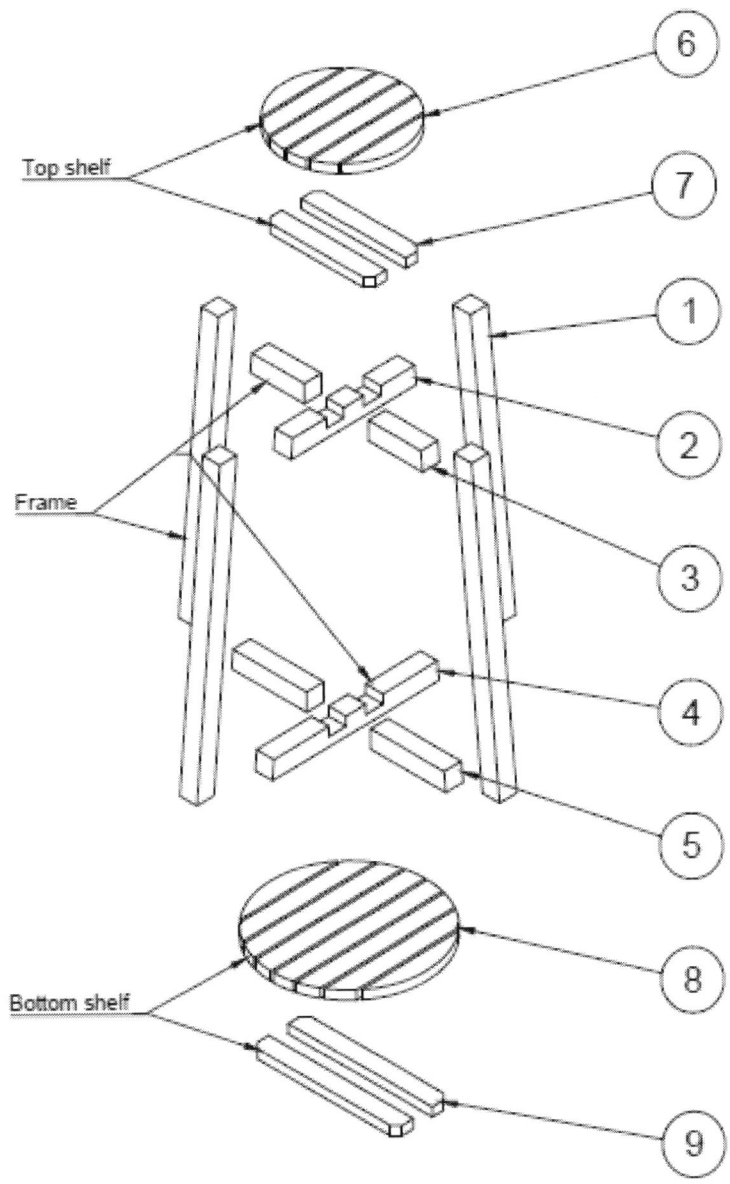

Step 1 - Notch the No.2 and 4 Pieces

1. To cut the notches in the No.2 and 4 pieces, first mark their locations as indicated below.

2. Make repeated cuts to the same depth using a miter saw so the notches appear like a comb.

3. Use a chisel to remove what's left over from the cuts.

4. Sand smooth using sandpaper.

5. Repeat for both notches on pieces No.2 and 4.

6. Ensure that the No.7 and No.9 pieces fit snugly in the notches (this is how the shelves will nest in the frame later).

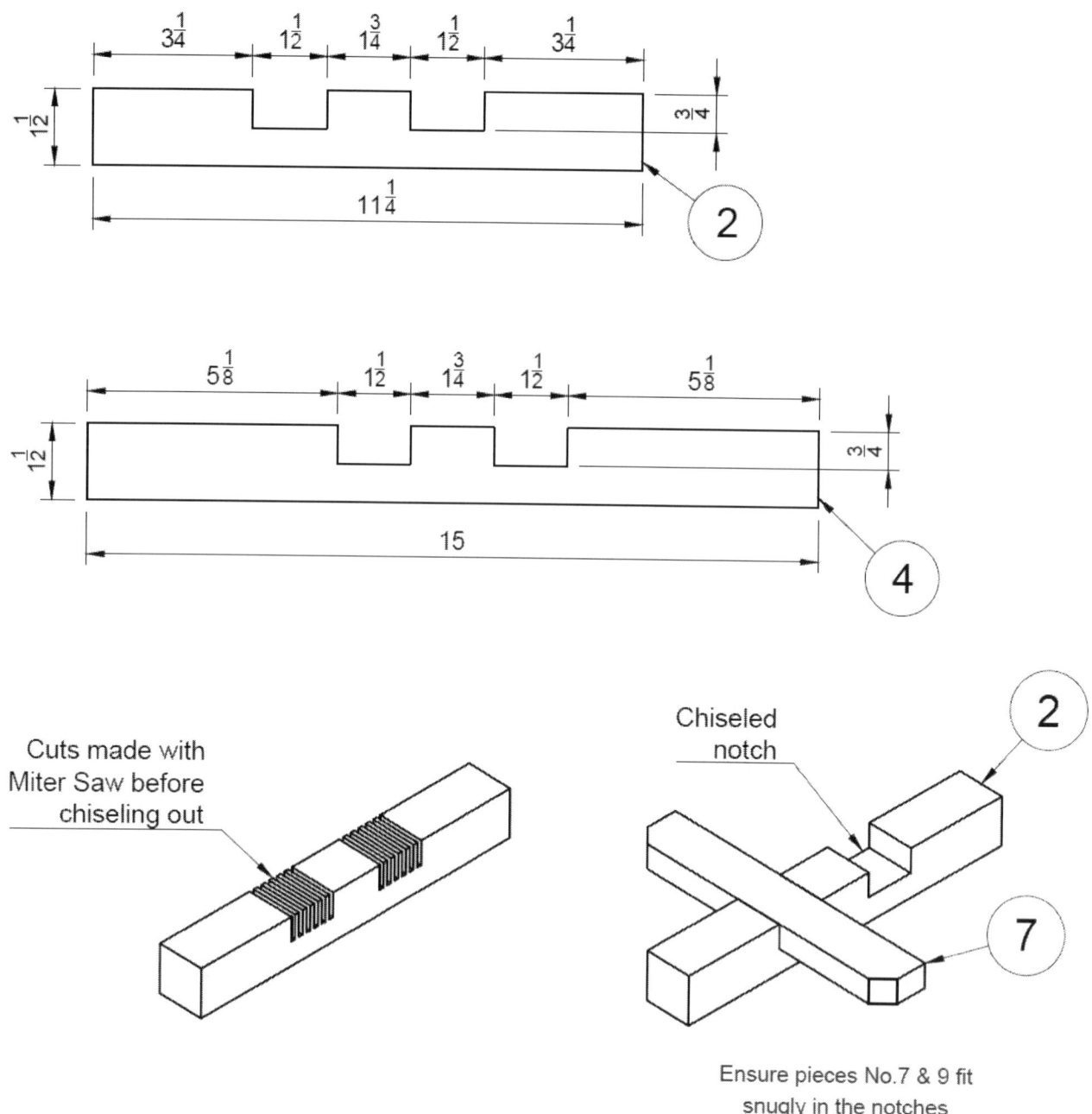

Step 2 - Make the Angled Cuts on the Frame Pieces

1. Gather all the pieces that make up the frame - pieces No.1(x4), 2, 3(x2), 4 and 5(x2).
2. Use a miter saw to cut the pieces to the lengths indicated below, making angled cuts as needed. For this example,
the cut angle is 5°; however, if you adjust the overall dimensions, the required angle may change.
3. Sand smooth the cut edges using sandpaper.

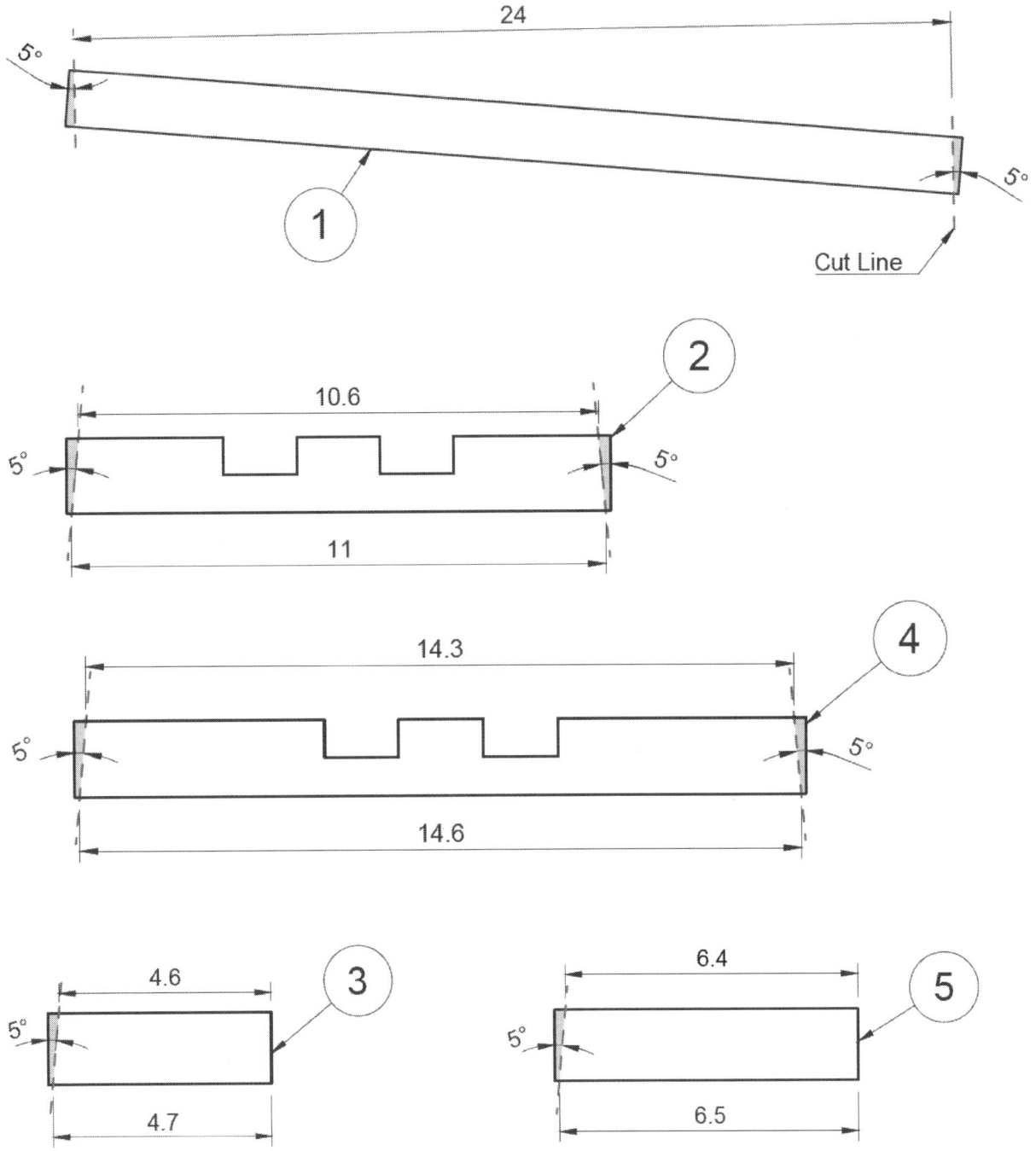

Step 3 - Drill the Pocket Holes

1. With a pocket hole jig, drill four pocket holes on the underside of pieces No.2, 3(x2), 4, and 5(x2) at the locations
shown below. The underside will be the side with the longest length on each piece.
2. The upper ends of the pocket holes will likely overlap on the shorter pieces, this is fine.
3. Sand smooth using sandpaper.

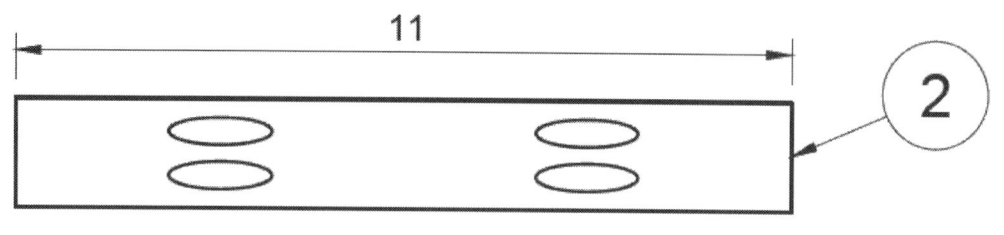

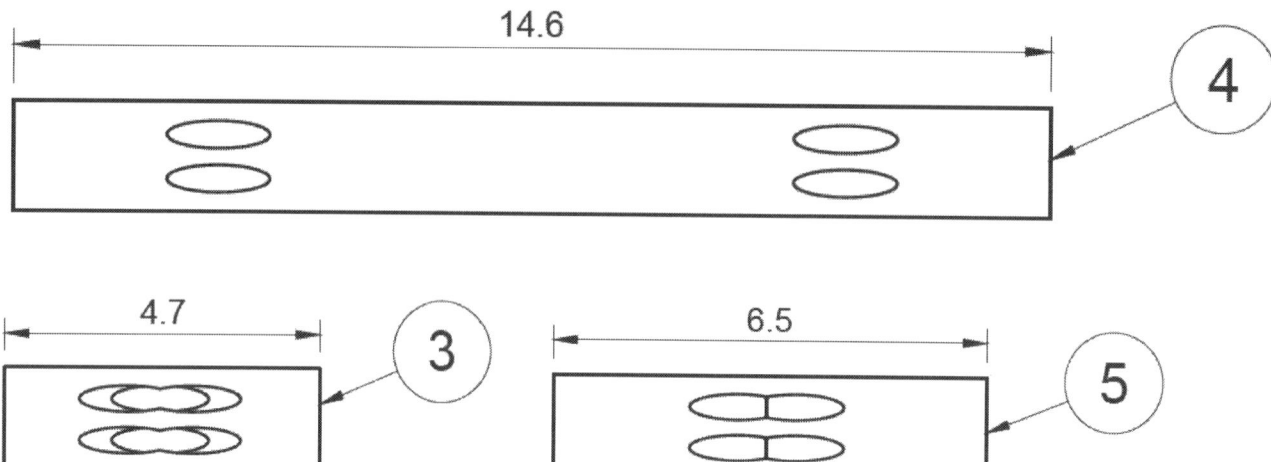

Step 4 - Begin Assembling the Frame

1. Lay on a flat surface pieces: No.1(x2), 2 and 4.

2. Align piece No.2 1-¼" from the top and piece No.4 1-½" from the bottom.

3. Secure together using 2-½" pocket-hole screws.

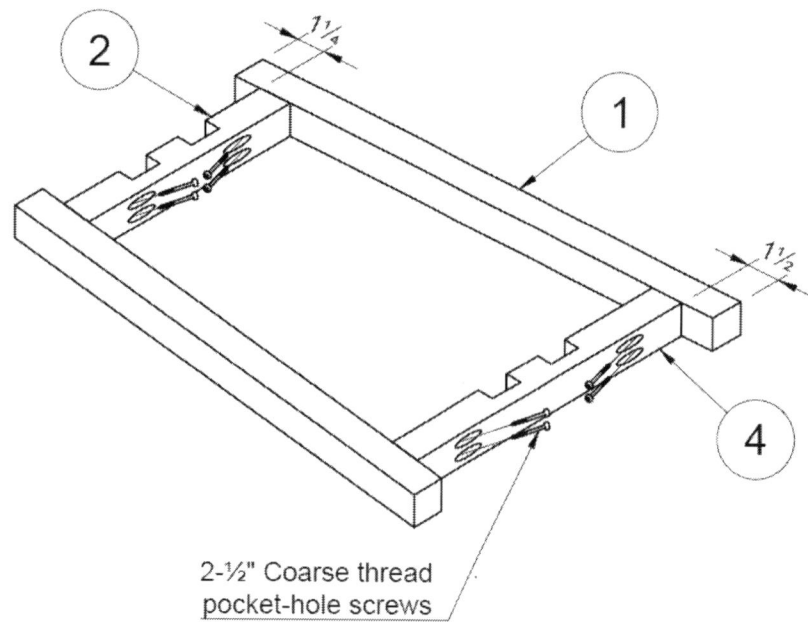

Step 5 - Secure Pieces No.3 and 5 to the Frame

1. Align pieces No.3 and 5 on the center of the Frame as shown below.
2. Secure together using 2-½" pocket-hole screws.

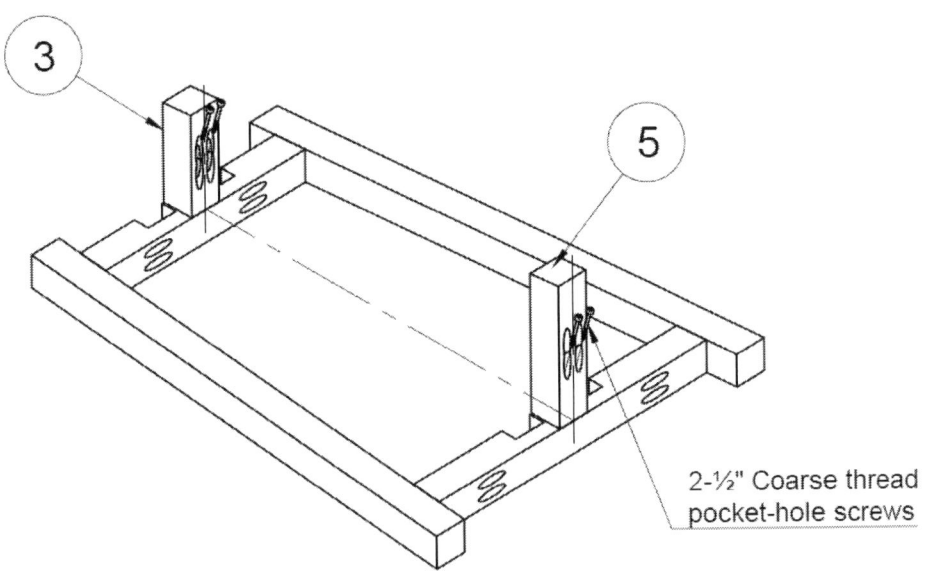

Step 6 - Attach a No.1 Piece to the Frame

1. Lay a No.1 piece on a level surface, then flip the frame upside down and align it in the same way as Step 3.
2. Secure together using 2-½" pocket-hole screws.

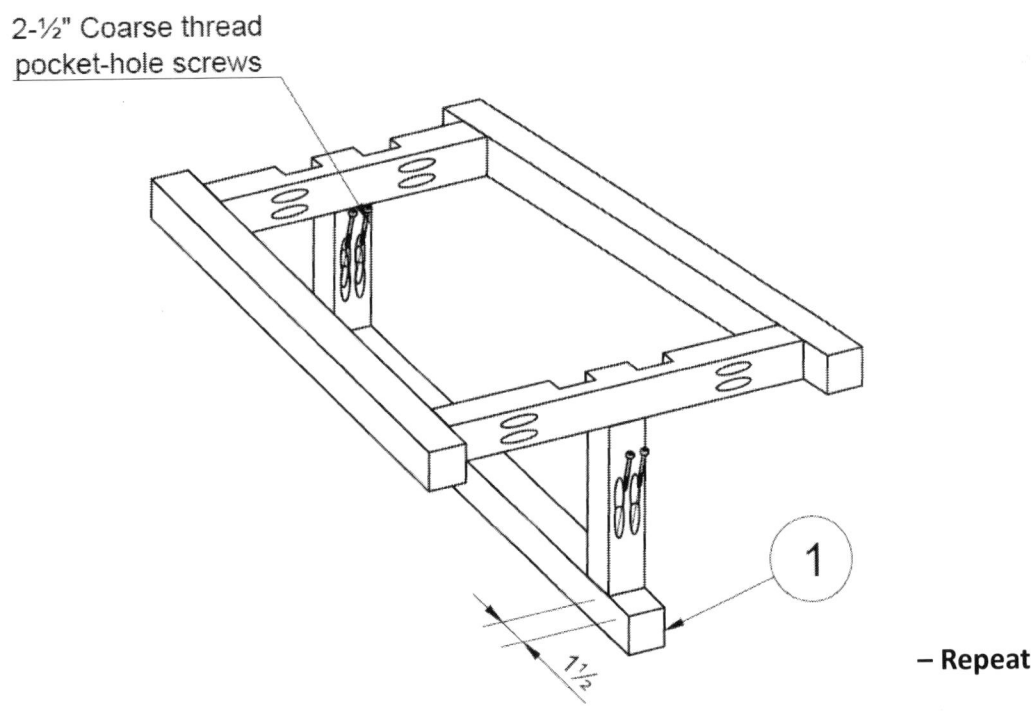

Step 7 – Repeat

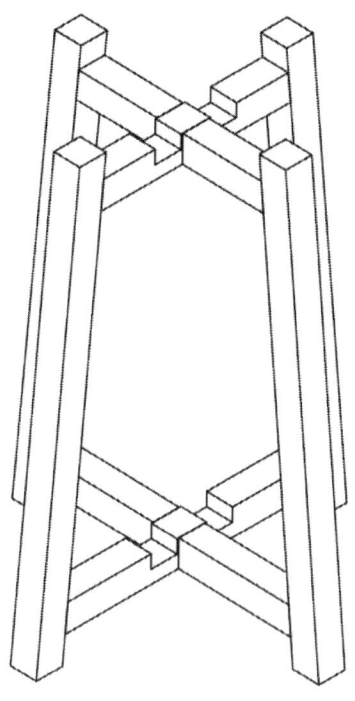

1. Repeat the same process as Steps 4-5 to finish assembling the frame.

2. Ensure the frame is stable. If it wobbles, sand down any necessary areas with sandpaper.

Step 8 - Prepare No.7 and 9 Pieces

1. Gather pieces No.7(x2) and No.9(x2).
2. Using a miter or jigsaw cut a ½"x ½" triangle of two corners of each piece.
3. Sand smooth cut edges with sandpaper.

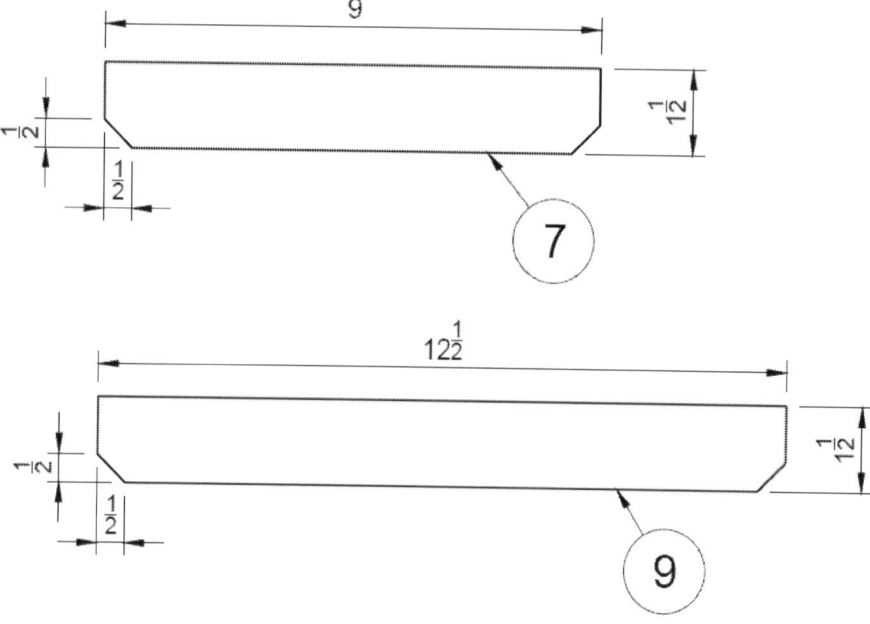

Step 9 - Lay out No.6 Pieces for the Top Shelf

1. On a flat and level surface lay out all the No.6 pieces with a ¼" gap between them all as shown below.
2. Using a spacer between the pieces can help keep them even, but precise dimensions aren't essential, as we'll be cutting this into a circle later.

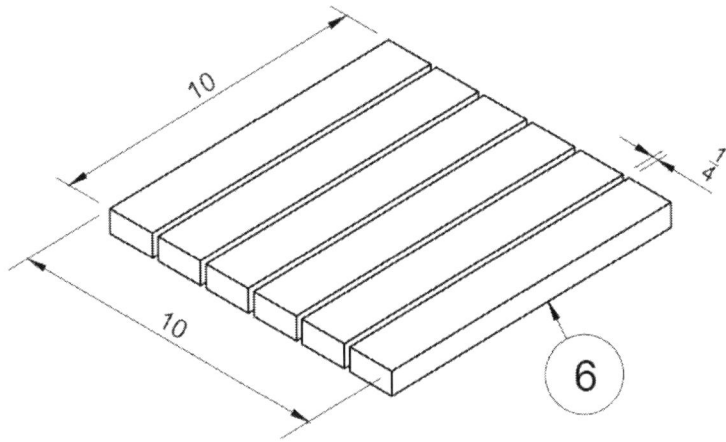

Step 10 - Join the Top Shelf Together

1. Align the No.7 pieces on top of the No.6 pieces in the positions shown below and secure them together using 1" wood screws. Start by fastening the outer No.6 pieces, then work inward.

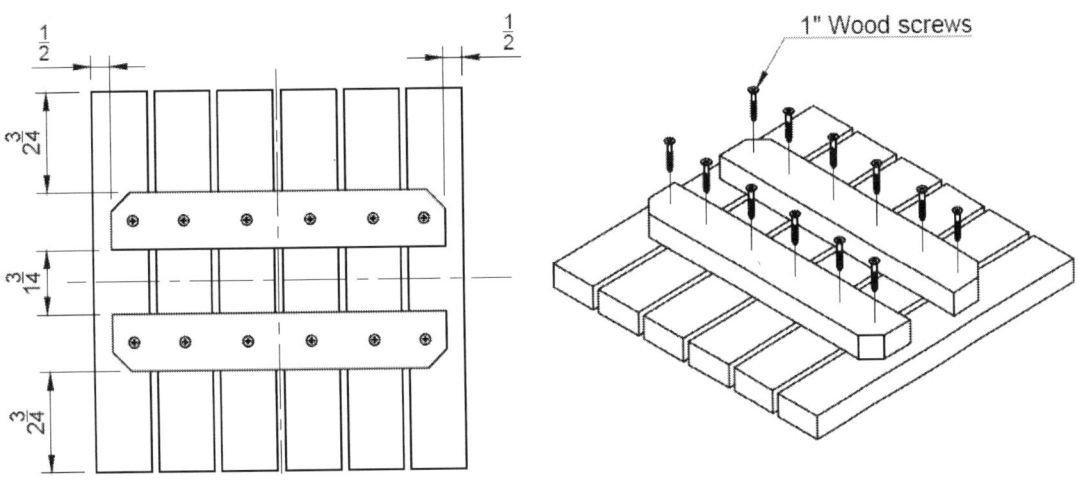

Step 11 - Cut the Top Shelf into a Circle

1. Mark with a pencil a 10" diameter circle on the top shelf.
2. Carefully cut out the circle using a jigsaw.
3. Sand cut edges smooth with sandpaper.

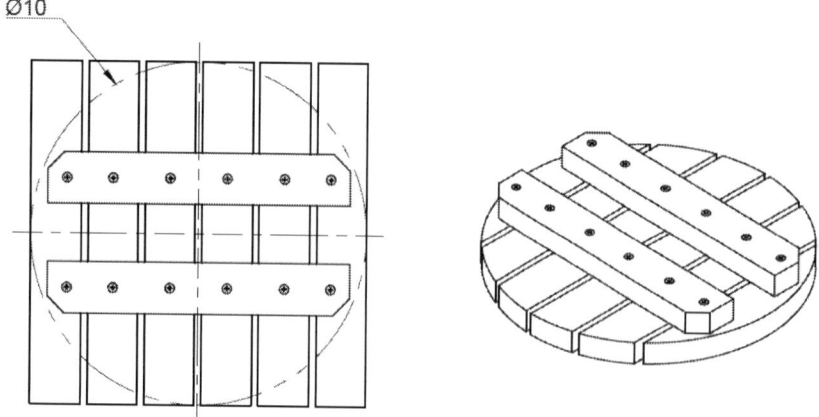

Step 12 - Join the Bottom Shelf Together

1. Repeat the process used in Step 10 to join the No.8(x8) pieces together for the bottom shelf. See the overall dimensions and spacing below.

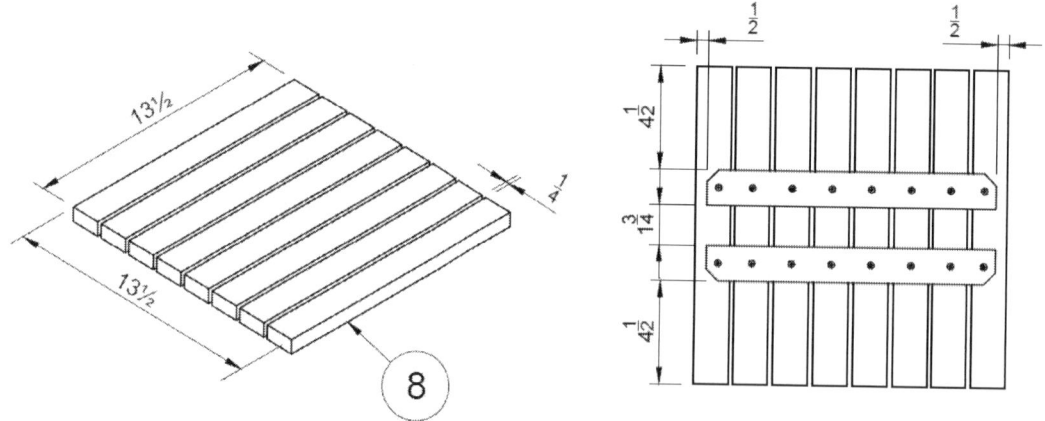

Step 13 - Cut the Bottom Shelf into a Circle

1. Mark with a pencil a 13-½" diameter circle on the bottom shelf.

2. Carefully cut out the circle using a jigsaw.

3. Sand cut edges smooth with sandpaper.

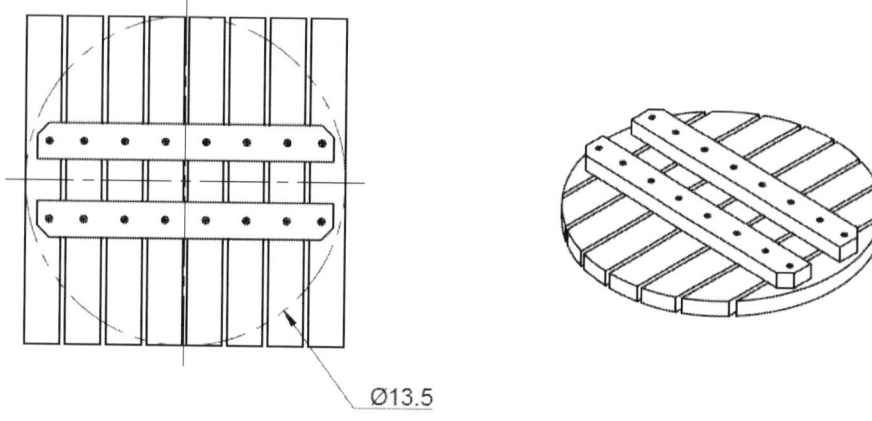

Step 14 - Finish and Assemble

1. Push the Top and Bottom Shelves onto the Frame into the notches we cut in Step 1.

2. Take the time to smooth any rough areas and even out the joints using sandpaper.

3. Finish with your chosen paint or stain, and allow them to dry.

4. Enjoy!

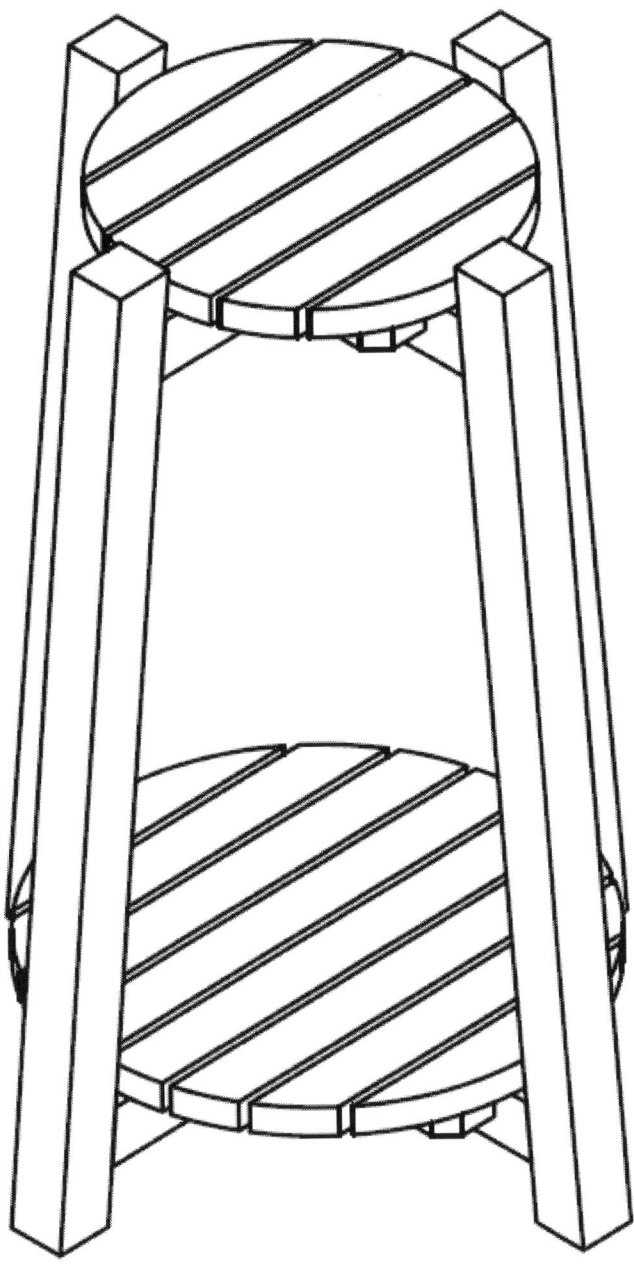

DIY Birdhouse

5-½"W x 8-¾"D x 15"H

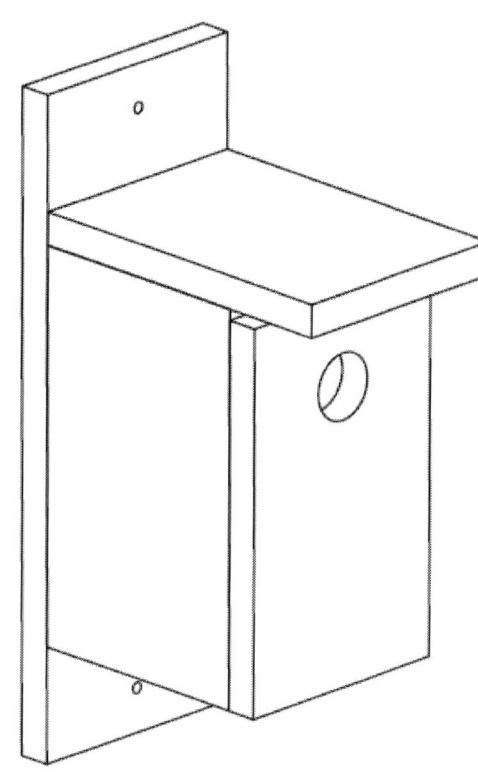

Materials

x1 Board, 1x6", 6' Length (use a wood suitable for outdoor use such as cedar or pine)

Hardware

x16 1-¼" Wood Screws (suitable for outdoor use)

x1 1x6", 6' Length

Tools

Miter Saw

Electric drill

1-½" Forstner Drill Bit

Tape measure

Sandpaper

Cut List and Parts

x1 Bottom, ¾" x 5, 4" Length

x1 Top, ¾" x 5-½", 8" Length

x1 Front, ¾" x 5-½", 8-¾" Length

x2 Side, ¾" x 5-½", 9" Length

x1 Back, ¾" x 5-½", 15" Length

x1 1x6", 6' Length

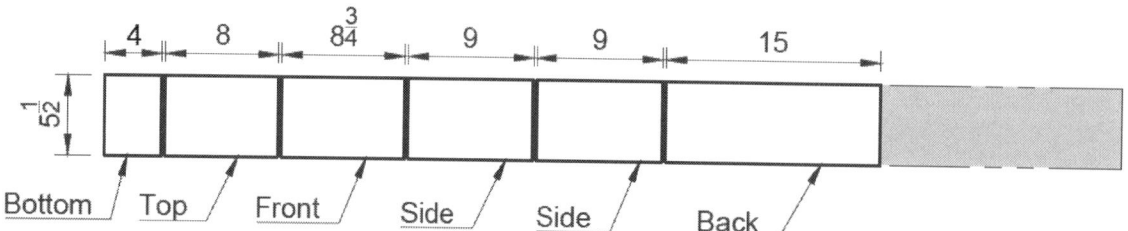

Exploded Diagram

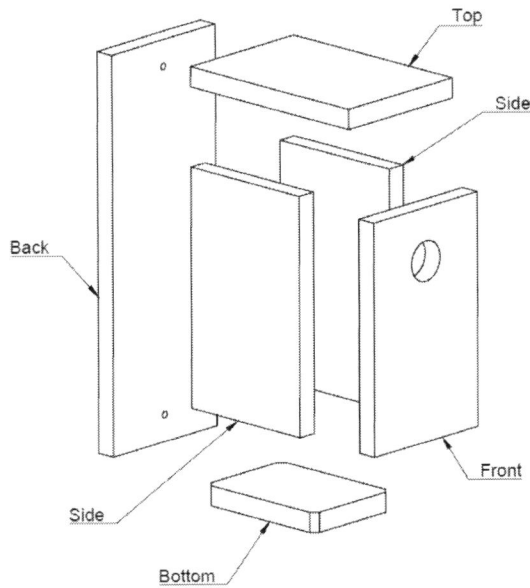

Step 1 - Drill the Bird Entry Hole

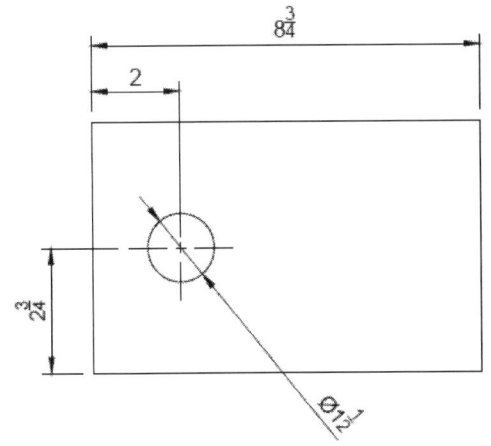

1. Using a 1-½" forstner drill bit, drill a 1-½" hole in the Front piece in the location indicated below.

2. Sand smooth using sandpaper.

Step 2 - Assemble the Front to the Sides

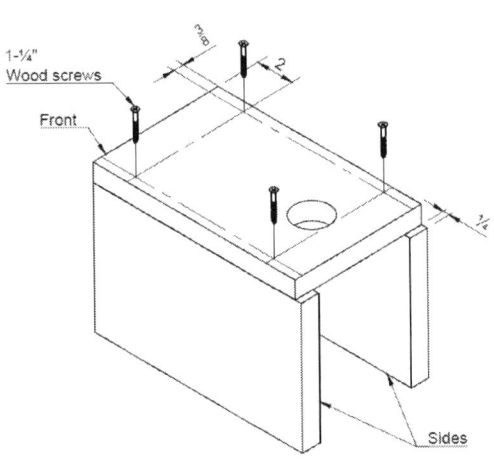

1. Arrange the two sides and the front on a flat surface as shown. Ensure all edges are aligned except the top where you should leave a ¼" gap for ventilation.

2. Using x4 1-¼" wood screws, join the 3 pieces together

Step 3 - Prepare the Base

1. To allow for drainage in the birdhouse, cut a ¼"x ¼" triangle off each corner of the base.

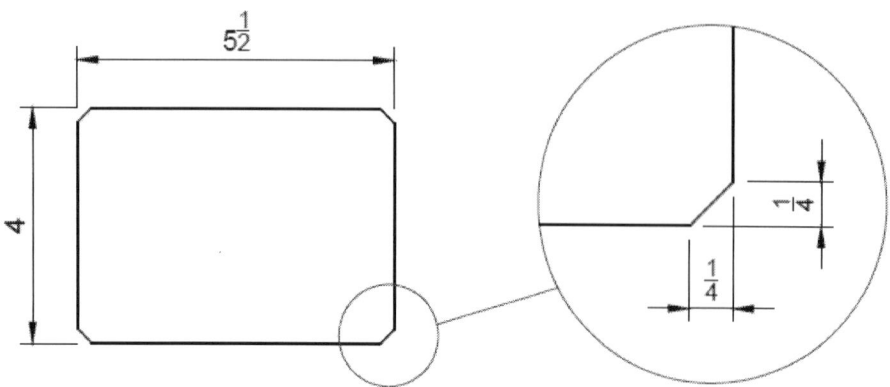

Step 4 - Attach the Base

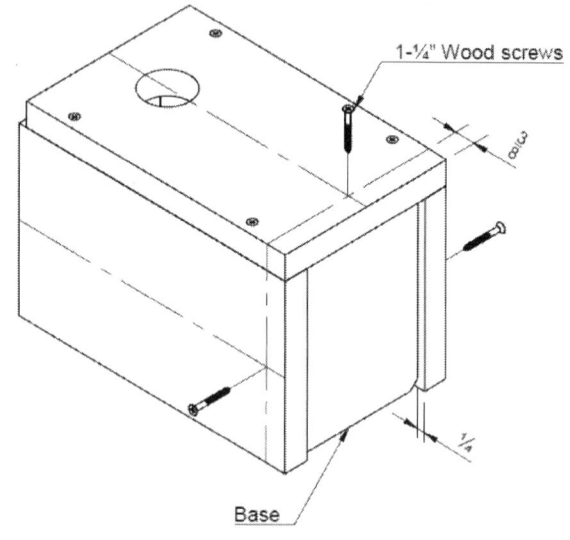

1. Slide the Base into the assembled Front and Sides. Ensure the back of the Base is flush with the back of the Sides.

2. Set the Base back ¼" from the bottom of the birdhouse, this will help with water run off.

3. Secure with x3 1-¼" wood screws.

Step 5 - Prepare the Back

1. Depending on your later method for hanging the birdhouse, drill 2 pilot holes in the locations shown.

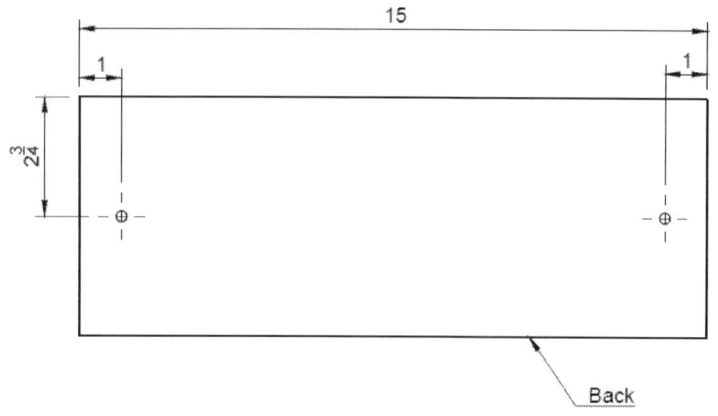

Hanging Options:

Option 1: Using long wood screws, screw the birdbox directly to a tree or post using the pre-drilled pilot holes.

Option 2: Drill a larger hole in the top of the Back piece, use this to hang the birdhouse over a nail.

Step 6 - Join the Back

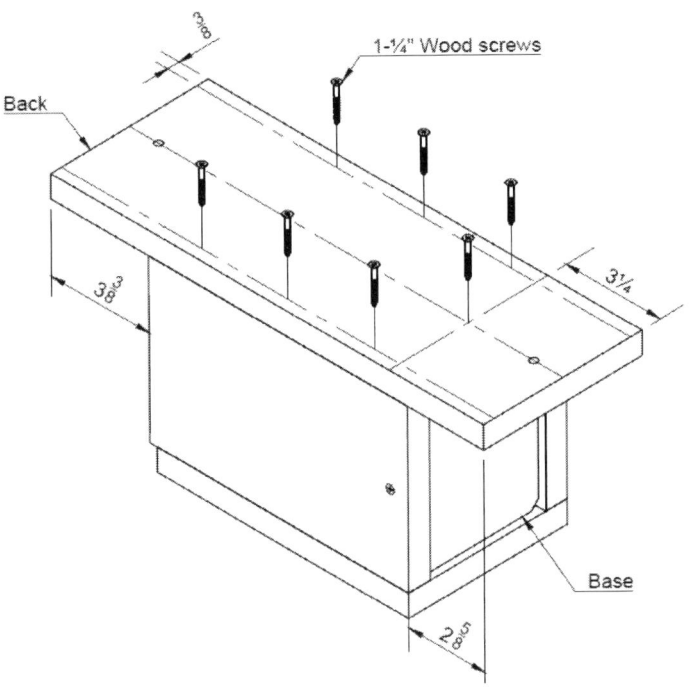

1. Align the Back on the assembled birdhouse using the dimensions below. After the Top is added the birdhouse will be central on the Back.
2. Secure with x7 1-¼" wood screws.

Step 7 - Attach the Top

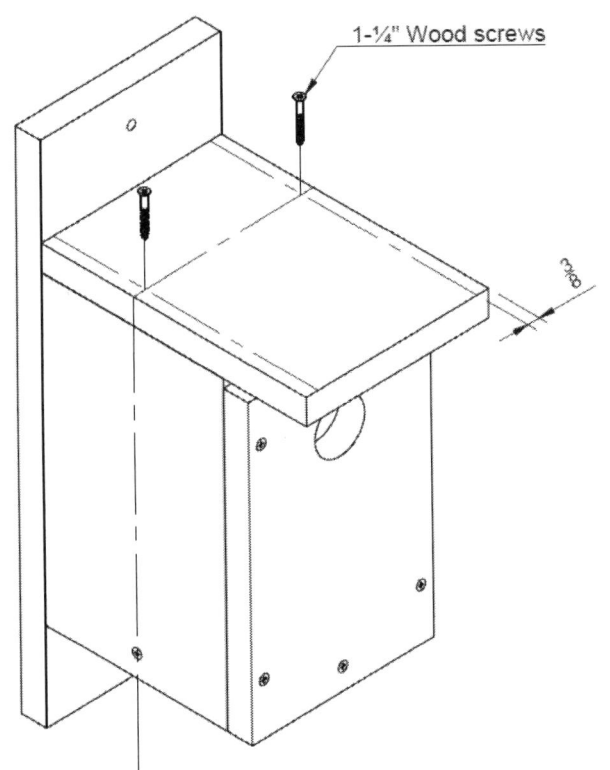

1. Place the Top on the top of the birdhouse.
2. Secure with x2 1-¼" wood screws. For later cleaning and maintenance these screws can be unscrewed to open the birdhouse.

Step 8 - Finish

1. Depending on the wood you used, either leave the birdhouse untreated or apply the paint or stain of your choice.
2. Hang up and enjoy!

DIY Chicken Feeder

15-½"W x 15-½"D x 6-½"H

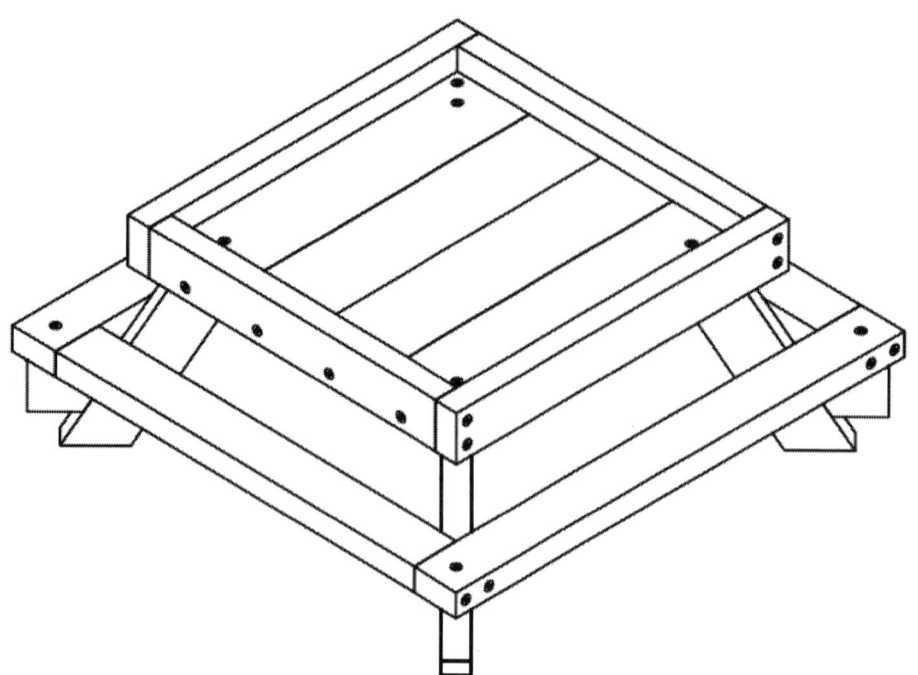

Materials

x1 Board, 1x3", 6' Length
x2 Board, 1x2", 6' Length

Hardware

x28 1-¼" Wood Screws
x8 2" Wood Screws

Tools

Miter Saw
Electric drill
Clamps
Tape measure
Sandpaper

Note: Use boards suitable for outdoor use and apply proper treatments to ensure durability

Cut List and Parts

x4 Table Top Slats, ¾" x 2-½", 10" Length	x2 Bench 2, ¾" x 1-½", 12-½" Length
x2 Trim 1, ¾" x 1-½", 11-½" Length	x4 Angled Leg, ¾" x 1-½", 7" Length
x2 Trim 2, ¾" x 1-½", 10" Length	x4 Bench Support, ¾" x 1-½", 2-¼" Length
x2 Bench 1, ¾" x 1-½", 15-½" Length	

x1 1x3", 6' Length

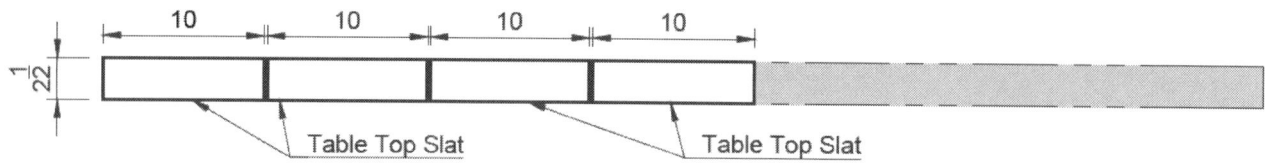

128

x1 1x2", 6' Length

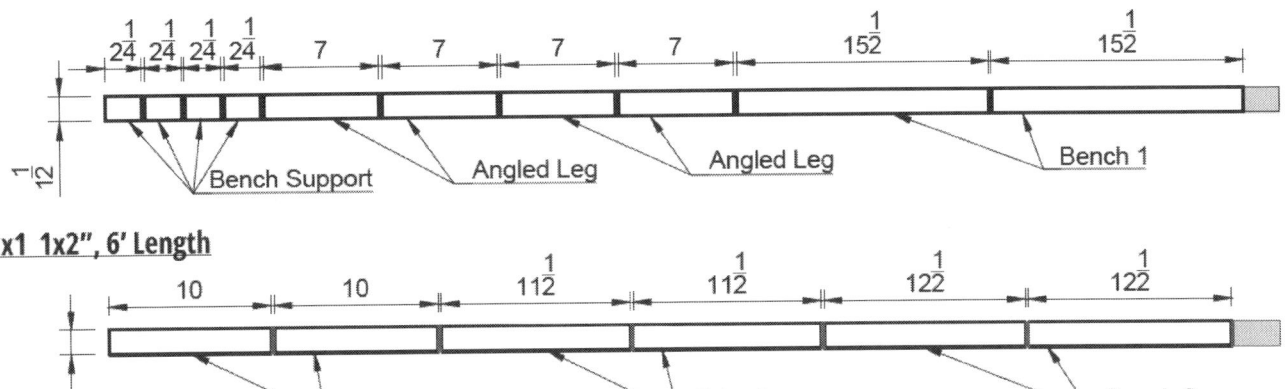

x1 1x2", 6' Length

Exploded Diagram

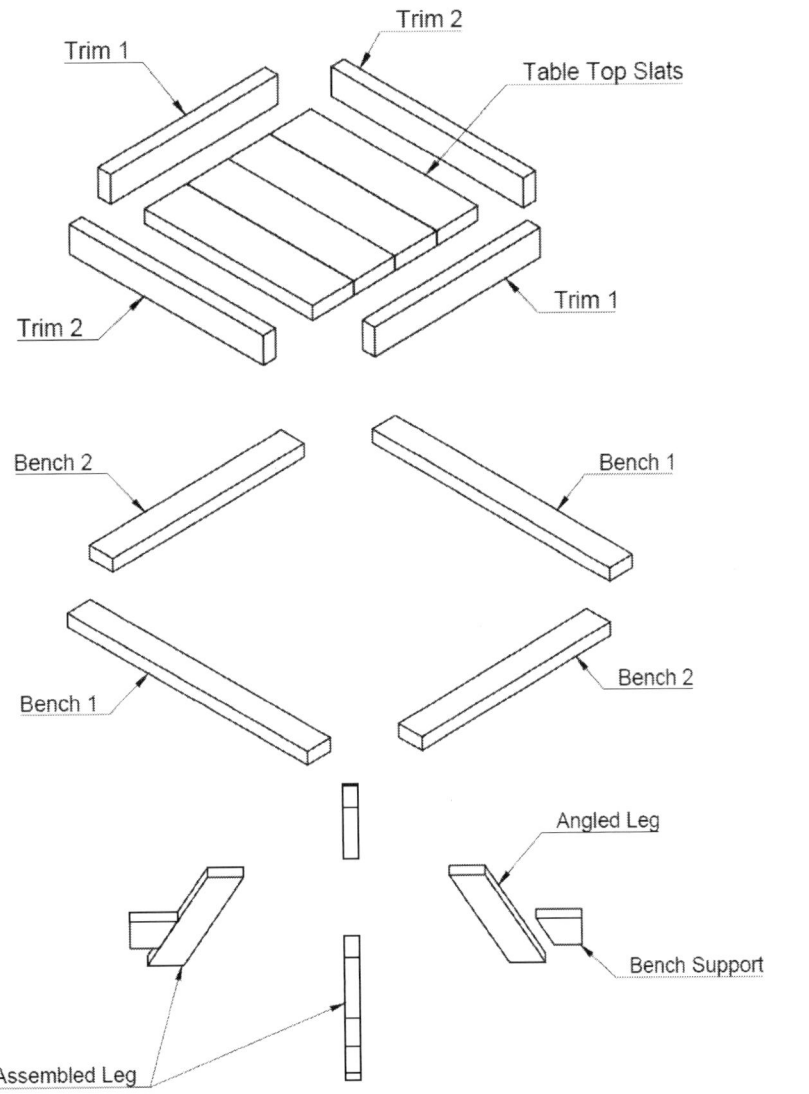

Step 1 - Assemble the Table Top

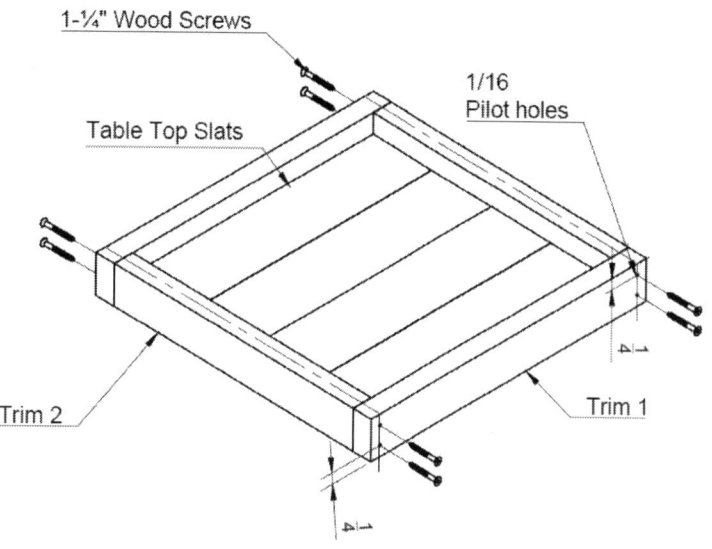

1. On a flat and level surface lay out all the Table Top Slats and the Trim pieces No.1 and 2 as shown below.
2. Clamp everything in place making sure the sides are square.
3. Drill four 1/16" pilot holes in each Trim 1 piece, ensuring they are evenly spaced and aligned with the center of the Trim 2 pieces.
4. Secure together with 1-¼" wood screws.

Step 2 - Assemble the Slats to the Trim

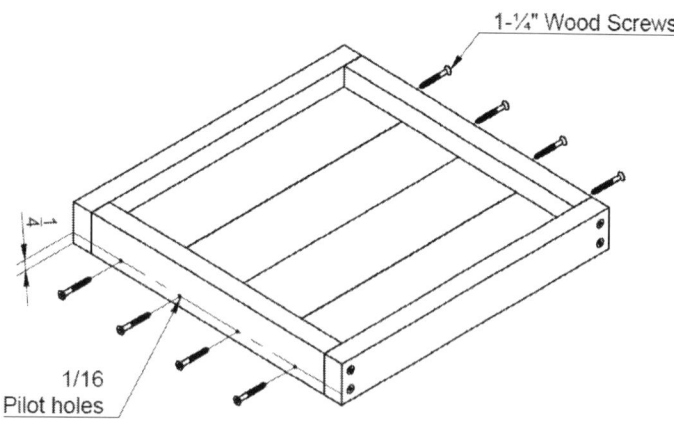

1. Drill four 1/16" pilot holes through the Trim 2 pieces, make sure they are evenly spaced and aligned with the center of each Table Top Slat.
2. Secure together with 1-¼" wood screws.

Step 3 - Assemble the Bench

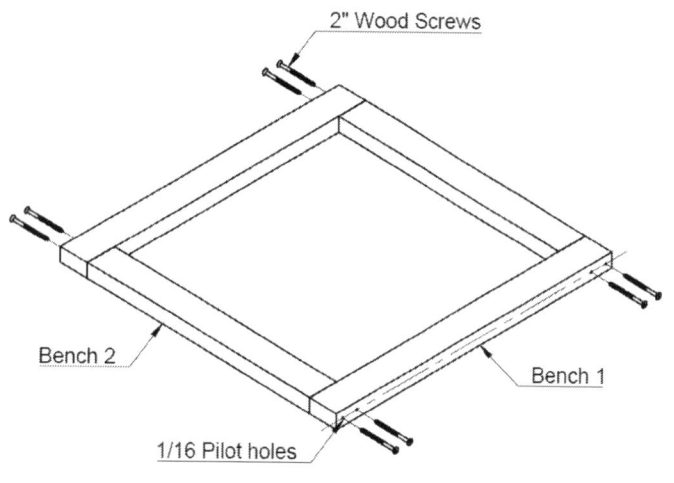

1. Arrange all the Bench pieces on a flat surface as shown. Ensure all edges are square and clamp together.
2. Drill four 1/16 pilot holes in each Bench 1 piece as indicated.
3. Join the four pieces with eight 2" wood screws.

Step 4 - Prepare the Legs

1. Gather the pieces that make up the Legs - x4 Angled Leg and x4 Bench Support pieces.
2. Mark out and use a miter saw to cut them to the lengths indicated below, making angled cuts as needed.
3. Sand cut edges smooth with sandpaper.

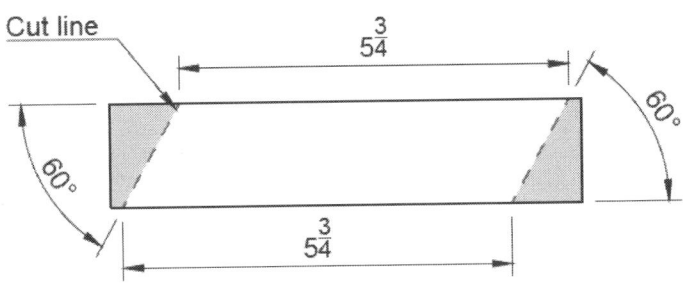
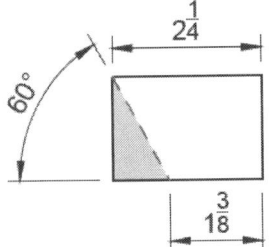

Cutting Pattern for the Angled Legs

Cutting Pattern for the Bench Supports

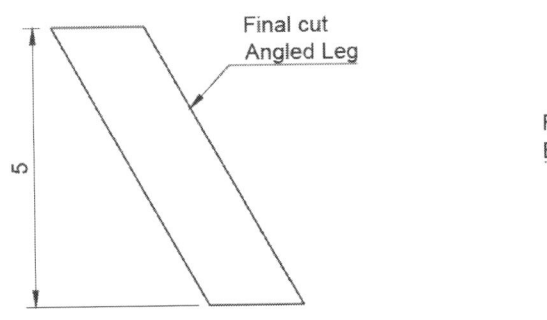
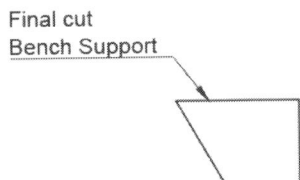

Step 5- Assemble the Legs

1. Lay an Angled Leg and a Bench Support on a level surface, position the Bench Support 1" above the bottom of the leg.
2. Secure together using a 1-¼" wood screw.
3. Repeat to assemble all four legs.

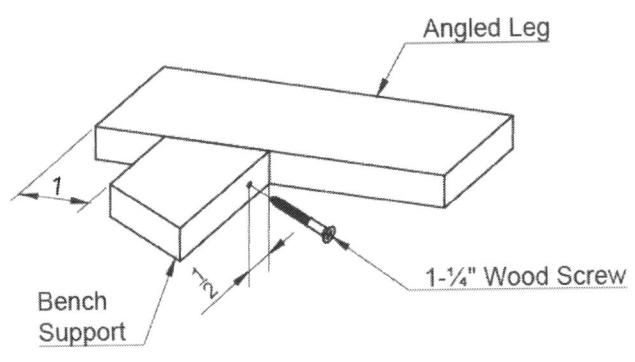
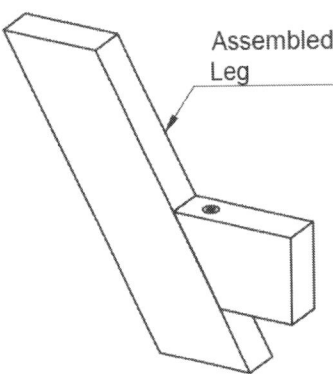

Step 6 - Join the Legs to the Bench

1. Align the front edge of a Leg with the underside corner of the Bench.
2. Drill a 1/16 pilot hole through the top of the Bench in the position indicated below.
3. Secure with a 1-¼" wood screw.
4. Repeat to attach all Legs to the Bench.

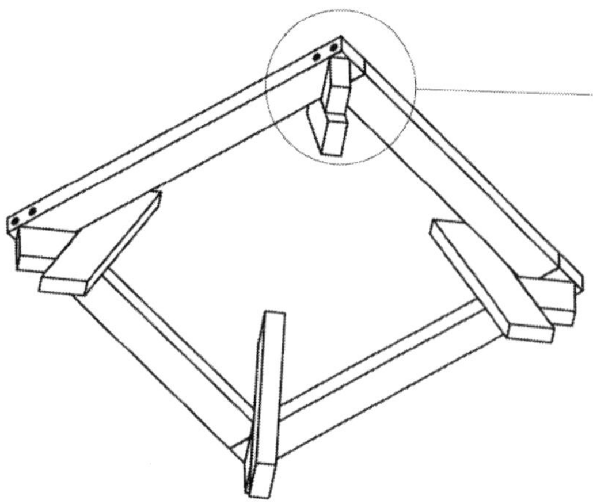

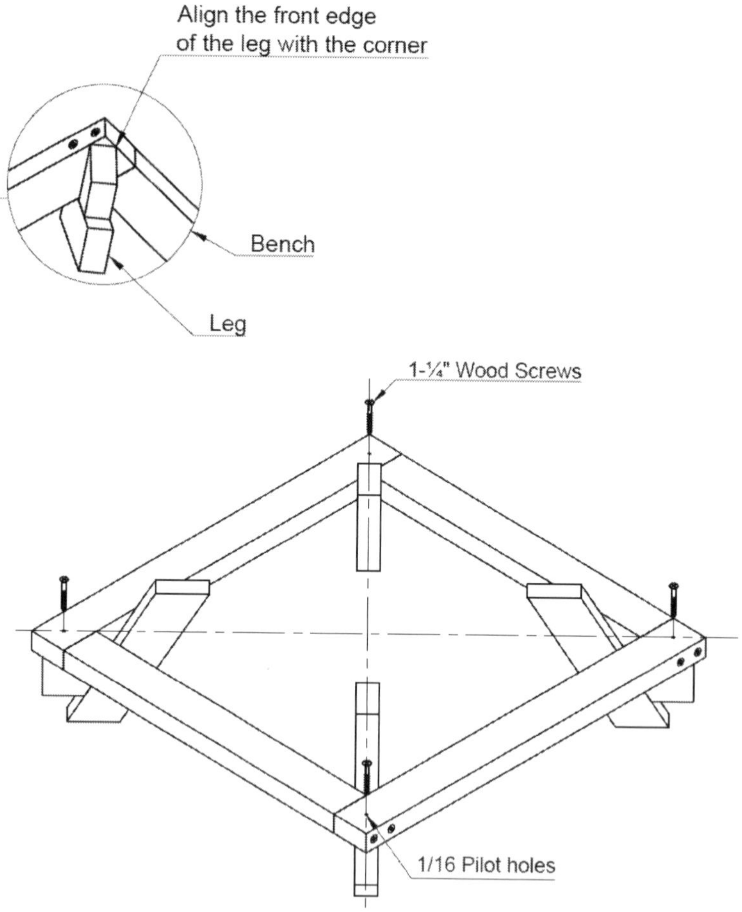

Step 7 - Join the Table Top to the Legs

1. Center the assembled Table Top on top of the assembled Bench and Legs as shown below.
2. Secure with x2 1-¼" wood screws, in each leg.

Top View of Chicken Feeder

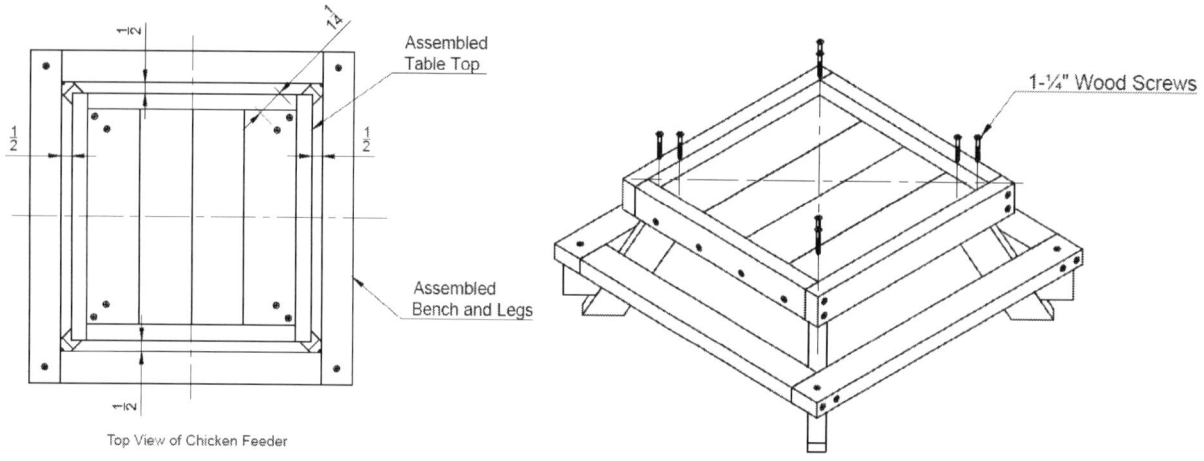

Step 8 - Finish

1. Depending on the wood you used, either leave the Chicken Feeder untreated or apply the 'Chicken Safe' paint or
stain of your choice.
2. Enjoy!

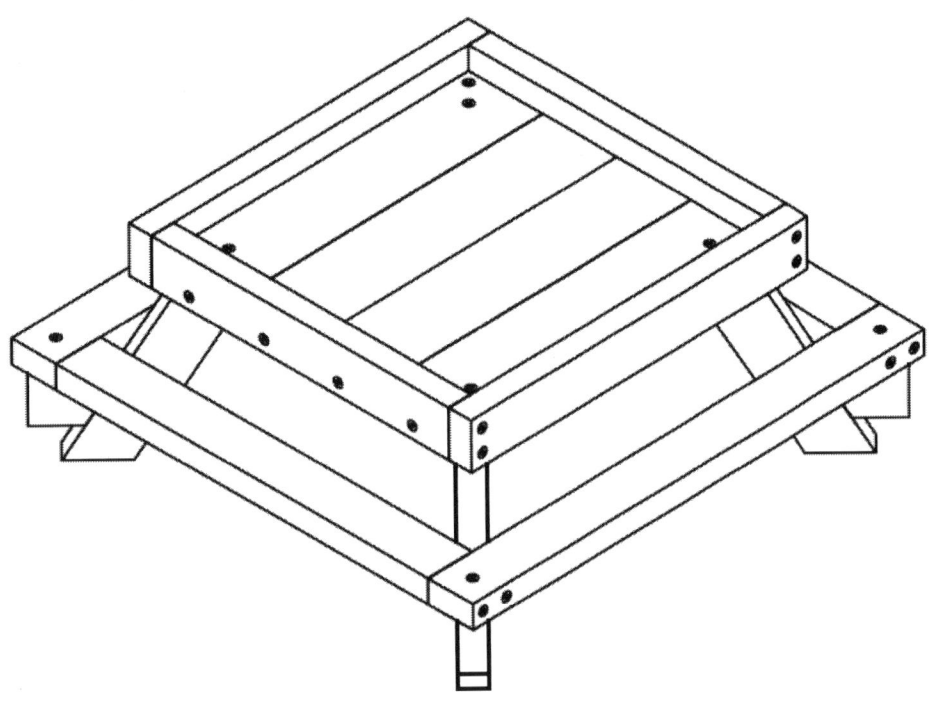

DIY Picnic Table

28.5"Wx55"Dx30"H

Materials

x5 Board, 2x6", 8' Length

x1 Board, 2x6", 6' Length

x1 Board, 2x4", 8' Length

x1 Board, 2x4", 6' Length

Hardware

x8 2-½" Coarse thread pocket-hole screws

x16 2½" Wood Screws

x16 7/16" Hex bolts, 3-¾" length

x32 7/16" Washers

x16 7/16" Nuts

Note: Use boards suitable for outdoor use and apply proper treatments to ensure durability.

Tools

Miter saw

Electric drill

Pocket-hole jig

Spanner or Wrench

Clamps

Tape measure

Sandpaper

Cut List and Parts

x4 Leg, 1-½" x 5-½", 33" Length

x5 Table Top Slat, 1-½" x 5-½", 55" Length

x2 Leg Brace, 1-½" x 5-½", 28" Length

x2 Leg Connector, 1-½" x 3-½", 26" Length

x1 Central Connector, 1-½" x 3-½", 26" Length

x2 Cross Brace, 1-½" x 3-½", 26-½" Length

x4 2x6", 8' Length

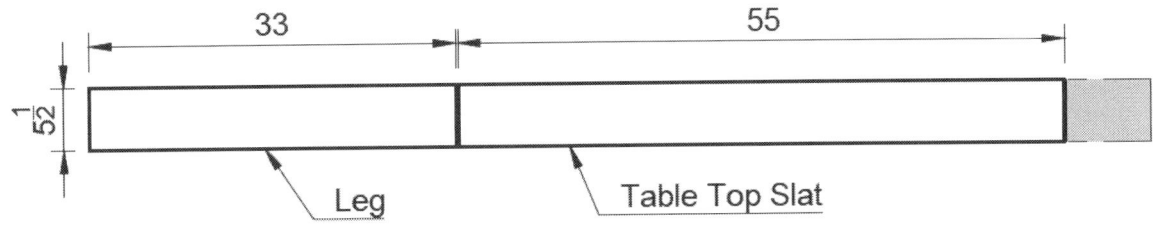

x1 2x6", 8' Length

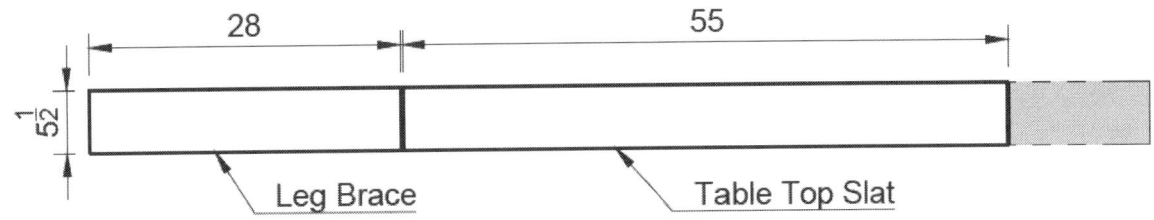

x1 2x6", 6' Length

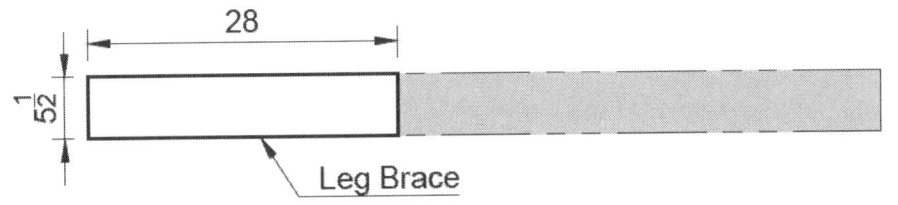

x1 2x4", 8' Length

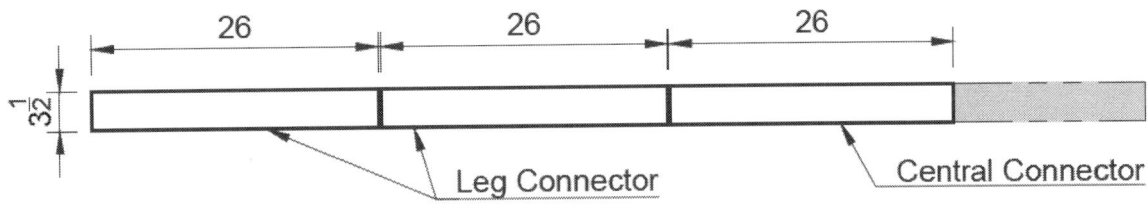

x1 2x4", 6' Length

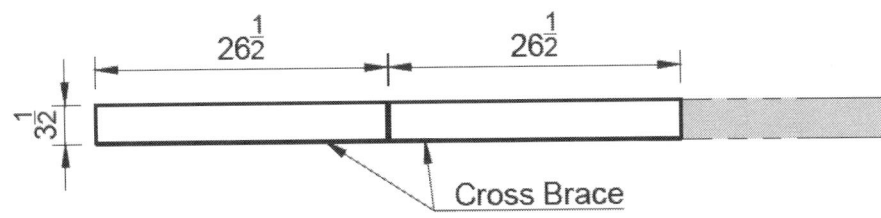

Exploded Diagram

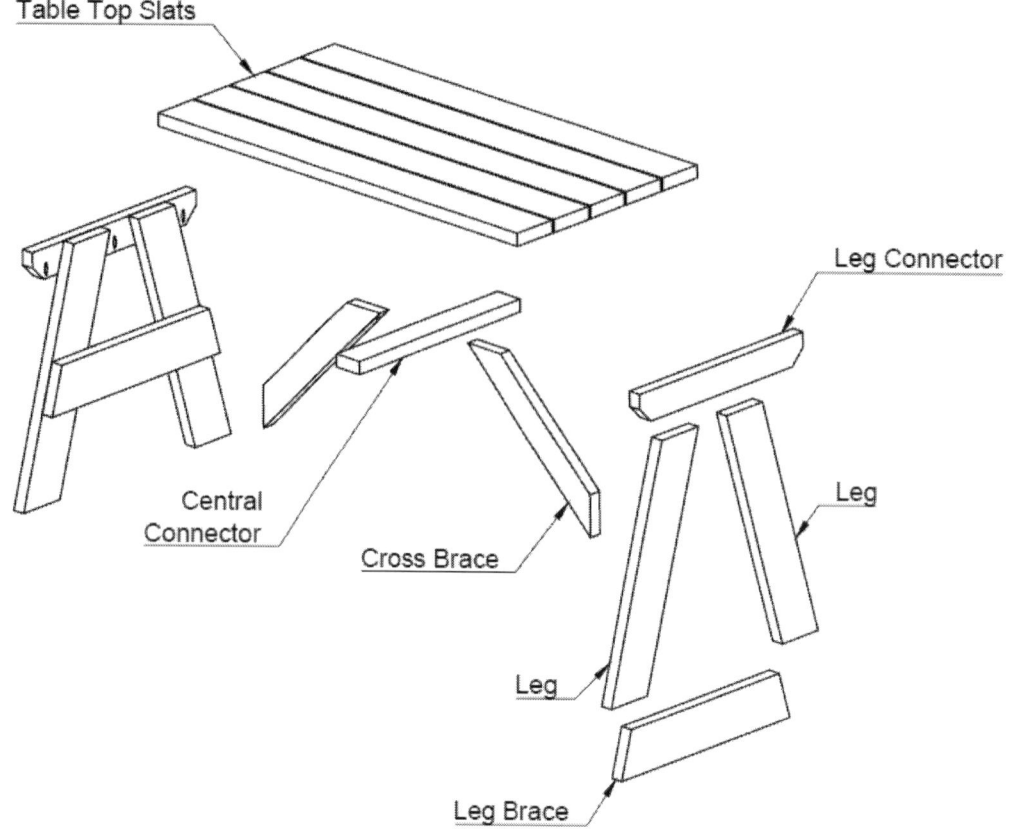

Step 1 - Assemble the Table Top

1. On a flat and level surface lay out all the Table Top Slats with a ¼" gap between them all as shown below.

2. Center the Central Connector on the Table Top Slats and secure them together using 2-½" wood screws. Start by fastening the outer Slats, then work inward.

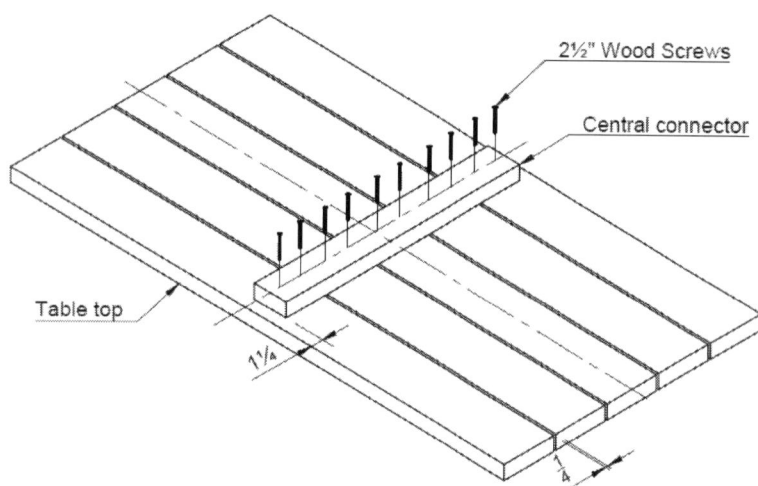

Step 2 - Prepare the Leg Connectors

1. Using a pocket-hole jig, drill 4 pocket-holes in the locations shown below on both Leg Connector pieces, the holes should line up at the approximate center of each Table Top Slat.
2. As a decorative feature, then cut a 1-¾" triangle off the bottom corners.
3. Sand smooth using sandpaper.

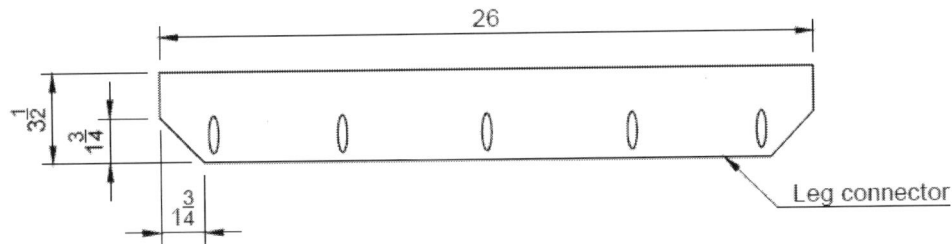

Step 3 - Secure the Leg Connectors to the Table Top

1. Align the Leg connectors with the pocket-holes facing in, on the underside of the table top in the positions shown below.
2. Secure with 2-½" pocket-hole screws.

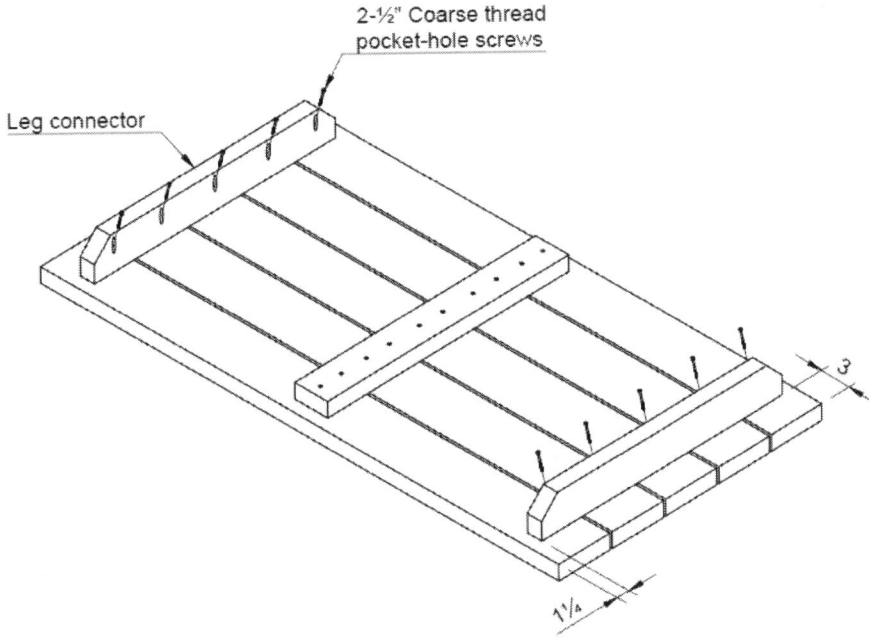

Step 4 - Prepare the Legs

1. Mark out and use a miter saw to cut the Leg pieces to the length indicated below, making angled cuts as needed.

For this example, the cut angle is 17°; however, if you adjust the overall dimensions, the required angle may change.

2. Sand cut edges smooth with sandpaper.

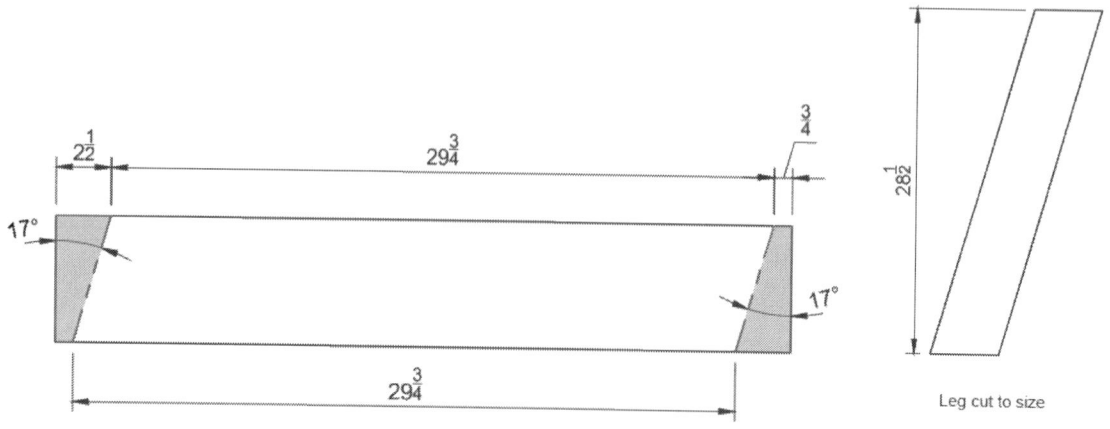

Step 5 - Join the Legs to the Table Top

1. Start by aligning two Legs on the underside of the table top in the positions indicated below, clamp securely in place.

2. Mark and drill ½" diameter holes through the Legs and Leg Connectors at once. Drill two holes per leg, ensuring they are evenly spaced and roughly centered vertically on the Leg Connectors.

3. Fasten the Legs to the Leg Connectors using 7/16" hex bolts, nuts and washers, tightening them with a suitable spanner or wrench.

4. Repeat until all the Legs are fastened securely.

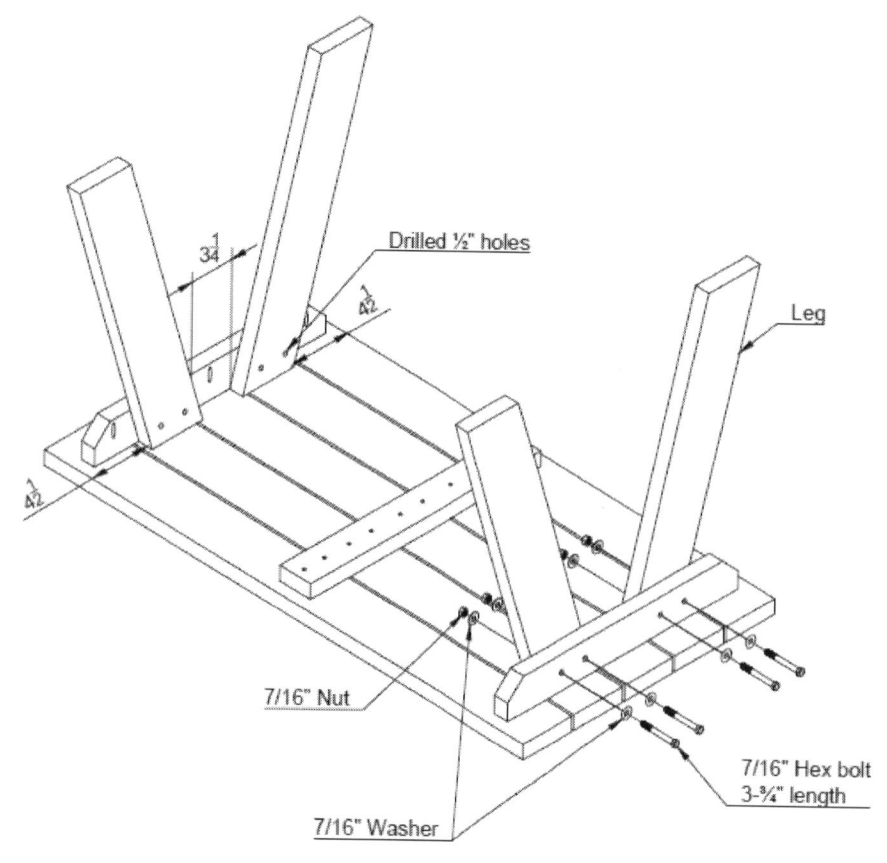

Step 6 - Prepare the Leg Braces

1. In order to get the correct angle and length, lay each Leg Brace over the Legs in the position shown below and mark the angles that needs to be cut.
2. Cut to size using a Miter saw.
3. Sand smooth cut edges using sandpaper.
4. Repeat for both Leg Braces.

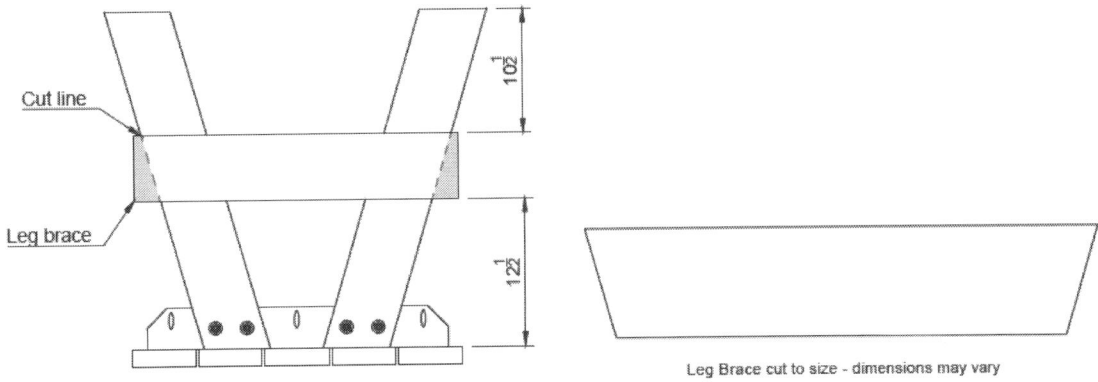

Leg Brace cut to size - dimensions may vary

Step 7 - Join the Leg Braces to the Legs

1. Start by aligning your Leg Brace on the Legs in the position from Step 6, clamp securely in place.
2. Mark and drill ½" diameter holes through the Leg Brace and Legs at once. Drill two holes per leg, ensuring they are evenly spaced and roughly centered vertically on the Leg Brace.
3. Fasten the Legs Brace to the Legs using 7/16" hex bolts, nuts and washers, tightening them with a suitable spanner or wrench.
4. Repeat until both the Leg Braces are fastened securely.

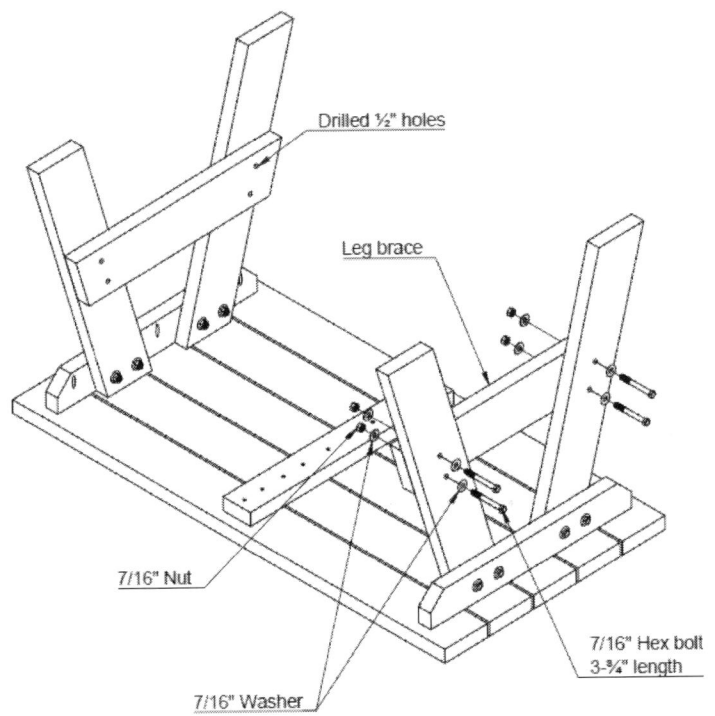

Step 8 - Prepare the Cross Braces

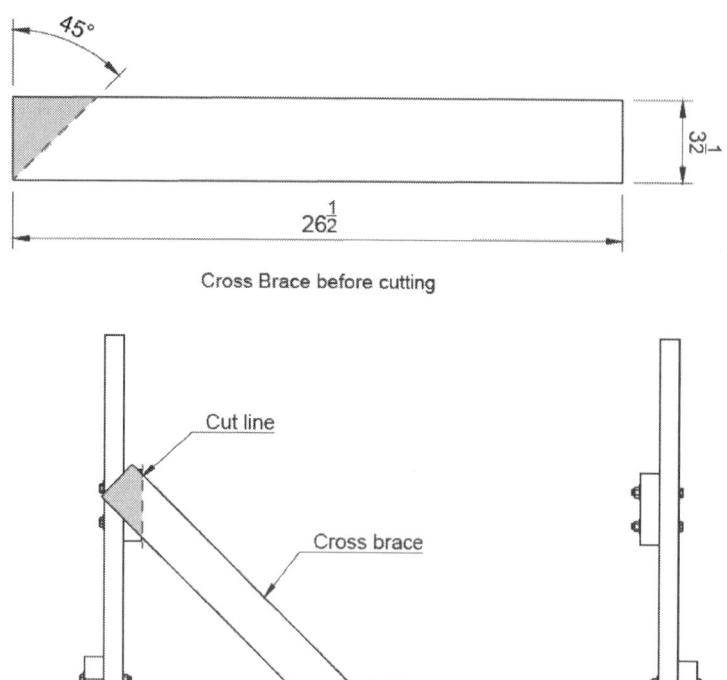

1. Mark out and cut a 45° angle on a Cross Brace using a Miter Saw.
2. Lay the Cross Brace against the assembled picnic table as shown in the picture to find the correct angle and length to cut.
3. Cut to size using a Miter saw.
4. Sand smooth cut edges using sandpaper.
5. Repeat for the other Cross Brace.

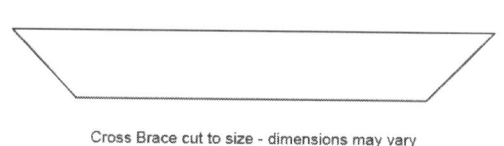

Cross Brace cut to size - dimensions may vary

Step 9 - Secure the Cross Brace to the Table Top

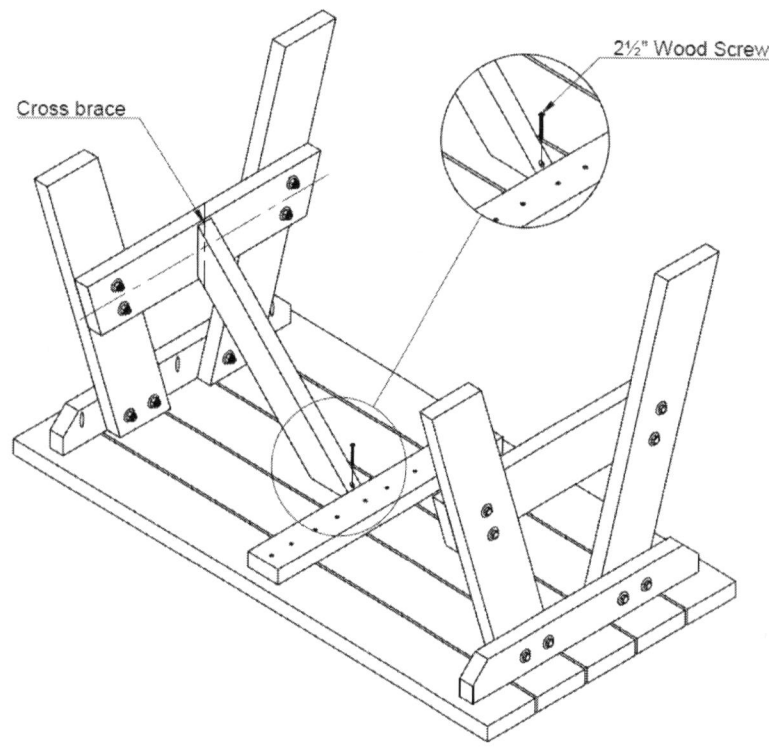

1. Center the Cross Brace on the underside of the picnic table.
2. Secure the Cross Brace to the table top using one 2-½" wood screw in the position indicated in the picture. Double check that in the position you are screwing them together that the screw won't pierce through to the table top.

Step 10 - Secure the Cross Brace to the Leg Brace

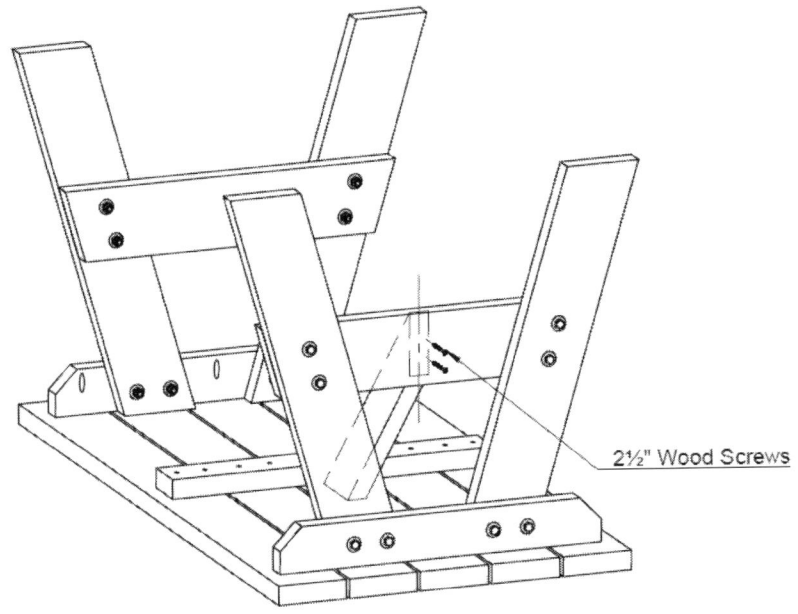

1. Secure the Cross Brace to the Leg Brace using two 2-½" wood screws. Ensure the screws are evenly spaced and roughly centered vertically on the Leg Brace. Again make sure that the screws won't pierce through the Cross Brace before screwing them together.

Step 11 - Repeat

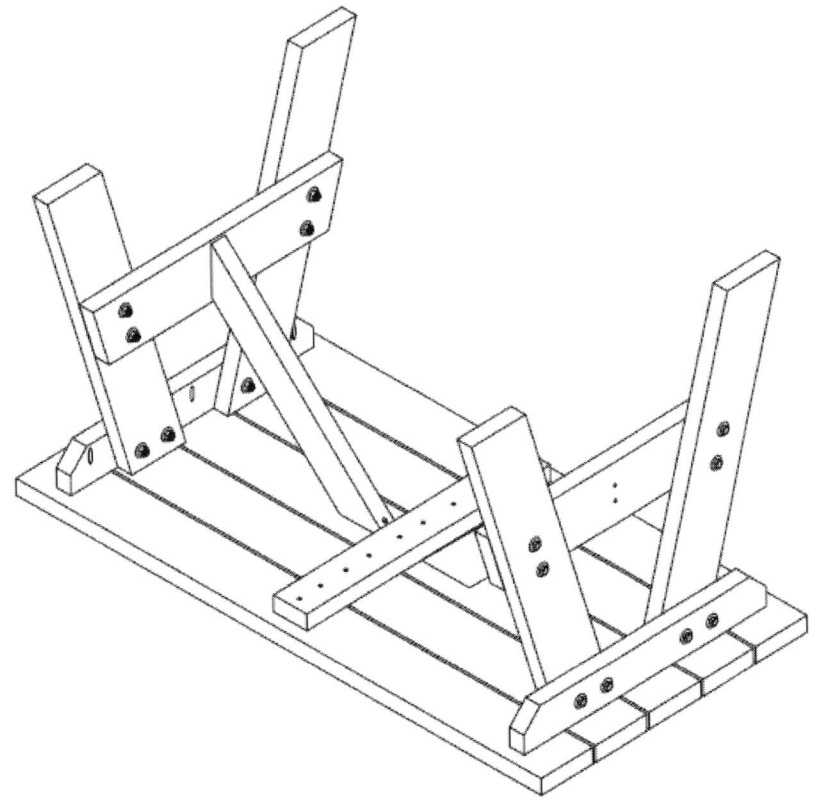

1. Repeat Steps 9 and 10 to attach the second Cross Brace.

Step 12- Flip Over and Finish

1. Flip the table the right way up, this will be a two-person job.
2. Depending on the wood you used, either leave the picnic table untreated or apply the paint or stain of your choice.
3. Enjoy!

DIY Outdoor Chair

24"W x 24-½"D x 33"H

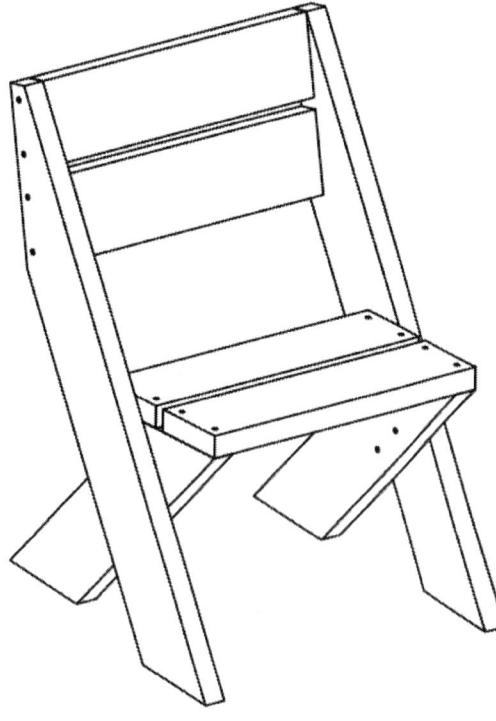

Materials

x2 Board, 2x6", 8' Length
x1 Board, 2x6", 6' Length

Hardware

x18 2-½" Wood Screws (suitable for outdoor use)

Tools

Miter Saw
Electric drill
Tape measure
Sandpaper

Cut List and Parts

x2 Long Leg, 1-½" x 5-½, 43-3/8" Length
x2 Short Leg, 1-½" x 5-½, 24-7/8" Length
x4 Slat, 1-½" x 5-½, 21" Length

x1 2x6", 8' Length

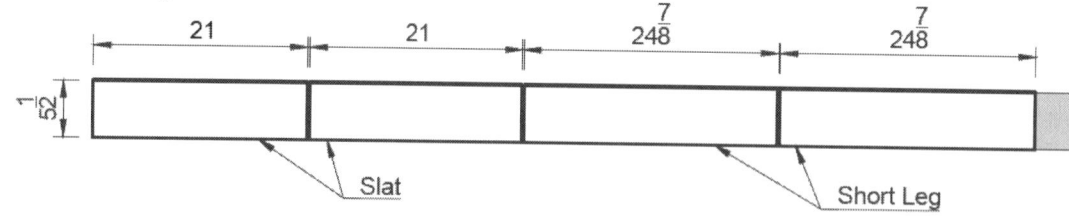

x1 2x6", 8' Length

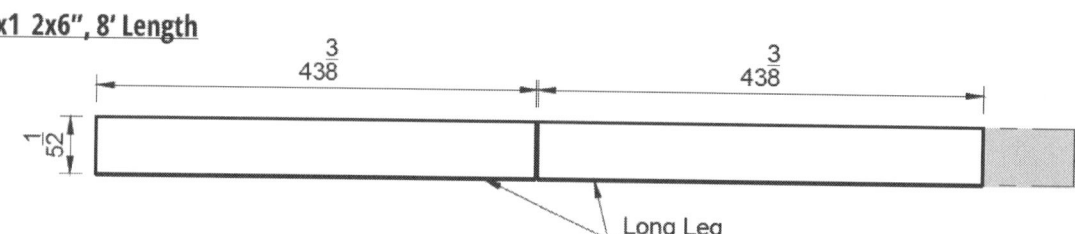

x1 2x6", 6' Length

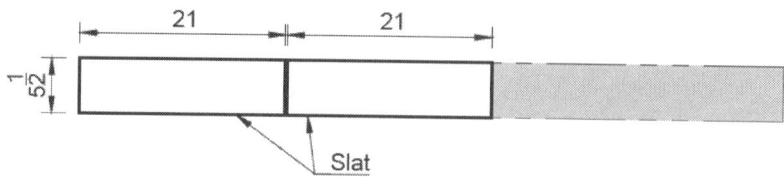

Exploded Diagram

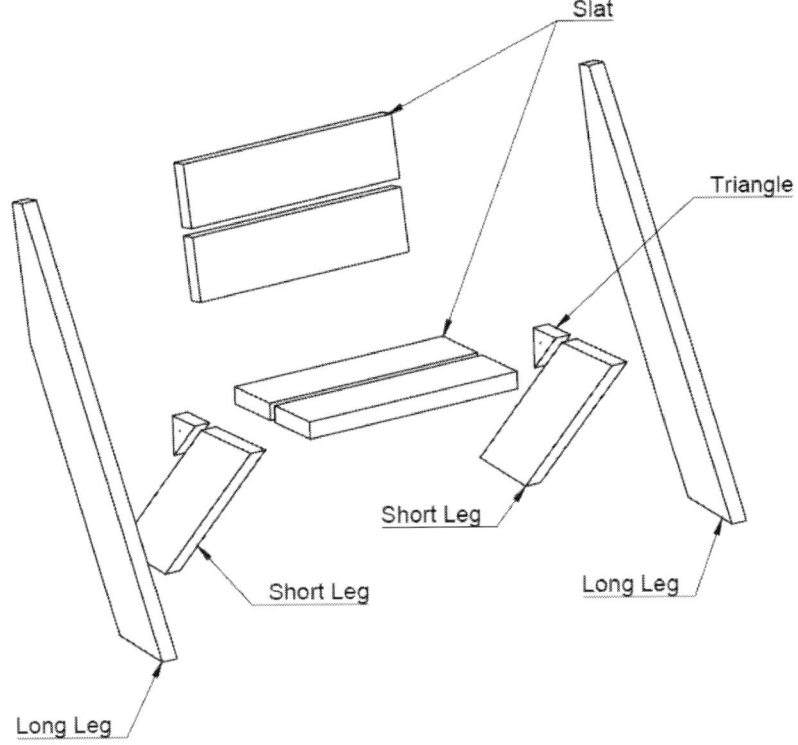

Step 1 - Prepare the Short Leg

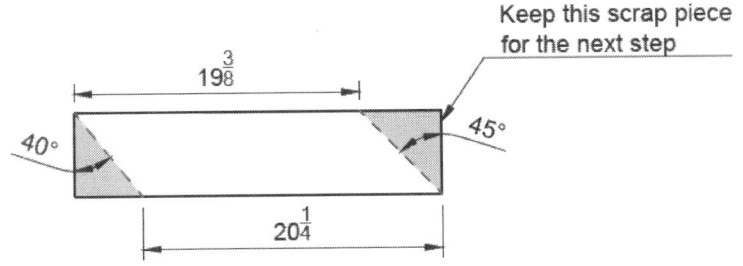

1. Lay the two Short Legs on a flat surface and mark out a 40° angle on the bottom edge and a 45° angle on the top edge, this is where the seat will be.
2. Cut to size using a miter saw, keeping the 45° scrap pieces for Step 2.
3. Sand smooth cut edges using sandpaper

Step 2 - Make 2 Triangles from the Scrap Pieces

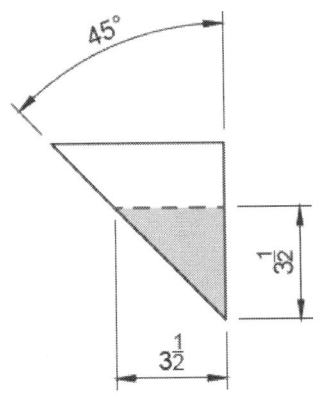

1. Mark out 3-½"x 3-½" triangles on the 45° scrap pieces.
2. Cut to size using a miter saw, keeping your fingers well away from the blade.
3. Sand cut edges smooth using sandpaper.

Step 3 - Prepare the Long Leg

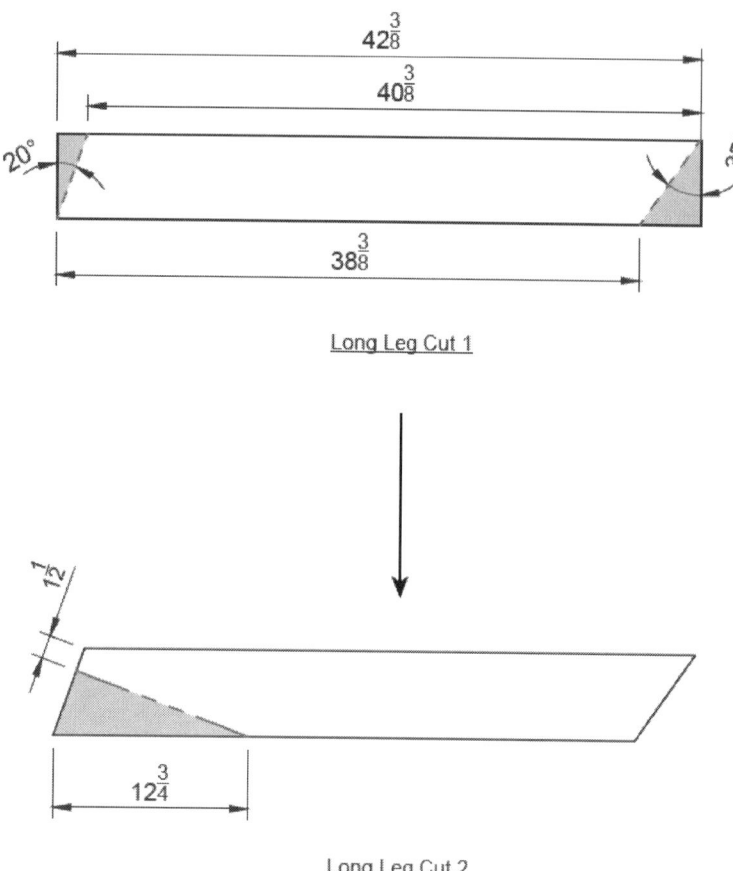

Long Leg Cut 1

Long Leg Cut 2

1. Lay the two Long Legs on a flat surface and mark out a 35° angle on the bottom edge and a 20° angle on the top edge.
2. Cut to size using a miter saw.
3. Next, mark out the distances as shown below for Cut 2, this is where the backrest will be later.
4. Cut to size using a miter saw.
5. Sand smooth cut edges using sandpaper.

Step 4 - Assemble the Legs

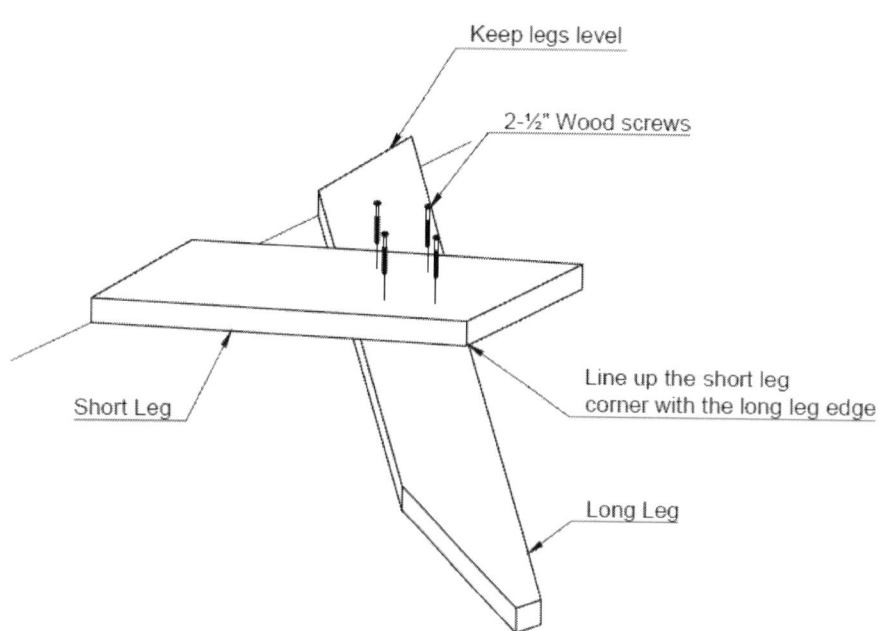

1. Place one short leg and one long leg on a flat surface, positioning them against a square edge to keep the bottoms aligned and level.
2. Align the corner of the short leg with the long leg edge as shown below.
3. Secure together using four 2-½" wood screws.

144

Step 5 - Attach the Triangle

1. Before attaching, drill a pilot hole in the position indicated below.
2. Lay the triangle on top of the long leg, aligning with the top edge of the short leg.
3. Secure together using a 2-½" wood screw.

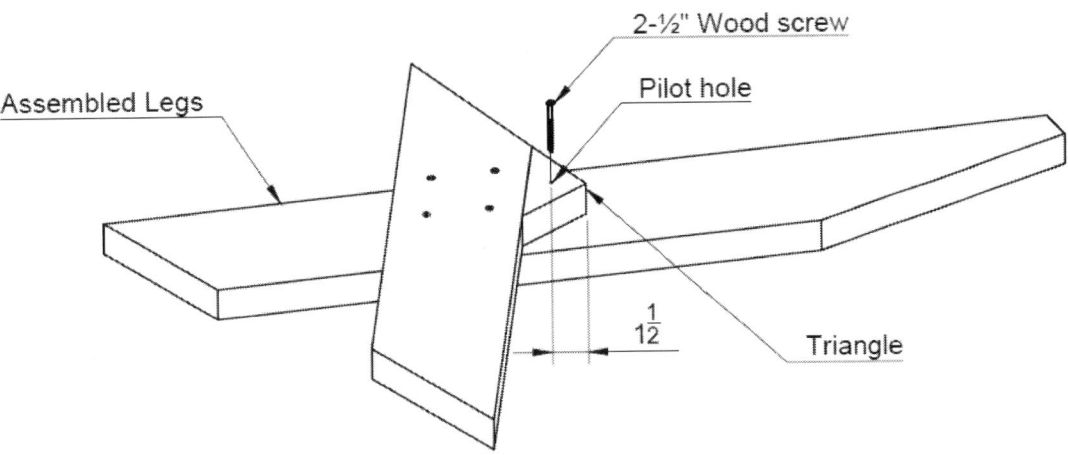

Step 6- Repeat

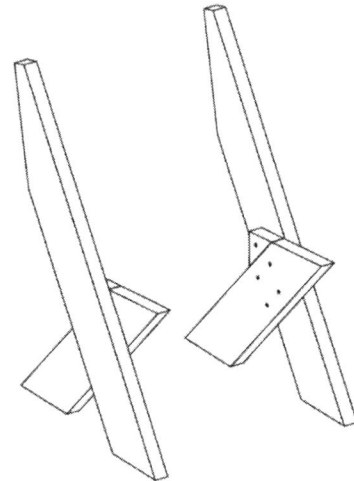

Repeat Steps 4 and 5 to assemble the other leg,
make sure the second leg is a mirror image of the first.

Step 7 - Attach the Seat

1. Align a slat with the front edges of the short legs, place a second behind it leaving a ¾" gap between the slats.
2. Attach each slat to the legs with four 2-½" wood screws. Drill the screw closest to the front of the chair at a slight angle to prevent it from going through the short leg.

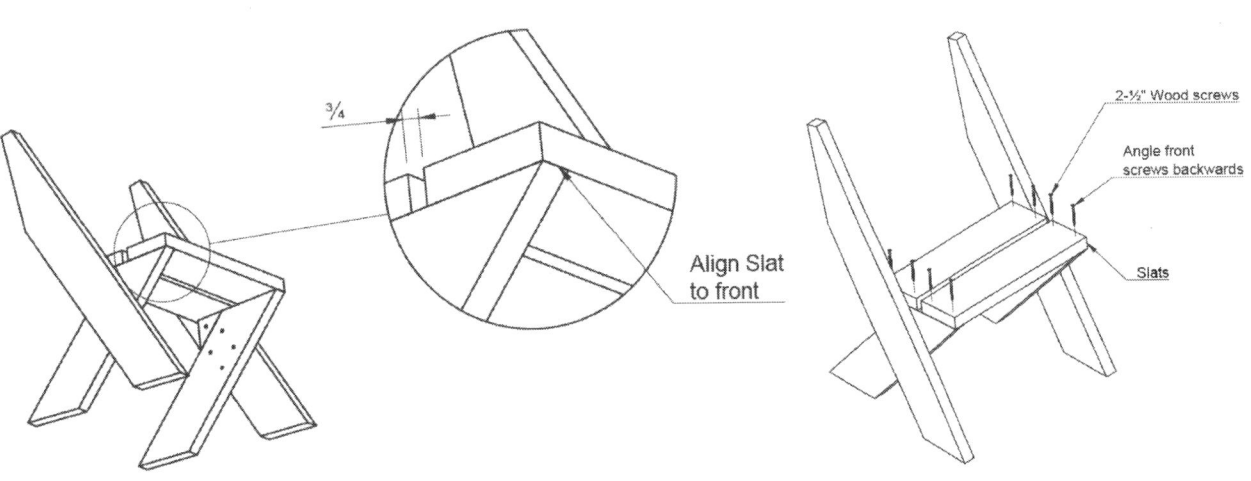

Step 8 - Join the Backrest

1. Place the chair on its side and align a slat so it is square with the top edge and angled to match the back of the long leg.

2. Push in the second slat, leaving a ¾" gap.

3. Attach each slat with four 2-½" wood screws through the sides of the long legs.

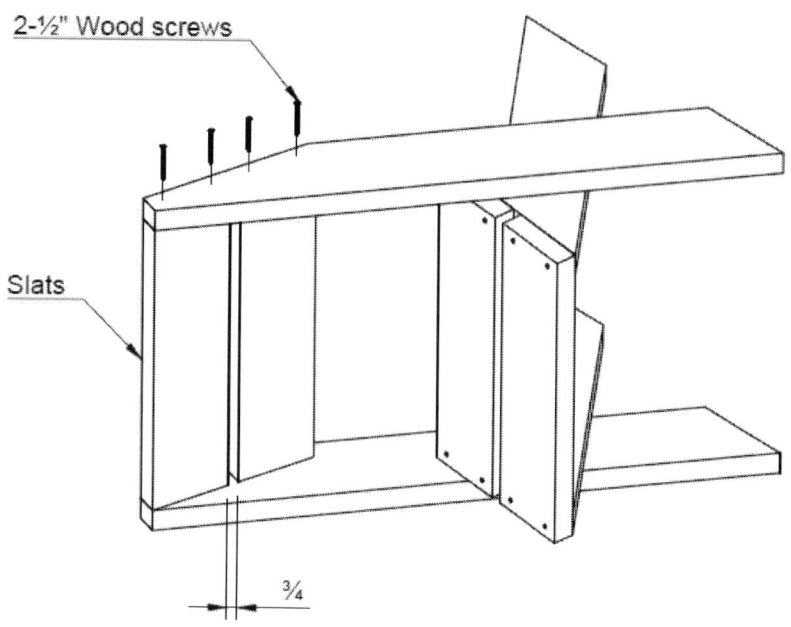

Step 9 - Finish

1. Depending on the wood you used, either leave the chair untreated or apply the paint or stain of your choice.

2. Enjoy!

DIY Storage Cabinet

35"Wx19"Dx40"H

Materials

x1 Pine Board, 2x2", 8' Length
x1 ¾" Plywood Sheet, 4x8'
x1 ¾" Plywood Sheet, 5x5'
x1 ¼" Plywood Sheet, 5x5'

Hardware

x44 1-¼" Coarse thread pocket-hole screws
x12 2-½" Coarse thread pocket-hole screws
x10 2" Wood Screws
x9 1-¼" Wood Screws
x32 5/8" Finishing Nails
x3 Drawer/Door Pulls (Handles)
x2 Drawer Slides
x4 Concealed Cabinet Hinges

Tools

Miter saw
Jigsaw or Table Saw
Electric drill
Pocket-hole jig
Tape measure
Sandpaper

Cut List and Parts

x1 No.1, ¾" Plywood, 35"x19"	x2 No.10, ¾" Plywood, 15-3/8"x17"
x2 No.2, ¾" Plywood, 31-½"x5"	x2 No.11, ¾" Plywood, 29"x5"
x1 No.3, ¾" Plywood, 33-½"x18"	x2 No.12, ¾" Plywood, 16"x5"
x1 No.4, ¾" Plywood, 33"x18"	x1 No.13, ¼" Plywood, 30-½"x16"
x1 No.5, ¾" Plywood, 31-½"x18"	x1 No.14, ¼" Plywood, 31-¼"x6-½"
x1 No.6, ¾" Plywood, 25-¼"x18"	x2 No.15, 1-½"x1-½", 23-¾" Length
x2 No.7, ¾" Plywood, 25"x15-1/8"	x4 No.16, 1-½"x1-½", 5-½" Length
x1 No.8, ¾" Plywood, 31-½"x5"	x2 No.17, 1-½"x1-½", 11" Length
x1 No.9, ¼" Plywood, 33"x26-¾"	

x1 ¾" Plywood, 5x5'

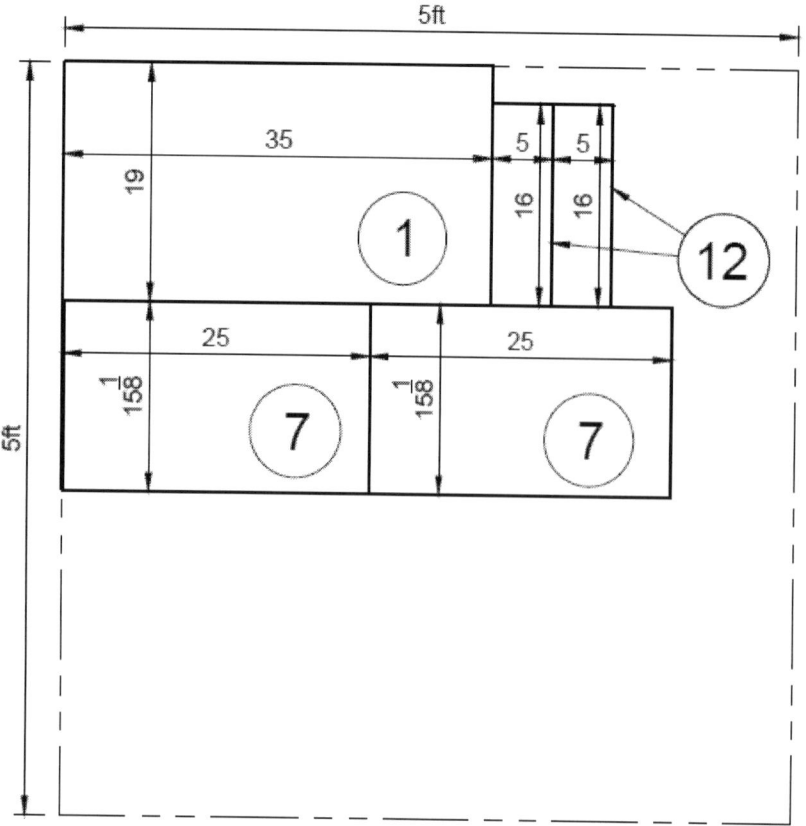

x1 ¾" Plywood, 4x8'

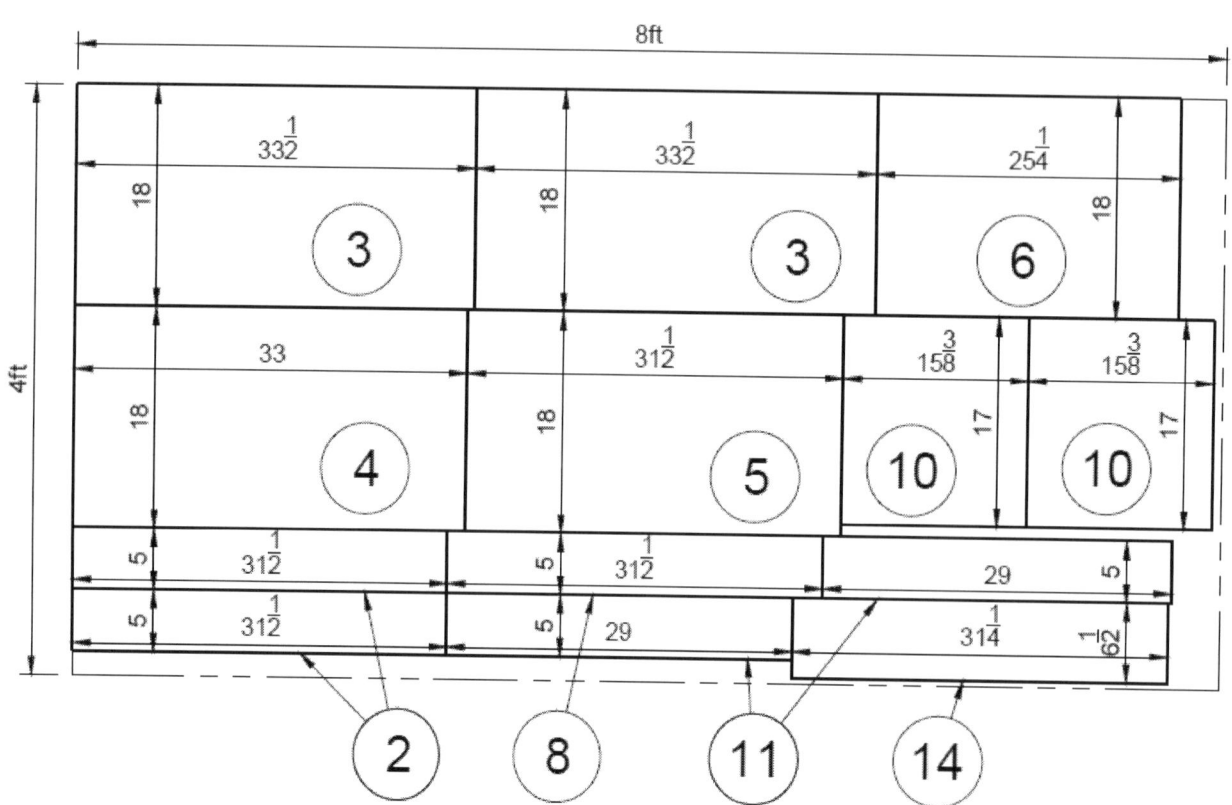

x1 ¼" Plywood, 5x5'

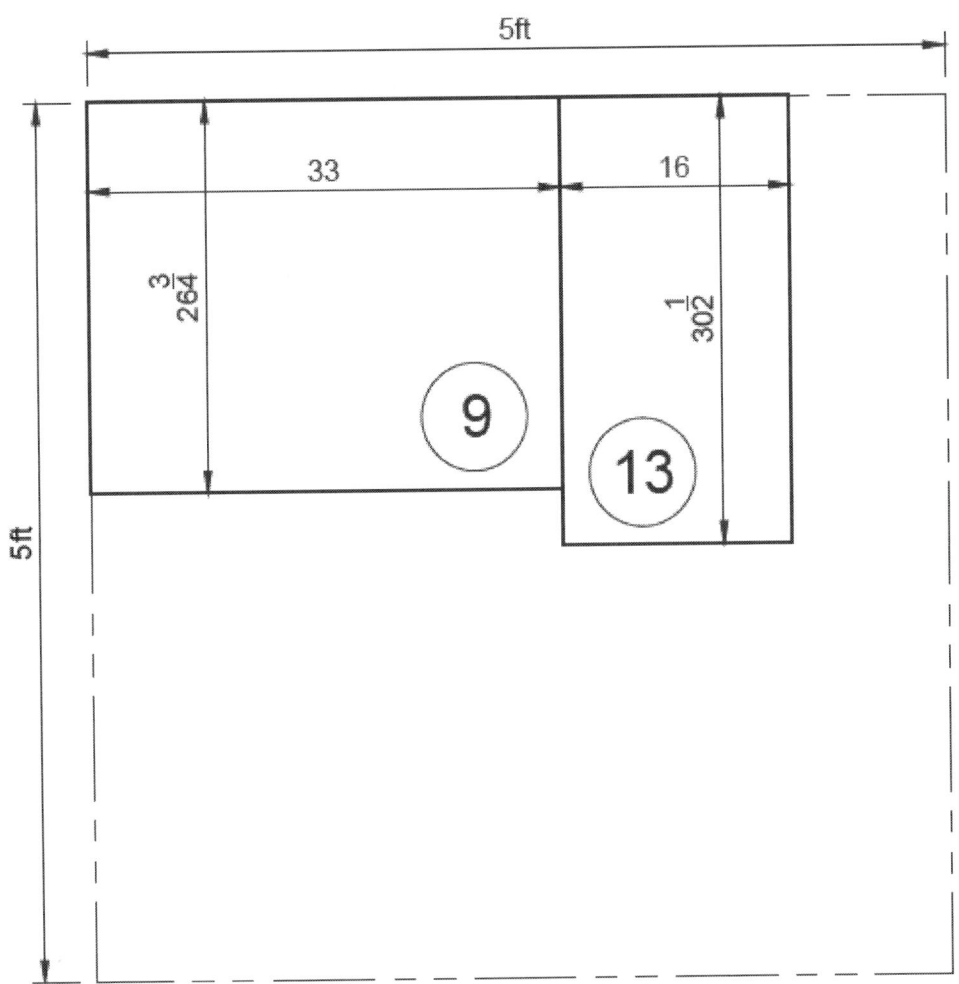

x1 2x2, 8' Length

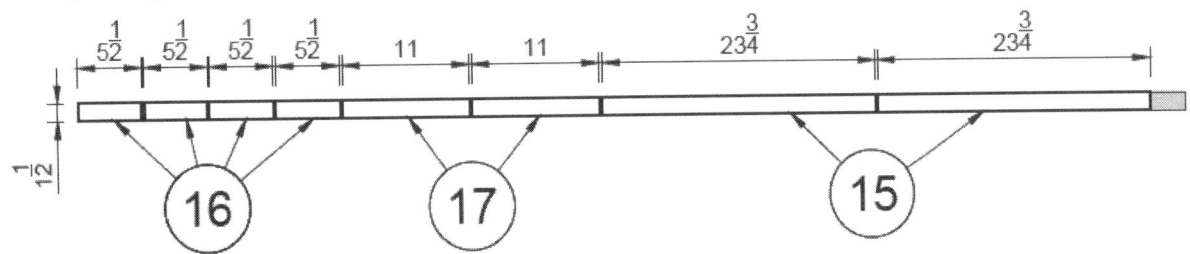

Exploded Diagram

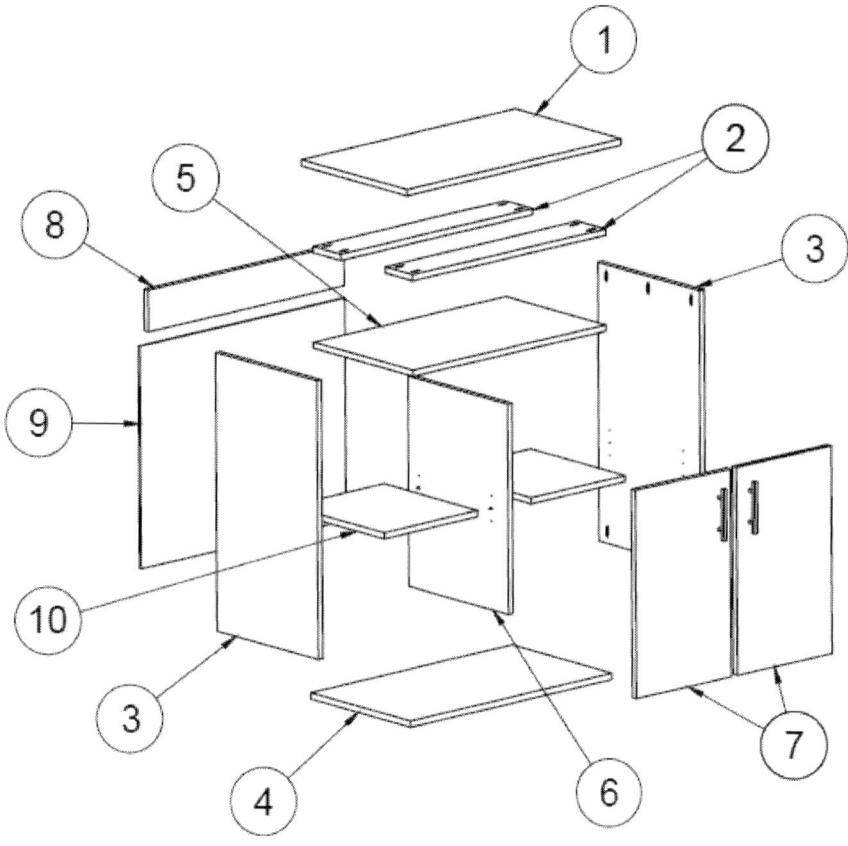

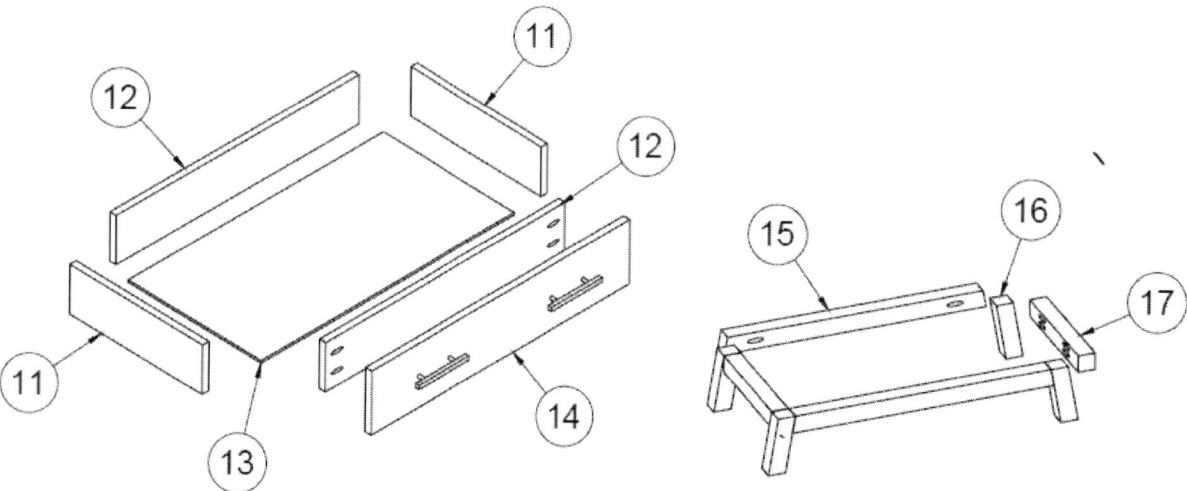

Exploded diagram of the drawer components

Exploded diagram of the base components

Step 1 - Begin Assembling the Carcass

1. Prepare the No. 3 (carcass side) pieces by drilling pocket-holes in the indicated locations with a pocket-hole jig.
2. Next, drill six 1/8" diameter holes, 0.3" deep, for the shelf pins for the adjustable shelves.
3. Sand smooth with sandpaper.
4. Lay the No.4 (carcass base) piece on a flat surface and align the No.3 pieces flush with the edges as shown below.
5. Secure with six 1-¼" pocket-hole screws.

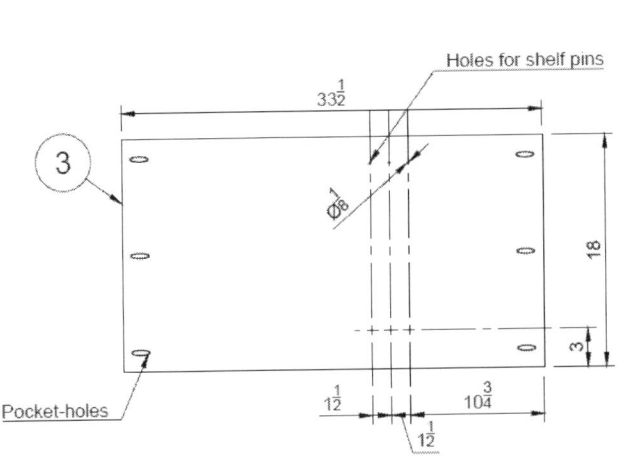
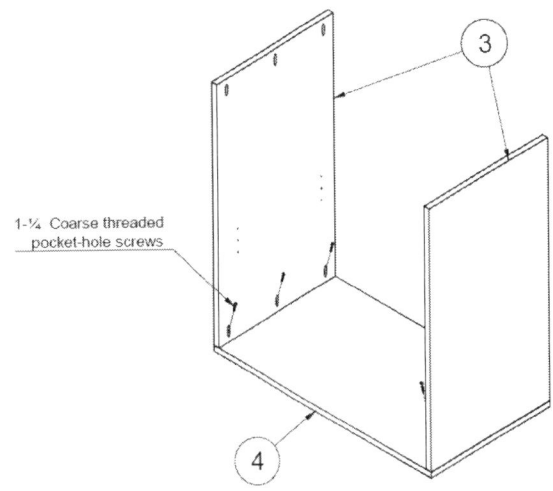

Step 2 - Assemble No.2 Pieces to the Carcass

1. Prepare the two No.2 (carcass top) pieces by drilling pocket-holes in the indicated locations with a pocket-hole jig.
2. Sand smooth using sandpaper.
3. Align the No.2 pieces flush with the outside edges of the carcass and secure using eight 1-¼" pocket-hole screws.
4. Double check at this stage that the carcass is square by measuring the diagonals, adjust if needed.

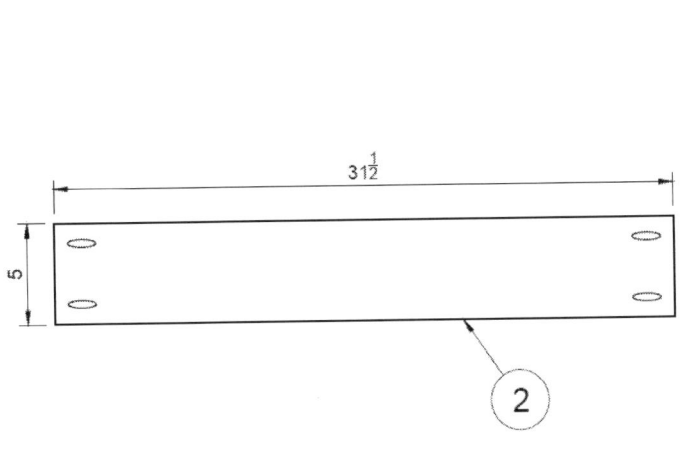
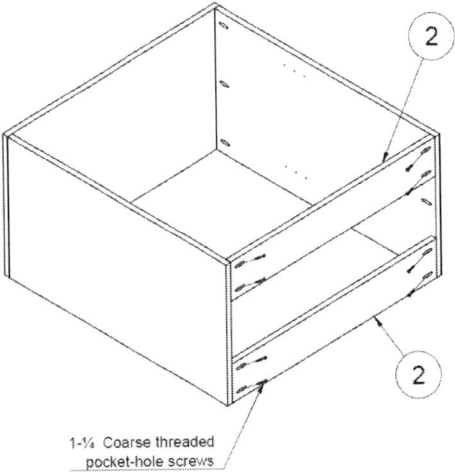

Step 3 - Join the Top to the Carcass

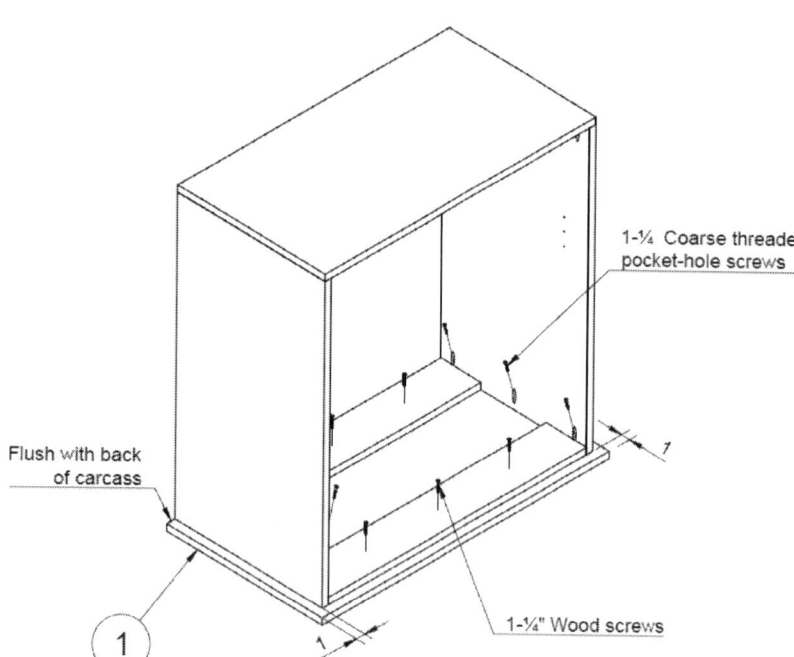

1. Turn the carcass upside down and place it on top of the No. 1 (Top) piece, leaving a 1" gap on all sides except the back, which should be flush with the carcass.
2. First secure using six 1-¼" pocket-hole screws in the pre-drilled holes in the top of the No.3 pieces.
3. Next using six 1-¼" wood screws, secure the underside of the top of the carcass to the No.1 piece as shown in the picture.

Step 4 - Join Piece No.5 to the Carcass

1. Prepare the No.5 (horizontal divider) piece by drilling pocket-holes in the indicated locations with a pocket-hole jig.
2. Align it inside the carcass making sure it is flush to the front and back. You can use the No.6 piece as guide to help mark its position.
3. Secure with six 1-¼" pocket-hole screws.

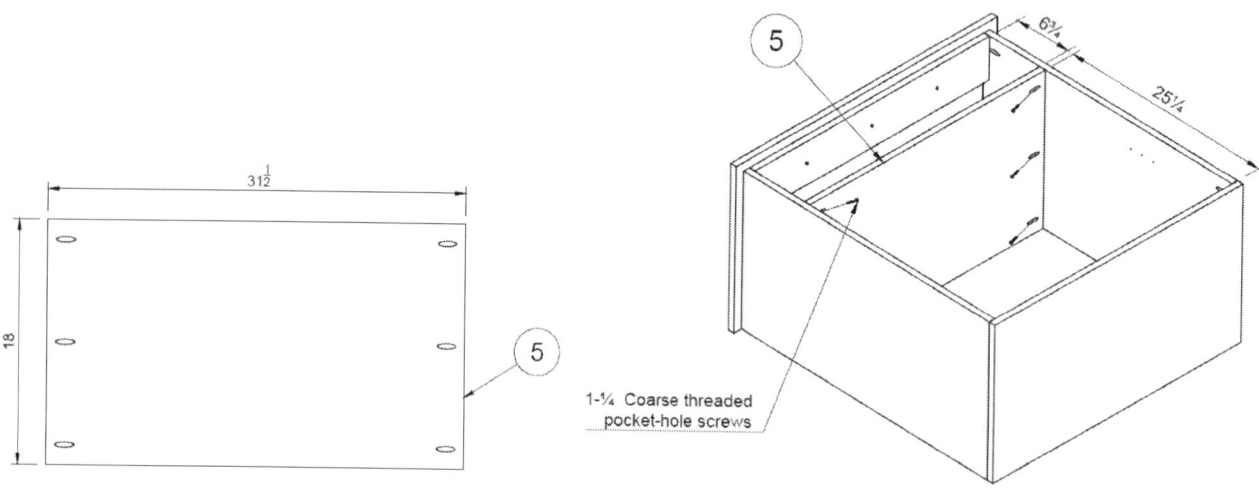

Step 5 - Join Piece No.6 to the Carcass

1. Prepare the No. 6 (vertical divider) piece by drilling pocket-holes in the indicated locations with a pocket-hole jig.
2. Next follow the same process as in Step 1 to drill the shelf pin holes in both sides of the piece.
3. Sand smooth with sandpaper.
4. Center it inside the carcass making sure it is flush to the front and back.
5. Secure with six 1-¼" pocket-hole screws.

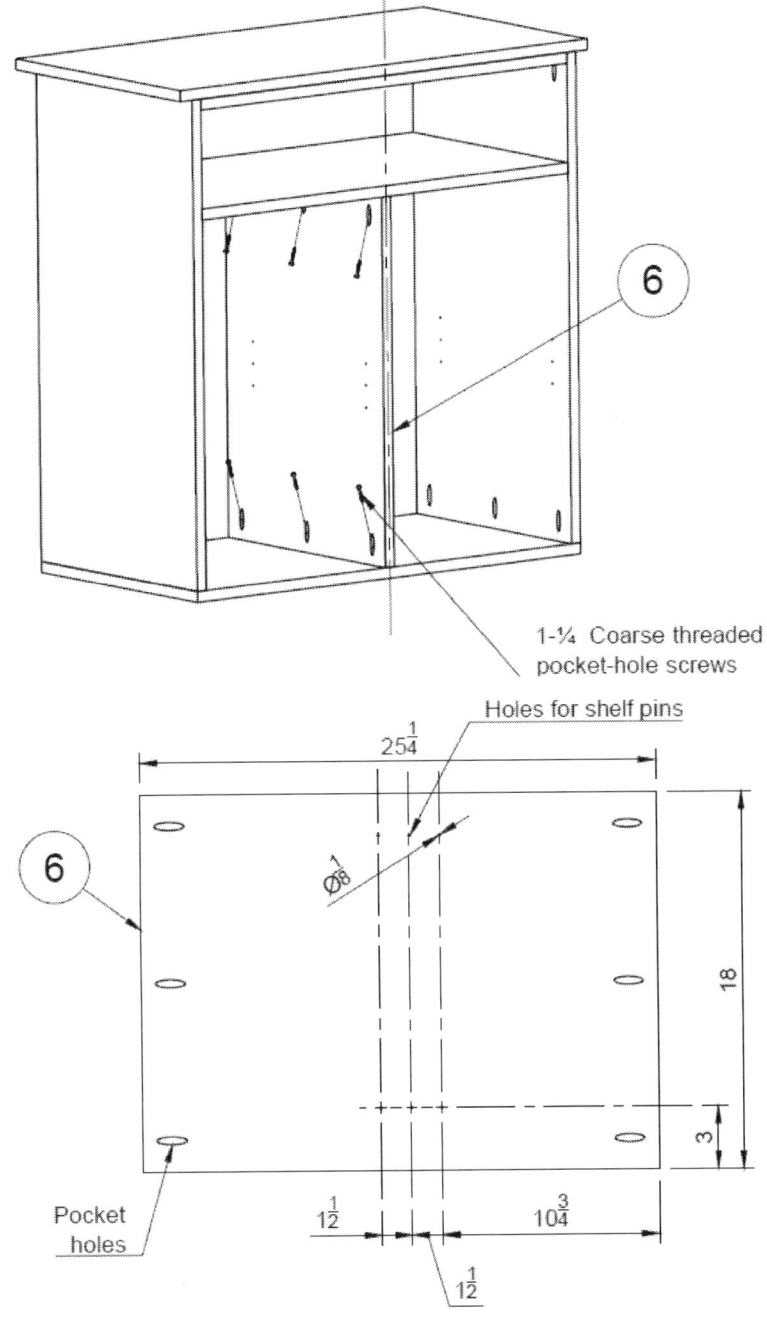

Step 6 - Assemble the Drawer Box

1. Prepare the two No. 12 pieces by drilling pocket-holes in the indicated locations with a pocket-hole jig.
2. Sand smooth with sandpaper.
3. Align all the No.12 and No.11 pieces on a level surface, ensuring the edges are flush, the box is square and the pocket-holes are on the outside.
4. Secure together using eight 1-¼" pocket-hole screws to make the drawer box.

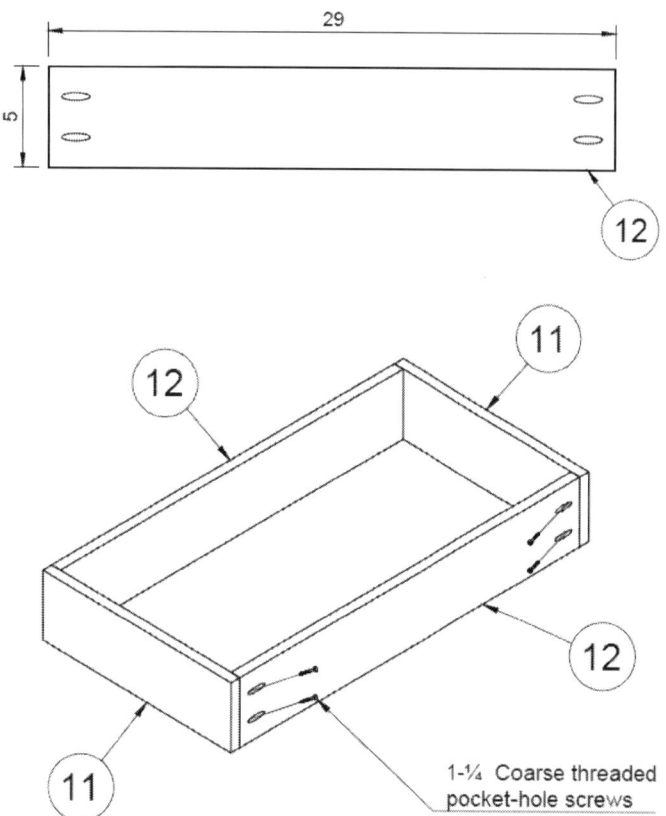

Step 7 - Add the Drawer Base

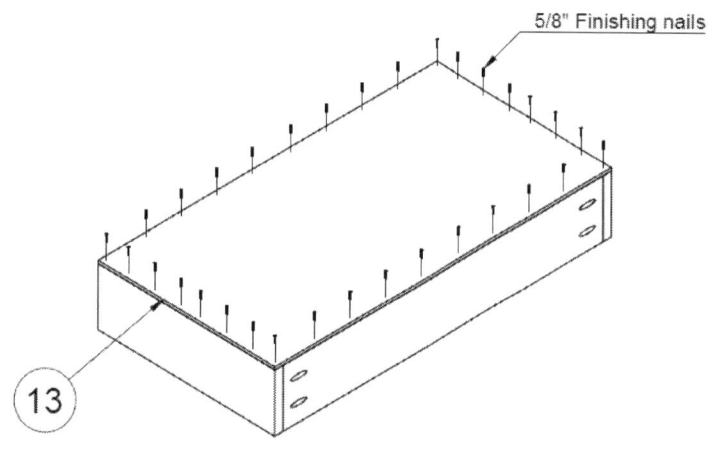

1. Lay the No.3 piece on the underside of the drawer box so it is flush on all sides.
2. Secure together using finishing nails or a staple gun.

Step 8 - Attach the Drawer Slides to the Carcass

1. Screw the drawer slides into the carcass at the location shown, make sure you leave enough space for the drawer front. Dimensions may vary with different drawer slides models.

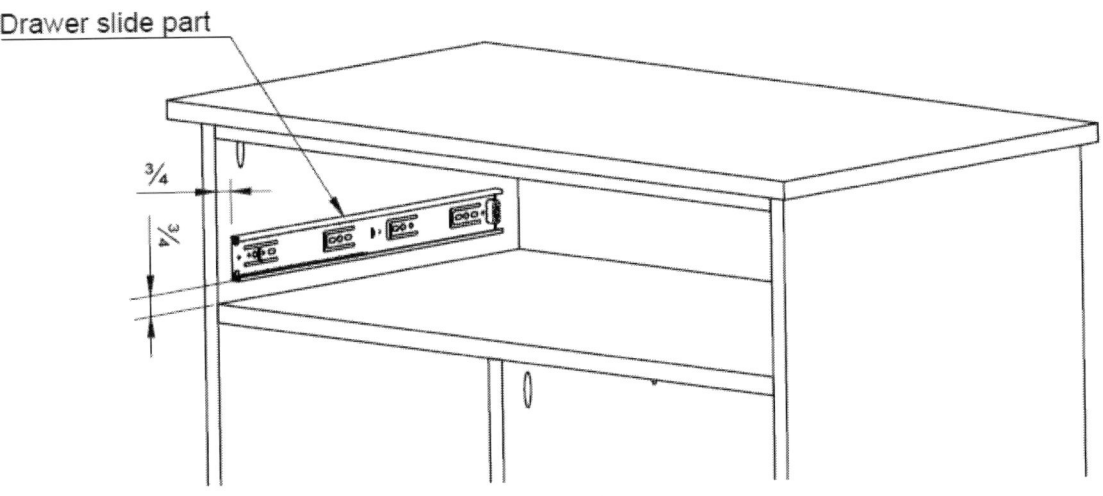

Step 9 - Attach the Drawer Slides to the Drawer Box

1. Reassemble the drawer slides to the sides of the carcass and slide the drawer box in halfway. Use a ¼" scrap piece of plywood to raise it by ¼".
2. Pull out the drawer slide to meet the front edge of the drawer box and attach with two screws on each side.
3. Remove the drawer box from the carcass and add the remaining screws to securely attach the drawer slide.

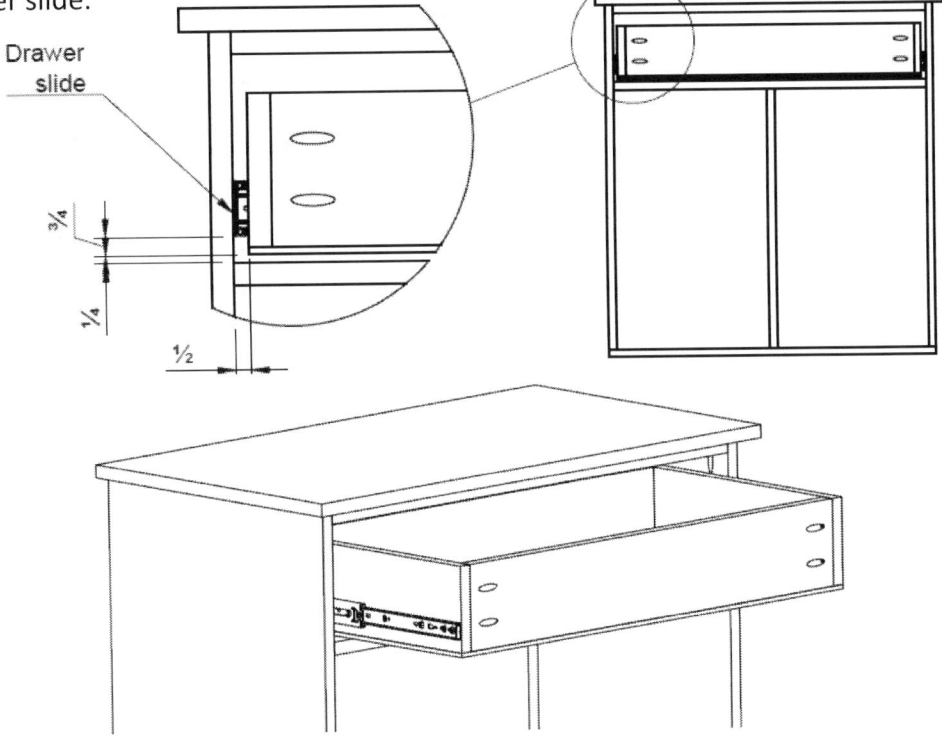

Step 10 - Add the Back to the Carcass

1. Prepare the No. 8 (carcass drawer back) piece by drilling pocket-holes in the indicated locations with a pockethole jig.
2. Sand smooth with sandpaper.
3. Push the No.8 piece into the back of the carcass in the position as shown below, make sure it's flush and secure using four 1-¼" pocket-hole screws.
4. Secondly, align the No.9 piece to the bottom and sides of the back of the carcass and attach using finishing nails or a staple gun.

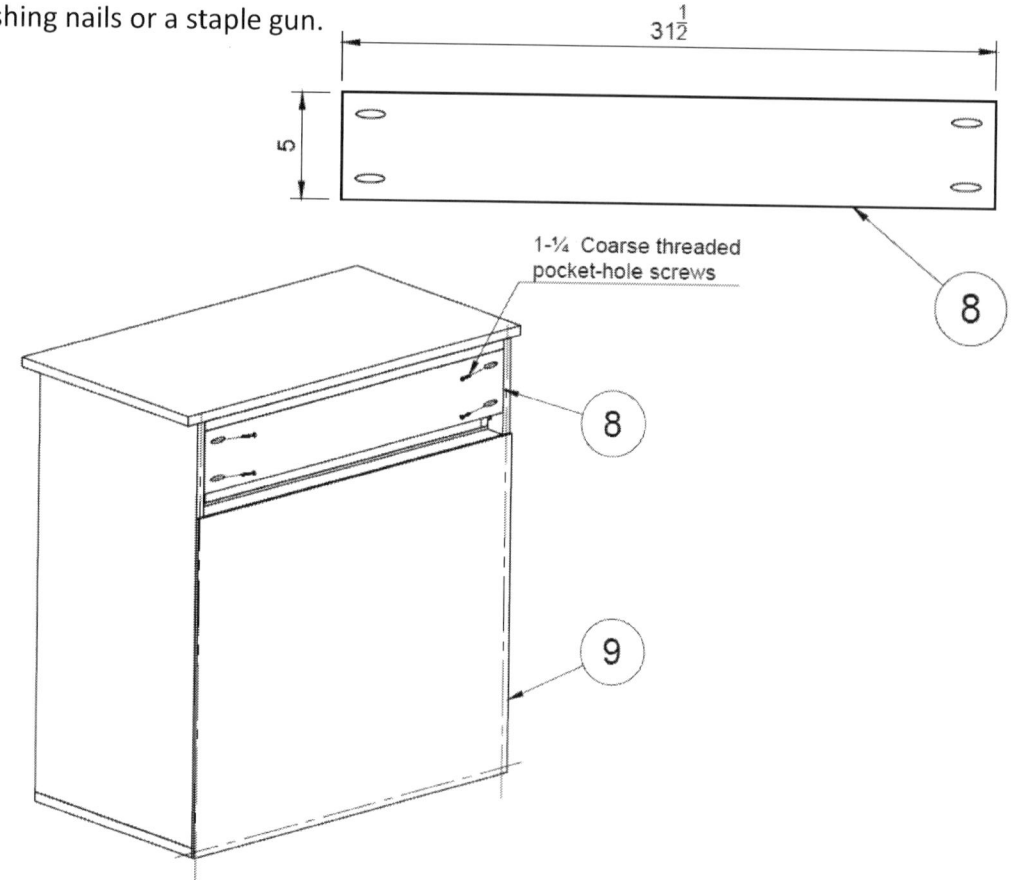

Step 11 - Prepare the Base Pieces

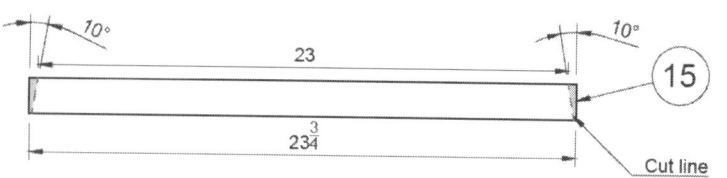

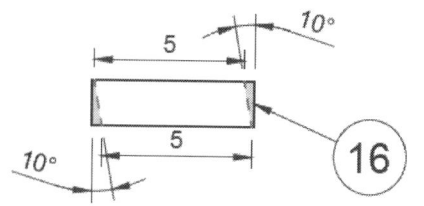

1. Use a miter saw to cut the No.15 and 16 pieces to the lengths indicated, making angled cuts as needed. For this example, the cut angle is 10°; however, if you adjust the overall dimensions, the required angle may change.
2. Sand smooth the cut edges using sandpaper.

Step 12 - Drill Pocket Holes

1. Drill pocket holes in the indicated locations with a pocket-hole jig on pieces No.15 and 17.
2. Sand smooth with sandpaper.

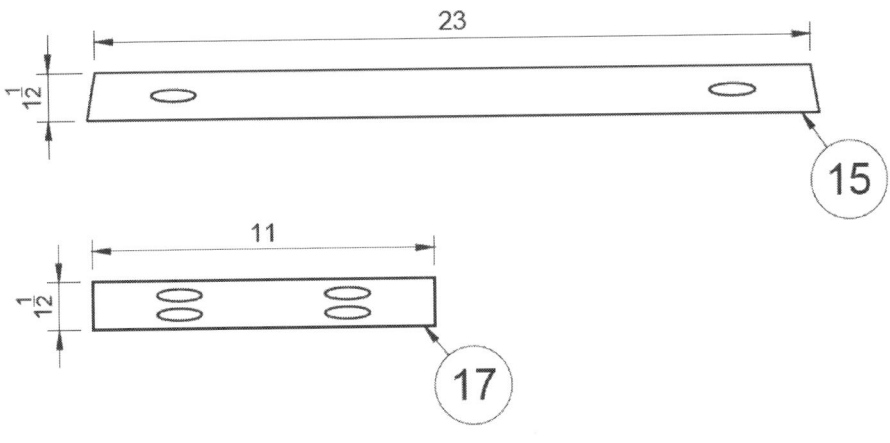

Step 13 - Assemble the Base

1. On a flat and level surface lay out all the No.6 pieces with a ¼" gap between them all as shown below.
2. Using a spacer between the pieces can help keep them even, but precise dimensions aren't essential, as we'll be cutting this into a circle later.

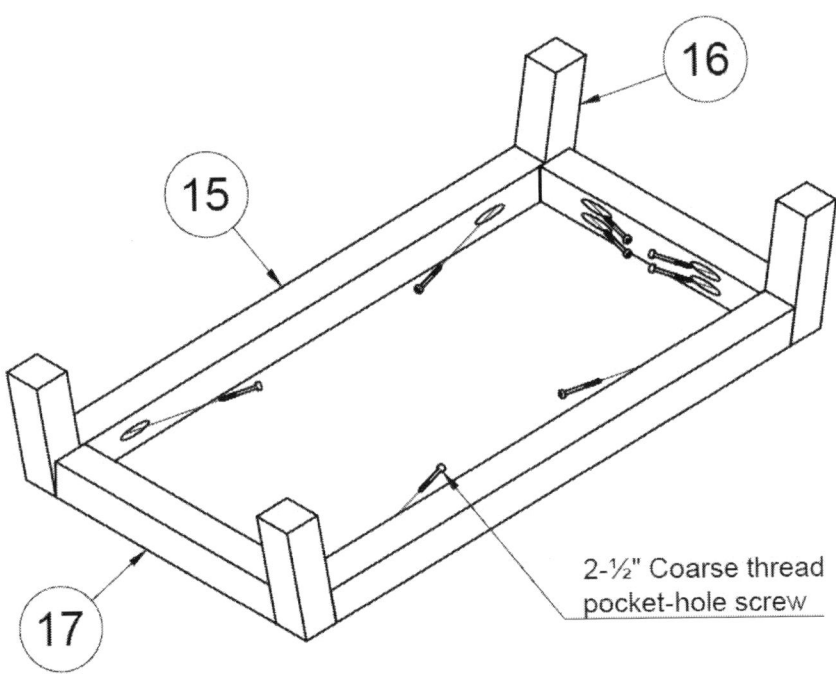

2-½" Coarse thread pocket-hole screw

Step 14 - Finish

1. Finish the assembled carcass, drawer box, base, drawer front (No.14) and door fronts (No.7) with your chosen paint or stain, and allow them to dry.

Step 15 - Assemble the Base to the Carcass

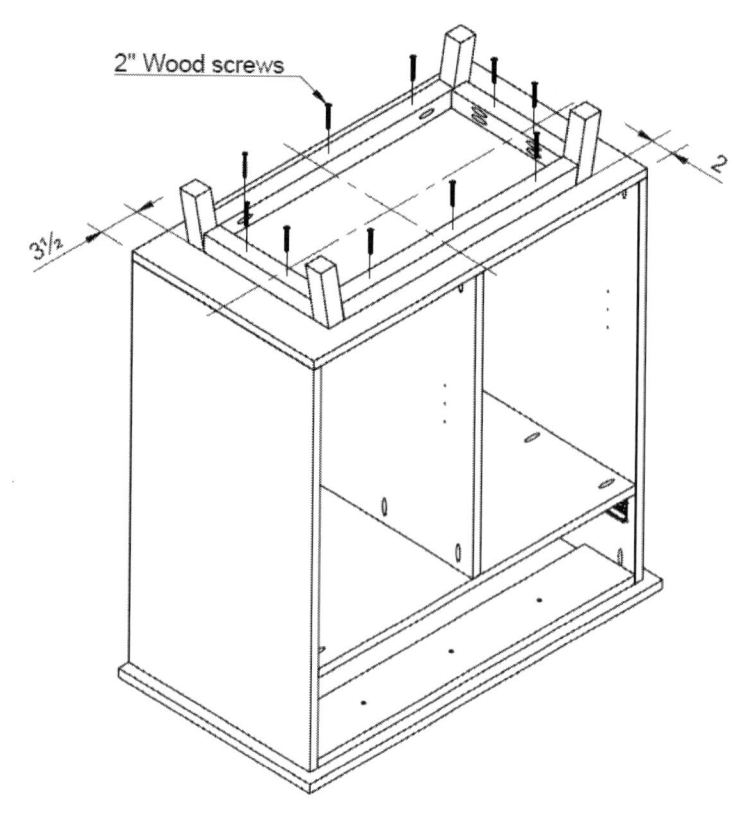

1. Flip the carcass upside down and center the base on the bottom as shown below.
2. Secure using ten 2" wood screws.
3. Turn the cabinet the correct way up.

Step 16 - Add the Drawer Front

1. Slide the drawer box all the way inside the cabinet.
2. Mark and drill the locations of the drawer pull hardware on the front of the No.14 piece (drawer front).
3. Push the drawer front inside the front of the cabinet, aligning it as below (you might need to use shims).
4. Using the screws for the hardware, screw the drawer front to the drawer box.

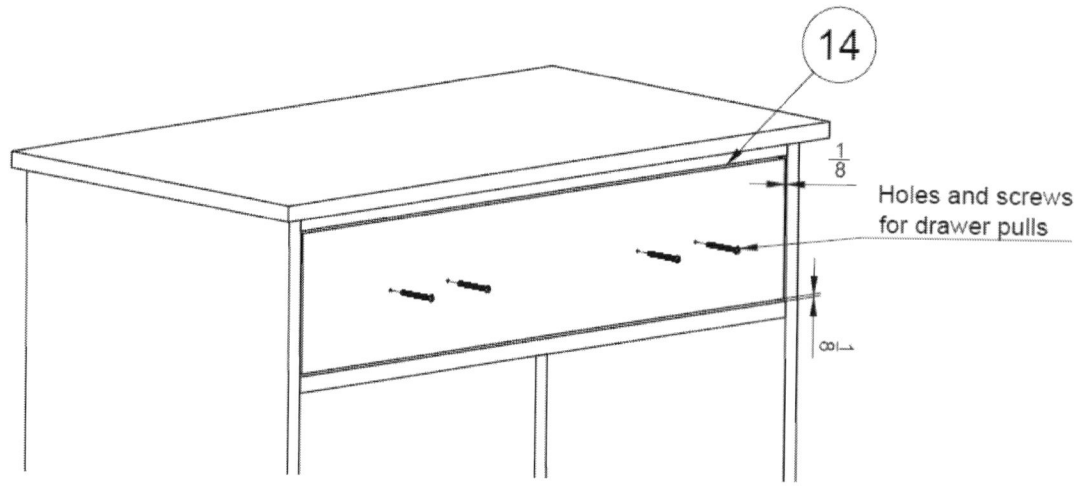

Step 17 - Add the Drawer Pulls

1. Now that the drawer front is correctly aligned on the drawer box, remove the drawer from the cabinet and properly secure the drawer box to the front using thee 1-¼" wood screws.
2. Remove the screws from Step 15 and use them to attach the drawer pulls.

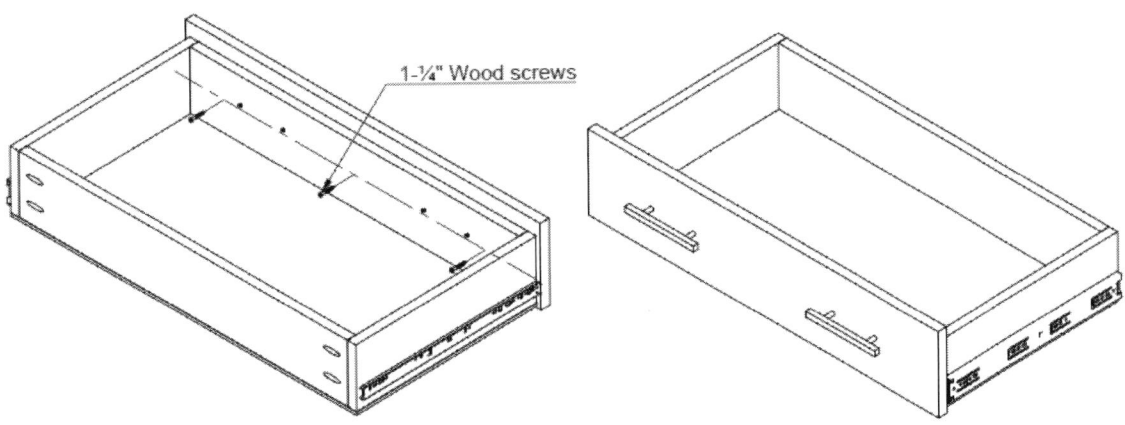

Step 18 - Add the Shelves and Attach the Doors

1. Using concealed hinges join the No.7 pieces (doors) to the inside of the cabinet. Follow the instructions from the
hinge manufacturer in regards to their positioning.
2. Add the door pulls to the doors.
3. Add four shelf pins in the inside of each side of the cabinet and slide in the No.10 pieces (shelves).
4. Enjoy!

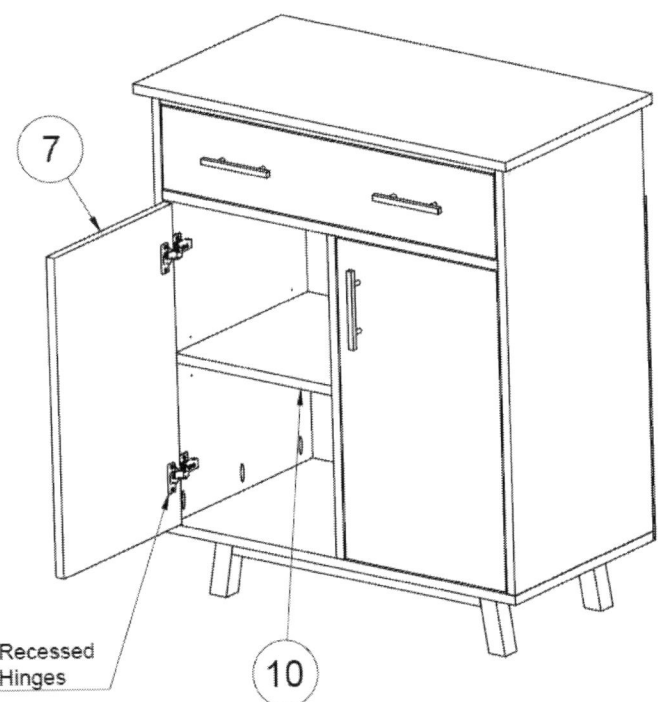

Extra Content

Uncover a treasure trove of extra content and additional resources waiting for you to explore and enjoy.

Scan the QR code to access everything:

https://www.boundlesspublishingpress.com/woodworking

Made in the USA
Columbia, SC
30 March 2025